Inside the 'Inclusive'
Early Childhood Classroom

CHILDHOOD STUDIES

Gaile S. Cannella
General Editor

Vol. 5

The Childhood Studies series is part of the Peter Lang Education list.
Every volume is peer reviewed and meets
the highest quality standards for content and production.

PETER LANG
New York • Bern • Frankfurt • Berlin
Brussels • Vienna • Oxford • Warsaw

Karen Watson

Inside the 'Inclusive' Early Childhood Classroom

The Power of the 'Normal'

PETER LANG
New York • Bern • Frankfurt • Berlin
Brussels • Vienna • Oxford • Warsaw

Library of Congress Cataloging-in-Publication Data

Names: Watson, Karen, author.
Title: Inside the 'inclusive' early childhood classroom:
the power of the 'normal' / Karen Watson.
Description: New York: New York, 2017.
Series: Childhood studies, Vol. 5 | ISSN 2379-934X (print) | ISSN 2379-9358 (online)
Includes bibliographical references and index.
Identifiers: LCCN 2017000804 (print) | LCCN 2017009244 (ebook)
ISBN 978-1-4331-3433-3 (hardcover: alk. paper)
ISBN 978-1-4331-3432-6 (pbk.: alk. paper) | ISBN 978-1-4331-4037-2 (ebook)
ISBN 978-1-4331-4038-9 (epub) | ISBN 978-1-4331-4039-6 (mobi)
DOI 10.3726/b10726
Subjects: LCSH: Children with disabilities—Education (Early childhood)
Inclusive education.
Early childhood education.
Mainstreaming in education.
Classification: LCC LC4019.3 .W37 2017 (print) | LCC LC4019.3 (ebook)
DDC 371.9—dc23
LC record available at https://lccn.loc.gov/2017000804

Bibliographic information published by **Die Deutsche Nationalbibliothek.**
Die Deutsche Nationalbibliothek lists this publication in the "Deutsche
Nationalbibliografie"; detailed bibliographic data are available
on the Internet at http://dnb.d-nb.de/.

Contents

Acknowledgements

I would like to sincerely thank the three early childhood centres, the directors, staff and families who kindly agreed to support this classroom project and allowed me to occupy some space in their classrooms for many weeks. I particularly want to thank the children in the settings who generously shared their ideas with me. I also want to thank all the children I have worked with over many years who I think about often and who have provided me with the passion and the fortitude to complete this project.

I am forever indebted to Zsuzsa Millei and Eva Bendix Petersen for the research and writing support they provided to me in completing the doctoral study that led to this book. Their knowledge, friendship and critical feedback made this work possible. I would also like to thank Gaile Sloane Cannella for giving me the opportunity and encouragement to write this book. Thank you to the Faculty of Education at the University of Newcastle, Australia, for their support and allowing me the time and space to write.

Thank you to my family who have always supported me in my work. To my parents, Ann and Arthur Healy, thank you for your unwavering interest and encouragement. The influence of both the Scannell and Healy families continue to shape me and the work that I do. Thank you to my five children, Sam, Matilda, Oliver, Clementine and Elliot, who have endured my passionate rantings and remain my constant inspiration. To my partner in life, Rocket, a huge thank you for listening to my ideas early in the morning, all through the day and often into the night. Thank you for keeping things in perspective. "Don't forget to smell the roses".

Portions of this book have been previously published in the following;

Watson, K., Millei, Z., & Petersen, E. B. (2015). 'Special' non-human actors in the 'inclusive' early childhood classroom: The wrist band, the lock and the scooter board. *Global Studies of Childhood, 5*(3), 266–278.

Watson, K. (2016). 'Silences' in the 'inclusive' early childhood classroom: Sustaining a 'taboo'. In E. B. Petersen & Z. Millei (Eds.), *Interrupting the psy-disciplines in education* (pp. 13–31). New York, NY & London: Palgrave Macmillan.

Watson, K. (2016). Talking tolerance inside the 'inclusive' early childhood classroom. Bank Street *Occasional Papers Series* 36, *Part II*. Retrieved from https://www.bankstreet.edu/occasional-paper-series/36/part-ii/talking-tolerance-insixe/

Introduction

Questioning My 'Truth' about Inclusion

The Story of David

In 1999, I took up a position as a teacher in an early intervention service, in a rural town, in New South Wales, Australia. The service, like many others, provided assessment, referral, multidisciplinary networking, therapy sessions and transition to mainstream services, for children with a medical or psychological diagnosis, or an assessed developmental delay. With the knowledge from my newly acquired Masters of Special Education, I was considered 'qualified' to identify and classify disability, make an assessment (not a diagnosis, as this was, and is, the prerogative of the medical professional) of the child, and program for appropriate remediation and therapy. As a mainstream teacher, I had been robustly informed by scientific knowledge and the 'truth' of child development. With a Masters degree, I now had the special education knowledge of the medical, psychological and behavioural sciences. I positioned myself, within these discourses, as someone who could assist a child with any diagnosis, and support the family in understanding their child's diagnostic characteristics. Giving support to those *in need* of help was an expected practice for a teacher in my position. Managing a new diagnosis in early intervention required sensitivity and sympathy, and as a teacher I needed and wanted to show empathy for the family and for their diagnosed child.

David (not his real name) arrived at the early intervention service at the age of three with a diagnosis of 'severe autism'. A paediatrician advised David's parents that he would never function like other 'normal' children, as his disability was profound. He would never love them as other children love their parents. He would not communicate and learn like other children. They were devastated by this medical pronouncement and were distraught on the first day I met with them. They were told that early detection and intervention were crucial for his development, which is advice consistent with so much of the literature in the field (Boyd, Odom, Humphreys, & Sam, 2010; Daniels, Halladay, Shih, Elder, & Dawson, 2014; Dempsey, 2012; Guralnick, 2011; Macy, Marks, & Towle, 2014; Underwood, Valeo, & Wood, 2012). I sensed in them some hope for their son, as they enrolled him in my early intervention program.

Over the next few years, David attended the service twice a week. I did regular home visits and supported the family, giving them ideas about ways of 'helping' David and their household. David's behaviours made family life quite difficult for his parents and siblings. The family positioned me as an 'expert' and I used both medical and special education knowledge to build an understanding of David and *his* autism. David did not communicate with words, so we set about trying, with minimal success, to use various social communication strategies and devices. Communication, verbal and non-verbal, have an important focus in special education literature (Kaale, Fagerland, Martinsen, & Smith, 2014).

David's diagnosis attributed many of his behaviours to anxiety, often resulting in unpredictable outbursts. Anxiety is commonly reported as a characteristic of autism (Green *et al.*, 2013). I tried to *manage* this behaviour by identifying his 'anxiety triggers' (Ozsivadjian, Knott, & Magiati, 2012) thereby minimising its occurrence. My interventions were expected to somehow *remediate* David's differences to the 'normal', or at least lessen his diagnostic characteristics and unmanageable behaviours. I positioned David as severely autistic according to the DSMIV (American Psychiatric Association, 2000) and I positioned his parents as needing my support, as David's behaviours were very challenging. I continued to read all I could about 'autism' in the research literature. I attended conferences and talked to many 'experts' in the field. Autism, at this time, was a diagnosis considered to be on the rise (Hertz-Picciotto & Delwiche, 2009) with more children arriving at early intervention with this label. I always thought and hoped, that more of this 'scientific' knowledge would provide the solution to David's problems, and deliver better ways to *help* him with *his condition*.

David's transition to a mainstream 'inclusive' classroom was not questioned by me, or his parents at the time, as it was expected that he would attend the local early childhood setting and later attend his local primary school. After all the need for inclusion had been 'naturally' established and expected as prescribed in policy and 'best practice' (Odom, Buysse, & Soukakou, 2011). His part-time transition gradually occurred over a few months. During this time, I assessed David's needs and the needs of the 'including' classroom, and organised the special support that would be needed. Support and preparation for the teachers and the classroom are presented as imperatives in the literature (Diamond, Hestenes, Carpenter, & Innes, 1997; Odom, 2000; Odom *et al.*, 2006). We were all 'concerned' about David and the prospect of his inclusion.

My role in his transition program focused on educating the centre's staff about David and his diagnostic characteristics. A lack of teacher training, special knowledge and confidence is reported as one of the main barriers to successful inclusion (Carrington, 1999; DeVore & Russell, 2007; Diamond & Carpenter, 2000; Hollingsworth, Boone, & Crais, 2009; Rafferty & Griffin, 2005) and so my role was to improve the 'including' teachers' knowledge. I consulted and collaborated with the staff and other professionals regularly and we shared our knowledge and particular strategies in a co-ordinated fashion. Collaboration between professionals, in multi-disciplinary teams, is regarded as fundamental for the child's progress and inclusion (Vakil, Welton, O'Connor, & Kline, 2009). David's parents wanted him to have a mainstream experience and have opportunities just like other children. Rafferty and Griffin (2005) contend that parents of children with disabilities want them to have social experiences with their "typically developing peers" (p. 174) in 'inclusive' environments. As David's teacher and advocate, I took up the position that he had the right to these experiences.

Unravelling 'Knowing'

For almost a decade, I was as an early intervention teacher. After 20 years as a mainstream early childhood teacher, I moved into the more specialised field with an educated enthusiasm to 'try and help'. The knowledge of child development and developmental psychology exclusively informed my practice. This narrative about David represents just one of many similar experiences I had during my teaching years. I share this story because it exposes how embedded I was in understanding my role, according to 'special' education knowledge, and practice prescriptions. The core of my work was pinpointing a diagnosis, as this ostensibly offered a thorough understanding of a child. A diagnosis drew attention to a child's deficiencies and differences, when compared to other undiagnosed, or perhaps not yet diagnosed children. A diagnosis offered explanations and justifications for a child's unusual or disruptive behaviours, or perceived 'milestone' discrepancies. It provided 'essential' information for making decisions about planning the child's 'necessary' remediation, therapy programs, and possible transition strategies into mainstream settings. Procuring a diagnosis, dispensed by paediatricians or psychologists, created opportunities, as it occasioned government funding which was crucial for the operation of services, subsidising the support teachers needed in an 'inclusive' mainstream classroom.

My knowledge and teaching practice was built on clinical and 'scientific' 'truth', and my understandings of the child were entrenched within 'the medical model of disability'. I did not know at the time that my knowledge, and my formidable allegiance to it, produced considerable constraints and limitations on the children I had taught. I lament the unquestioning and uncritical way I performed as a teacher and how I positioned myself. In this context, the sanctioned medical and 'special' education knowledges and practices, positioned David and his family, his teachers and the classroom in particular ways. From these positions we *all* grappled with our 'mission' of trying to remediate David, so that he could be successfully transitioned into a mainstream early childhood classroom and into a better life.

The story of David I hope communicates my strong emotional attachment to him and his family, as well as a sense of responsibility, obligation and concern for him, and for the many other children that I worked with. Concern for children with disabilities is repeatedly expressed by teachers, educators and other professionals who work in the field. This concern to some extent is built around trying to do ones best for the child, so they are not left behind. During my teaching years I met hundreds of children and families. It was in my relationship with David that I started to ask many questions about inclusion, the role of a diagnosis and my educated knowledge. I started to feel and see the effects of the 'medical model of disability'.

David's Exclusion

Despite all the knowledge, advocacy and preparation, David became too problematic for the 'including' classroom and after much consultation with staff and family he was asked to not attend. David was positioned as too unpredictable, too disruptive and too 'dangerous' to be in the presence of the 'including' group of 'normal' children. The parents of the 'normal' children had concerns about

David's attendance. They feared for their child's safety. The early childhood centre staff too were anxious and apprehensive around David. David's exclusion it seemed was founded on fear. Parents' hesitant attitudes about inclusionary practices, as well as staff concerns and anxieties, are consistently reported in the literature (Gilman, 2007; Grace, Llewellyn, Wedgwood, Fenech, & McConnell, 2008). David needed to be separated from the class group permanently, so that it could remain safe and secure.

Even though the medical model provided us all with surplus information about David's diagnosis, its deficit-driven perspective (Billington, 2000; Oliver, 1996; Purdue, 2009; Slee, 2010) and prescriptions did not help to bring him into the group. The expert scientific 'truth' about David and *his* diagnosis did not bring about his inclusion. David nevertheless continued to regularly attend the early intervention service until he was six. He was then enrolled in a segregated special unit at his local primary school. Inclusion for David into the mainstream education system was never realised. At the time I was devastated for David and his family, as his exclusion seemed so unjust. I had failed David and his family, and many of the other children in this situation needing my help.

David's story of exclusion is possibly not the experience of all children with a diagnosis who attend 'inclusive' settings, but my experiences as a teacher raised many questions about the notion of inclusion. How could inclusion for children like David be achieved? Was it achievable? What haunted me most was the idea that David's exclusion seemed, to some extent, to be founded on fear. How did fear come to inform 'inclusive' practice?

This story conveys the certainty of the vision that I had in my position as an 'expert', where there was no room for uncertainty or other possibilities. Central to my positivist thinking was a view of the world as knowable and ordered, firmly entrenched in modernity and a grand quest for rationality and normality. Slowly this certainty, this 'truth', began to unravel as I experienced years of disappointment, where many children were not included, partially included, or only physically included. In recent years, through my doctoral study, my modernist perspective has changed significantly, and any sense of certainty and universality is now disrupted by the project of postmodernity, where there is no absolute knowledge and no reality to be uncovered. Unlike the medical and developmental models, that regard the individual as unitary, fixed and deficient, the postmodern subject is viewed as "decentred, contingent and heterogeneous and fluid" (Dahlberg, Moss, & Pence, 2013, p. 25) and cannot be known objectively. How could this thinking change understandings of the processes of inclusion?

How did David and other children come to be excluded? In my experience, David was one of only a few children to be formally excluded, but in many 'inclusive' classrooms, the other children I worked with were often left out, rejected, separated and ignored. How do these classrooms come to be this way? Who or what decides; who is in and who is out? Who are in the 'including' group? How does exclusion happen in the classroom, what is the role of the including group?

In this introduction, I have attempted to explain some of the history and motivation behind the classroom project that evolved into this book. Early childhood education and early intervention in Australia have a long tradition and commitment to 'inclusive' practice. From my experience as a teacher in the field, I know how dedicated educators are, and how hard they work to do their best for the children in their care. In writing this book, there is absolutely no intention to pass judgement on the people in the project, or those who work diligently in classrooms everywhere. I am not offering a critique of the actions of the teachers or the children in the classrooms as they work and play. The practices, words and actions of all participants are informed by firmly embedded knowledges that shape, inform and surround them. These discipline knowledges are so established in the early childhood classroom, that they have become a powerful truth that we all feel we must abide by. It is the knowledges that I critique here and not the participants. I am very grateful to the children and the educators who participated in this project for allowing me to spend time with them. I do not wish my reading of their practices to reflect badly on them, as we all operate within the discourses available to us.

My teaching methods in early childhood operated under these 'regimes of truth' (Foucault, 1977) for many years. This project, however, took up alternative ways of understanding the words and actions performed in the classroom by the children. My different reading of practices has been shaped by poststructural perspectives, steering an examination of how knowledges, in particular those produced in the medical and scientific disciplines, exercise power in the classroom, as they create certain and privileged ways of being and doing. These disciplines, and the practices that they produce, are interrogated here, as they have for the most part, become taken-for-granted, naturalised and automatic.

I do not in any way wish to present my changed understanding as a new 'truth'. I hope instead that my writing here "could arouse, persuade and reproach its readers to see something other than their own view of the world" (Allan, 2010, p. 613). I aspire to 'unshackle the chains' that continue to hold educators to certain 'truths' that position particular children as Other via the undisputed and unexamined power of medical and scientific discourses. The purpose of this book is to challenge what has become our 'business as usual'. To share the idea that there are other ways to think about children, about 'inclusive' processes and about the effects of our everyday practices on everyone in the classroom.

Structure of the Book

The chapters that follow scrutinise and make uncomfortable conventional understandings and assumptions about inclusion from inside the classroom. Chapter one examines the meaning of inclusion and the need to make obvious the exclusion it is premised on. It presents the case for identifying the normal and interrogating it as a way of potentially doing things differently. Chapter two discusses the framework used in this project for investigating the 'inclusive' practices. Ethnography among children permitted the views from inside the classroom. As a poststructural researcher the chapter also reflects on my role as a researcher and my struggle with representation via reflexivity. Chapters three and four explore how the 'normal' is constructed within the classroom. Chapter three examines some of the multiple discourses that circulate in the classroom which are identified in the way the children use words and actions, as they produce, reproduce and maintain the 'normal'. Chapter four deals with the way non-human actors in their entanglement with human actors also powerfully contribute to the production of the 'normal'. Chapters five and six reflect on the noteworthy effects of the children's work in maintaining the category of the 'normal', with Chapter five interrogating the acceptable discourses of tolerance and Chapter six investigating how different forms of silence are taken up, as a sanctioned way to maintain social order and the 'normal'. Chapter seven reflects on Foucault's thesis *History of Madness* and the power of the 'normal', in the contemporary classroom, to divide and separate. This discussion focuses on fear, as a remnant of history that continues to shape the way the 'normal' position those who are Othered in the classroom. Chapter eight, as the final chapter, poses questions and raises attention to other possibilities for the 'inclusive' classroom, where ways of being are no longer fixed and compared, but instead fluid and diverse.

References

Allan, J. (2010). The sociology of disability and the struggle for inclusive education. *British Journal of Sociology of Education, 31*(5), 603–619.

American Psychiatric Association. (2000). *Diagnostic and statistical manual of mental disorders* (4th ed.). Washington, DC: Author.

Billington, T. (2000). *Separating, losing and excluding children: Narratives of difference.* New York, NY: Routledge Falmer.

Boyd, B. A., Odom, S. L., Humphreys, B. P., & Sam, A. M. (2010). Infants and toddlers with autism spectrum disorder: Early identification and early intervention. *Journal of Early Intervention, 32*(2), 75–98.

Carrington, S. (1999). Inclusion needs a different school culture. *International Journal of Inclusive Education, 3*(3), 257–268.

Dahlberg, G., Moss, P., & Pence, A. (2013). *Beyond quality in early childhood education and care: Languages of evaluation.* London: Routledge.

Daniels, A. M., Halladay, A. K., Shih, A., Elder, L. M., & Dawson, G. (2014). Approaches to enhancing the early detection of autism spectrum disorders: A systematic review of the literature. *Journal of the American Academy of Child & Adolescent Psychiatry, 53*(2), 141–152.

Dempsey, I. (2012). The use of individual education programs for children in Australian schools. *Australasian Journal of Special Education, 36*(1), 21–31.

DeVore, S., & Russell, K. (2007). Early childhood education and care for children with disabilities: Facilitating inclusive practice. *Early Childhood Education Journal, 35*(2), 189–198.

Diamond, K. E., & Carpenter, E. S. (2000). Participation in inclusive preschool programs and sensitivity to the needs of others. *Journal of Early Intervention, 32*, 81–91.

Diamond, K. E., Hestenes, L. L., Carpenter, E. S., & Innes, F. K. (1997). Relationships between enrolment in an inclusive class and preschool children's ideas about people with disabilities. *Topics in Early Childhood Special Education, 17*, 520–536.

Foucault, M. (1977). *Discipline and punish: The birth of the prison.* London: Penguin.

Gilman, S. (2007). Including the child with special needs: Learning from Reggio Emilia. *Theory into Practice, 46*(1), 23–31.

Grace, R., Llewellyn, G., Wedgwood, N., Fenech, M., & McConnell, D. (2008). Far from ideal: Everyday experiences of mothers and early childhood professionals negotiating an inclusive early childhood experience in the Australian context. *Topics in Early Childhood Special Education, 28*(1), 18–31.

Green, S. A., Rudie, J. D., Colich, N. L., Wood, J. J., Shirinyan, D., Hernandez, L., … Bookheimer, S. Y. (2013). Overreactive brain responses to sensory stimuli in youth with autism spectrum disorders. *Journal of the American Academy of Child & Adolescent Psychiatry, 52*(11), 1158–1172.

Guralnick, M. J. (2011). Why early intervention works: A systems perspective. *Infants & Young Children, 24*(1), 6–28.

Hertz-Picciotto, I., & Delwiche, L. (2009). The rise in autism and the role of age at diagnosis. *Epidemiology, 20*(1), 84–90.

Hollingsworth, H. L., Boone, H. A., & Crais, E. R. (2009). Individualized inclusion plans at work in early childhood classrooms. *Young Exceptional Children, 13*(1), 19–35.

Kaale, A., Fagerland, M. W., Martinsen, E. W., & Smith, L. (2014). Preschool-based social communication treatment for children with autism: 12-month follow-up of a randomized trial. *Journal of the American Academy of Child & Adolescent Psychiatry, 53*(2), 188–198.

Macy, M., Marks, K., & Towle, A. (2014). Missed, misused, or mismanaged: Improving early detection systems to optimize child outcomes. *Topics in Early Childhood Special Education, 34*(2), 94–105.

Odom, S. L. (2000). Preschool inclusion: What we know and where we go from here. *Topics in Early Childhood Special Education, 20*(1), 20–28.

Odom, S. L., Buysse, V., & Soukakou, E. (2011). Inclusion for young children with disabilities: A quarter century of research perspectives. *Journal of Early Intervention, 33*(4), 344–356.

Odom, S. L., Zercher, C., Li, S., Marquart, J., Sandall, S., & Brown, W. (2006). Social acceptance and rejection of preschool children with disabilities: A mixed-method analysis. *Journal of Educational Psychology, 98*, 807–823.

Oliver, M. (1996). *Understanding disability: From theory to practice.* New York, NY: Palgrave.

Ozsivadjian, A., Knott, F., & Magiati, I. (2012). Parent and child perspectives on the nature of anxiety in children and young people with autism spectrum disorders: A focus group study. *Autism, 16*(2), 107–121.

Purdue, K. (2009). Barriers to and facilitators of inclusion for children with disabilities in early childhood education. *Contemporary Issues in Early Childhood, 10*(2), 133–143.

Rafferty, Y., & Griffin, K. W. (2005). Benefits and risks of reverse inclusion for preschoolers with and without disabilities: Perspectives of parents and providers. *Journal of Early Intervention, 27*(3), 173–192.

Slee, R. (2010). Revisiting the politics of special educational needs and disability studies in education with Len Barton. *British Journal of Sociology of Education, 31*(5), 561–573.

Underwood, K., Valeo, A., & Wood, R. (2012). Understanding inclusive early childhood education: A capability approach. *Contemporary Issues in Early Childhood, 13*(4), 290–299.

Vakil, S., Welton, E., O'Connor, B., & Kline, L. S. (2009). Inclusion means everyone! The role of the early childhood educator when including young children with autism in the classroom. *Early Childhood Education Journal, 36*, 321–326.

1

Troubling Inclusion

Policy and Practice

The move toward 'inclusive' policy and practice in early childhood education in Australia, as in other parts of the world, is a relatively recent trend (Nutbrown & Clough, 2009). Although written about in the 1970s, inclusion for children with disabilities in mainstream classrooms only emerged as an option during the 1990s (Odom, 2000). Historically, the moves from the institutional care of disabled children to segregated educational settings, and then onto policies of integration of children into mainstream educational environments, opened additional possibilities for children. Inclusion replaced integration as a preferred model (UNESCO, 1994). This movement towards inclusion was introduced with the view to change existing structures and to potentially change the view of disability in society (Oliver, 2013; Purdue, 2009). "Supporters for inclusion argue that inclusive education respects the unique contributions of each child and supports the civic, social, and educational rights of all children in the normal daily life of the school" (Boldt & Valente, 2014, p. 202). The Australian Government's *Belonging, Being & Becoming: The Early Years Learning Framework for Australia* (Department of Education, Employment and Workplace Relations, 2009) introduced into early childhood education in 2009, supports the idea of "inclusive learning communities" (p. 15) where ability and disability are viewed as aspects of diversity. Inclusion for the most part is taken for granted as an appropriate practice in early childhood today.

Questioning the Notion and Practice of Inclusion

Inclusion is not well defined in education and assumptions around 'inclusive' practice commonly accept that inclusion has already commenced, or is somehow completed, with a shared meaning and understanding in existence among educators, families, communities and children. A 'benign commonality', with everyone thinking that they know what inclusion means, is dangerous (Graham & Slee, 2005). There is a hazardous familiarity about the term inclusion that conceals and overlooks difference. It avoids any confrontation with difference or any conversation about it. Teachers often speak of their 'inclusive' settings as places of harmony, where everyone fits in. Inclusion is often regarded as successful when the child with special needs is physically present (at least for some part of the day) and tolerated in the mainstream setting, without causing too much hassle or upheaval. The illusion of inclusion as a finished product (Slee & Allan, 2001) is also potentially problematic as the term, and its associated meanings and practices, continue to be challenging, undefined and elusive. Inclusion remains a contentious issue in many classrooms.

'Inclusive' early childhood education is described as "far from ideal" (Grace, Llewellyn, Wedgewood, Fenech, & McConnell, 2008, p. 18). The practices of special education that saturate the 'inclusive' classroom are robustly shaped by the psy-disciplines (Foucault, 1977); particularly psychology, developmental psychology and psychiatry. Using constant assessment and surveillance, these practices confine and isolate the diagnosed child, as work is carried out to 'correct' and contain the child's body and mind. Thought to support and to improve the lives of diagnosed children, these practices however, produce effects on inclusionary and exclusionary processes within the classroom. These effects have been typically passed over, as the diagnosis and the ideal of remediation, often takes precedence over the child's becoming identity.

Recent progressive policy reforms in education, as mentioned, have discontinued the practice of segregating and isolating children with special needs in separate institutions and/or classrooms, in an attempt to foster inclusiveness. Unfortunately, the discourses of special education, which circulate in the early childhood classroom, and compellingly inform practices in 'inclusive' education, have not undergone parallel reform (Slee, 2011). The unrelenting scrutiny, surveillance and remediation, that was once sanctioned in segregated special education, is still regarded as crucial for the diagnosed child, even though they are now in the mainstream setting. A prescribed level of development, or some resemblance of 'normal', is deemed obligatory within contemporary educational contexts. Assessments and modifications that were once carried out in separate spaces, or in different institutions, are now accomplished *in* the classroom, and termed 'inclusive'. The discourses and practices of special education, continue to separate and isolate *in* the classroom, and actively create a 'somewhere else' for the marked child to 'be', and potentially, to 'be cured'.

Looking Awry at Practices Inside 'Including' Classrooms

The questions I began to ask about inclusion challenged me to look and think otherwise. The knowledge produced via the medical model of disability no longer seemed to me to provide what was needed for inclusion. Understanding more about the diagnostic characteristics, and behaviours of the special child, did not change their position in the 'including' classroom. Looking at inclusion differently involved a significant shift. A shift that challenged and disrupted the truths that for years had provided me with a sense of certainty about children and about 'normal' development. The truths that insisted on the special remediation of those who were deemed to be 'not normal', or less than 'normal', so that inclusion could be better achieved. Inclusion relying heavily on everyone moving towards being the same.

The move away from the medical model of disability, initially, toward the social model of disability offered a changed view of disability, appreciating it as a culturally and socially constructed entity (Purdue, 2009). From this standpoint, disability is not the result of restraints caused by illness, delays or impairments, but emanates from wider societal discourses (Oliver, 1996). Within the social model, disability is considered the product of exclusionary social practices and is positioned as a form of oppression rather than a description of an individual's deficits (Slee, 2010). This model however applied, has not been overly successful in usurping the authority of medical knowledge or its interpretation in the classroom. It has not been able to shift knowledge bases or assumptions.

Poststructural Perspectives

A more significant shift for the 'inclusive' classroom involves an exploration of poststructural perspectives. Using a different theoretical lens to view the classroom, its inhabitants can be seen in an alternative light. As an 'inclusive' protagonist, turning the gaze of scrutiny, away from the individual child and their diagnosis, toward the 'including' group, changes understandings. By gazing in the direction of the 'already included', the investigation of processes and practices proceed from a reworked angle. For the most part the children *in* the classroom have avoided any examination of their role in 'inclusive' processes. By taking a look *inside* the classroom and interrogating the operations of the including group, the undiagnosed, also referred to as the 'normal', another analysis can be appreciated.

Questioning the power of normative discourses, and in particular scientific knowledges in the classroom, provides for a possible disruption to the way inclusive processes operate and are viewed. The effects of the discursive 'normal', on all the children and their becoming subjectivities, are regarded as significant. As the children go about their daily activities, they negotiate who they are and who they are not, positioning themselves as different, or the same as each other. How they view themselves and others, within the embedded classroom discourses, powerfully contributes to inclusive and exclusive processes. And so, thinking otherwise, I hope to provoke the reader to move traditional 'inclusive' educational gazing away from the inspection, dissection and labelling of the diagnosed child, toward the discursive context of the 'normal'. To view and scrutinise its operation, and examine the multiple effects it produces for children's subjectivities, in their everyday encounters with each other.

The Classroom Project

This project takes a look inside three early childhood classrooms. Each classroom was visited for two months, during a six-month long ethnography. The classrooms, located within early childhood centres, were situated in two regional urban centres of NSW, Australia. Approximately 75 children, aged between two and six years old, and 12 educators participated in the project, with observations and conversation contributing to most of the data created. Human actors, as well as a number of non-human actors, became implicated. While each classroom was unique in their own way, they all provided for the most part what might be described as a 'standard' preschool experience. A 'child-centred' pedagogy operated in each classroom, with adult planning and daily schedules managed for the most part by the teachers and staff. All the early childhood educators in this project are described as teachers, even though they have a variety of qualifications, as the children refer to all the adults who work in the centres in this way.

Each classroom had several children with a diagnosis enrolled. Overall, in the three classrooms there were 10 children with a variety of diagnosed disabilities or delays. There is no commentary on the children's diagnostic labels in this book. This is done intentionally, and for many, may be a source of frustration. Discursively produced labels and the associated homogenising characteristics that define and prescribe the diagnosed child and their behaviours, are not the focus of the project and are vigorously challenged. The child is marked by their diagnosis and the details of the diagnosis does not alter the child's marked position among the children. No matter what the diagnosis might have been, the child was deemed to be different. A diagnosis is described by Billington (2000) as a 'social disease', which he argues has lifelong repercussions for a child and their family. Making no mention of an individual's diagnosis is one way of disrupting acknowledgement of it.

Other Labels

There are a plethora of labels/terms used in education to describe particular children. In this book I use the terms: 'child with a diagnosis', 'marked child' or the 'not normal' child and alternatively 'child without a diagnosis', the 'unmarked child' or the 'normal' child. I have used other labels up to this point to show how the terminology such as 'diagnosis + child' (autistic David), can also refer to 'special needs child', 'child with special needs', 'disabled child', 'child with a disability'. The term often changes, but it seems the epistemology remains firmly the same. These labels locate the 'problems' associated with inclusive practice *in* the child. The word 'diagnosis' best describes for me how the child is marked by medical and psychological discourses. The child (with the diagnosis) is marked by the diagnosis bestowed on him or her by medical, psychological, psychiatric or educational professionals. These various terms, along with the diagnosis, confer certain 'truths' about the child and the inclusion process. In order to disrupt the work of 'diagnosis as usual', I use the terms 'child with a diagnosis' and 'child without a diagnosis' to underscore the ways a diagnosis positions the child in the setting.

Children's Understanding of Difference

These labels/words circulate in the early childhood setting and contribute to classroom understandings of who might be different. Young children's everyday experiences in the classroom and their encounters with difference, particularly race and gender have been well documented (Blaise, 2005; Connolly, Smith, & Kelly,

2002; Davies, 1989). Robinson and Jones-Diaz (2006) argue that young children are aware of diversity and difference from an early age and are very capable of identifying what they understand as the 'normal' or the right way to be. Young children actively draw on normalising discourses, around their own and others' identities and the homogenous group. They adjust their own behaviours and observe the behaviour of others around them and can decide whether or not they might be the same.

Children readily exclude peers based on their differences in their everyday interactions (Connolly *et al.*, 2002). They are not merely socialised by adults or passive in their encounters with others. They do not simply repeat understandings or descriptions about others they may have heard. Children are active participants in their own lives and in their interactions with others (James, Jenks, & Prout, 1998; James & Prout, 1997). Based on these understandings, children are positioned as 'stakeholders' and 'active agents' in the way 'inclusive' processes are examined in this book. Up until this point little research in early childhood education has looked at how young children mediate inclusion. This book opens up a dialogue about the processes of inclusion and exclusion among the children in the classroom. How do the group of children *in* the classroom understand themselves as included/excluded? How do they experience being part of the including group, the 'normal' and how do they negotiate their position and those that are positioned outside the 'normal'?

Theorising the 'Normal' in the Classroom

Understandings of the 'normal' in the early childhood classroom are governed by, and created within, medical and scientific knowledges, which have become so familiar that there is no longer any reflection on them, and the 'normal' has become a comfortable truth shared by all (Harwood & Rasmussen, 2004). Foucault (1977) describes the norm as "the new law of modern society" (p. 184) as it exercises power and gives muscle to a homogenous social body. The norm has the power to measure the gaps or differences between individuals. It is fashioned via techniques of surveillance, where "inspection functions ceaselessly. The gaze is alert everywhere" (Foucault, 1977, p. 195). Children in the classroom become objects under constant observation and scrutiny from adults and teachers. They are studied and monitored via "a notion of difference that is itself socially constructed" (Allan, 1996, p. 224). In the classroom, adults and teachers are not alone in this ceaseless inspection, as children are also attentive of the 'normal', and capable of observing and scrutinising each other.

The construction of a "developmental norm was a standard based upon the average abilities or performances of children at a certain age on a particular task" (Rose, 1999, p. 145). It has generated in the early childhood classroom, a 'desirable' standard. These calculations have presented a picture of what is 'normal' and what 'normality' looks like, enabling the 'normality' of any child to be assessed. This constructed knowledge has not come about from studying 'normal' children, but has come from the examination of the abnormal. It is around the abnormal that the conceptions of the 'normal' have taken shape. As Rose explains, "normality is not an observation but a valuation" (Rose, 1999, p. 133), it contains a judgement about what is desirable, and what should be achieved. The 'normal' grants power to scientific truth, as psychological judgements and comparisons are made about children, by their teachers, and by children, about themselves, and about others.

A Framework for Examining the Construction and Operations of the 'Normal'

A poststructural perspective troubles taken-for-granted assumptions of the 'normal' in the classroom. Well established knowledges that categorise and label individuals, produce and reproduce privilege, and privileged positionings. Equally they create subjugated positions. Subtle, and not so subtle, messages in these discourses reveal a constructed human hierarchy (Cannella, 1997), where some are produced as 'naturally' superior and others as 'naturally' inferior. A poststructural viewpoint disrupts these constructs, questioning the exercise of power and privilege that is generated.

The writing of French philosopher Michel Foucault has shaped this project, as the role of discourse and power are foreground in the constitution of subjects in the classroom. The subject is seen as an individual who is constructed within and by discourses. Discourse both constructs and constrains subjects, but it is through discourse that "human beings are made subjects" (Foucault, 1982, p. 326). The concept of discourse is broader than just language and is understood as social, material, historical and linguistic practices. Discourses are "practices that systematically form the objects of which they speak" (Foucault, 1972, p. 49). They are 'regimes of truth' that formulate how an object or subject is to be understood and supposed to be, a correct way of being (Millei & Petersen, 2015). The way children speak and learn in the classroom is steered by discourses, which reveal to them, how they should attend to the world, and make meaning from it.

Discourses shape the way the children come to know themselves and others as subjects, as they negotiate and renegotiate the multiple discourses in the classroom and the power relations that are produced. By focusing on the children's words and their silences, their actions and lack of actions, observations can be made about how they position themselves within the discourses. Discourses produce ways of doing, being and thinking for subjects and also ways of not doing, not being and not thinking. From this perspective, "the human subject is produced in the discursive practices that make up the social world as opposed to a pre-given psychological subject who is made social and socialised" (Walkerdine, 1999, p. 4). The subject is not fixed and not predetermined but fluid and changing. Discourses therefore govern the possibilities or impossibilities of subjectivities (Davies, 2006).

Becoming a subject is always situated and constrained by relations of power. An examination of power, and the form of power that makes individuals subjects, but in addition also marks them, is of interest in this book. Power that is productive, but also subjugates, is a power that circulates within discourses, but also, is exercised by discourses. There is nothing outside of power or free from power or the effects of its discipline to normalise (Foucault, 1975).

Using these conceptual tools of discourse, power and subjecthood, normative discourses are exposed in the classroom and their effects made visible. In analysing the data created, Foucauldian discourse analysis (Foucault, 1972) is utilised, as well as positioning theory (Harré & van Langenhove, 1999) and category boundary and maintenance work (Petersen, 2004; Davies, 1989). In discourse analysis, the multiple discourses that constitute the 'normal' are identified and explored. Discourses produce statements, and what discourses say or give voice to, and what they do, is closely examined. The statement is not studied as a linguistic unit (Foucault, 1972) as what is of greater interest is what the statement does, how it creates effects and what function it performs. Further to applying discourse analysis, positioning theory is used to explore the interactions between people, from their own standpoint, and as representatives or exemplars of a group (Harré & van Langenhove, 1999). Positions, taken up by people, are relational and having taken up one's position, one sees the world from that vantage point.

Drawing on a position's storylines, images, metaphors and concepts, it is also possible to position others and be positioned by others. As the children in the classroom take up a position, they identify with others who are similarly positioned, creating a category where membership is permitted to a particular kind of person, who knows how to belong and how to be correctly located as a member (Davies, 1993). Knowing how to belong and how to perform as a member, and how to maintain oneself that way, involves category boundary and maintenance work (Davies, 1989; Petersen, 2004). The category boundary work, performed in the classroom, makes visible the discursive inclusions and exclusions in social practices. This category boundary work "involves relative *legitimisations* of some acts, articulations and subjects and a relative *delegitimisation* of others" (Petersen, 2004, p. 28, author's emphasis).

Observed Effects of the Category Boundary Work of the 'Normal'

The poststructural interrogations of the operations of the 'normal' in the classroom exposes multiple effects. These significant effects on the children and their relations with each other are discussed throughout this book and present a genuine challenge for 'inclusive' classrooms. The effects in particular, of practices of tolerance and silence, taken up by the 'normal', as they negotiate around the diagnosed child, are detailed at length in the chapters that follow. As these effects were noted, and analysed during this project, what emerged was an overwhelming, but nevertheless, disconcerting level of segregation and separation of the marked child in the classroom. These practices can be traced back to centuries past, where separation of disease and subsequently 'madness', were considered crucial in protecting the 'normal' (Foucault, 2006). In the 'inclusive' classroom this separation, although not always physical, is enacted over and over again by the children and teachers in their words and actions, when they encounter a child with a diagnosis. A long history of separation of those Othered in education and in society, is residual in our current classroom discourses and practice.

For the most part, full segregation is no longer contemplated as being a part of contemporary practice. 'Inclusive' practice is policy. Nonetheless traces of a bygone era linger, and are made visible in this book. In taking an alternative interrogatory look at the 'normal' inside the 'inclusive' early childhood classroom, the powerful and productive effects of its operations become conspicuous. Practices of isolation, separation and exclusion, produced and sanctioned by the 'normal', as they encounter the 'not normal', exhibit unescapable resemblances to the past segregational activities. Enduring understandings from long ago infiltrate our classrooms, and shape our ways of knowing those who are positioned as 'not normal'.

Within these historical understandings of the Other, an element of fear was produced around 'madness' and 'unreason' (Foucault, 2006). According to Foucault, the image of 'madness' as a condition, has altered over time, but when a major shift occurred in its image in the 17th century, the world of 'madness' became the world of exclusion (Foucault, 1987). An exclusion based on fear. A fear that today, it seems, encircles modern constructions of those diagnosed and pathologised in our classrooms. The need to silence and separate, makes this fear observable.

It was fear that I witnessed, unknowingly, in my relationship with David and his family. His parents were fearful on the first day I met them, and although they displayed many emotions in the time we spent together, fear was a noteworthy constituent of their demeanour. This fear was complex but nevertheless palpable. I was sometimes fearful of David when he became upset and angry with me and my many attempts to remediate *his* deficits. David's mainstream teachers were fearful of him. The children and parents in the preschool also displayed fear in their actions and words and fear played a part in David's final exclusion from the classroom. Understanding how this fear is historically constructed, what effects it has, and how it is maintained by the power of the 'normal', could be a way of rethinking our practices. However, while current practices and discourses persist, and are reiteratively taken up by the children, and teachers in the classroom, 'inclusive' practice will remain problematic and elusive.

References

Allan, J. (1996). Foucault and special educational needs: A 'box of tools' for analysing children's experiences of mainstreaming. *Disability & Society, 11*(2), 219–234.

Australian Government Department of Education, Employment and Workplace Relations. (2009). *Belonging, being and becoming: The early years learning framework for Australia.* Retrieved June 6, 2010 from http://docs.education.gov.au/system/files/doc/other/belonging_being_and_becoming_the_early_years_learning_framework_for_australia.pdf

Billington, T. (2000). *Separating, losing and excluding children: Narratives of difference.* New York, NY: Routledge Falmer.

Blaise, M. (2005). *Playing it straight; Uncovering gender discourses in the early childhood classroom.* New York, NY: Routledge.

Boldt, G., & Valente, J. M. (2014). Bring back the asylum: Reimagining inclusion in the presence of others. In M. N. Bloch, B. B. Swadener, G. S. Cannella, & M. N. Bloch (Eds.), *Reconceptualizing early childhood care and education: A reader* (pp. 201–213). New York, NY: Peter Lang.

Cannella, G. S. (1997). *Deconstructing early childhood education: Social justice & revolution.* New York, NY: Peter Lang.

Connolly, P., Smith, A., & Kelly, B. (2002). *Too young to notice? The cultural and political awareness of 3–6 year olds in Northern Ireland.* Belfast: Community Relations Council.

Davies, B. (1989). *Frogs and snails and feminist tales: Preschool children and gender.* Sydney: Allen & Unwin.

Davies, B. (1993). *Shards of glass: Children reading and writing beyond gendered identities.* Sydney: Allen & Unwin.

Davies, B. (2006). Subjectification: The relevance of Butler's analysis for education. *British Journal of Sociology of Education, 27*(4), 425–438.

Foucault, M. (1972). *The archaeology of knowledge and the discourse on language.* New York, NY: Pantheon.

Foucault, M. (1975). *15 January 1975.* London: Verso.

Foucault, M. (1977). *Discipline and punish: The birth of the prison.* London: Penguin.

Foucault, M. (1982). The subject and power. *Critical Inquiry, 8*(4), 777–795.

Foucault, M. (1987). *Mental illness and psychology.* Berkeley, CA: University of California.

Foucault, M. (2006). *History of madness.* Oxon: Routledge.

Grace, R., Llewellyn, G., Wedgwood, N., Fenech, M., & McConnell, D. (2008). Far from ideal: Everyday experiences of mothers and early childhood professionals negotiating an inclusive early childhood experience in the Australian context. *Topics in Early Childhood Special Education, 28*(1), 18–31.

Graham, L. J., & Slee, R. (2008). An illusory interiority: Interrogating the discourse/s of inclusion. *Educational Philosophy and Theory, 40*(2), 277–293.

Harré, R., & van Langenhove, L. (Eds.). (1999). *Positioning theory: Moral contexts of intentional action.* Oxford: Blackwell Publishers.

Harwood, V., & Rasmussen, M. L. (2004). Studying schools with an ethic of discomfort. In B. Baker & K. Heyning (Eds.), *Dangerous Coagulations? The uses of Foucault in the study of education* (pp. 305–321). New York, NY: Peter Lang.

James, A., Jenks, C., & Prout, A. (1998). *Theorizing childhood.* Cambridge, UK: Polity Press.

James, A., & Prout, A. (Eds.). (1997). *Constructing and reconstructing childhood.* London: Falmer Press.

Millei, Z., & Petersen, E. B. (2015). Complicating 'student behaviour': Exploring the discursive constitution of 'learner subjectivities'. *Emotional and Behavioural Difficulties, 20*(1), 20–34. doi:10.1080/13632752.2014.947097

Nutbrown, C., & Clough, P. (2009). Citizenship and inclusion in the early years: Understanding and responding to children's perspectives on 'belonging'. *International Journal of Early Years Education, 17*(3), 191–206.

Odom, S. L. (2000). Preschool inclusion: What we know and where we go from here. *Topics in Early Childhood Special Education, 20*(1), 20–28.

Oliver, M. (1996). *Understanding disability: From theory to practice.* New York, NY: Palgrave.

Oliver, M. (2013). The social model of disability: Thirty years on. *Disability & Society, 28*(7), 1024–1026.

Petersen, E. B. (2004). *Academic Boundary Work: The discursive constitution of scientificity amongst researchers within the social sciences and humanities.* (PhD), University of Copenhagen, Copenhagen.

Purdue, K. (2009). Barriers to and facilitators of inclusion for children with disabilities in early childhood education. *Contemporary Issues in Early Childhood, 10*(2), 133–143.

Robinson, K. H., & Jones-Diaz, C. (2006). *Diversity and difference in early childhood education: Issues for theory and practice.* New York, NY: Open University Press.

Rose, N. (1999). *Governing the soul: The shaping of the private self* (2nd ed.). London: Free Association Books.

Slee, R. (2010). Revisiting the politics of special educational needs and disability studies in education with Len Barton. *British Journal of Sociology of Education, 31*(5), 561–573.

Slee, R. (2011). *The irregular school: Exclusion, schooling and inclusive education.* Oxon: Routledge.

Slee, R., & Allan, J. (2001). Excluding the included: A reconsideration of inclusive education. *International Studies in Sociology of Education, 11*(2), 173–191.

UNESCO. (1994). *The UNESCO Salamanca statement and framework for action on special educational needs.* Paris: UNESCO.

Walkerdine, V. (1999). Violent boys and precocious girls: Regulating childhood at the end of the millennium. *Contemporary Issues in Early Childhood, 1*(1), 3–23.

2

Doing Poststructural Ethnography Inside the 'Inclusive' Classroom

In order to interrogate the constitution of the 'normal' and its operations in the classroom, ethnography was chosen as the research methodology, as it offered me a way to spend more time inside the classroom. Ethnography, as a qualitative research process, aims to study in detail and in-depth, the everyday lives and practices of participants. It requires a long term engagement in the field in order to gain an insider's point of view, to understand how meanings are constructed (Geertz, 1973).

Ethnography *among* Children

Over the past decade or more, there has been a consensus in early childhood that researchers should move away from research *on* or *about* children and move instead to research *with* or *for* children (Christensen & James, 2008; Christensen & Prout, 2002; Mayall, 2002; Punch, 2002). Researchers have pondered different methods, including offering children a participatory role in research (Gallacher & Gallagher, 2008), so that researching *with* children can be achieved. The child research paradigm (Alderson, 2008; O'Kane, 2008) has tried to redress adult-child power relations in research, by attempting to 'empower' children by engaging them with prescribed participatory techniques. However, the notion that power is a commodity that can be acquired or relinquished (Gallacher &Gallagher, 2008) is challenged by Foucauldian theorising (1982), as power exists in actions, and in relations. What occurs in research is often beyond the control/power of the researcher. Moreover, children are capable of performing "beyond the limits prescribed by 'participatory' techniques" suggested in the research literature (Gallacher & Gallagher, 2008, p. 507).

Researching *among* children, the notion taken up in this classroom project, could be described as 'hanging out' amidst children, the researcher being a *part of the study*. Ethnography as a research method allows and demands the researcher spend time "within the patterns of the community life, moving in the spaces shaped by the community and taking part in its activities on its terms" (Traweek, 1988, p. 10). Time to collect firsthand accounts, to better understand how the classroom community, and the subjects in that community, produce and reproduce themselves in their everyday space and over time (Marcus, 1995). Spending time inside the classroom, affords the opportunity to understand how classroom narratives shape what the children understand about difference, but also what they find interesting and challenging, boring and funny, different and strange, the 'right' and the 'wrong' ways of 'being' and 'doing', and how people and things fit together or don't fit together (Traweek, 1988).

A poststructural ethnographer wants to gather "information about how the group [or groups] maintains its boundaries and guides its own members toward acceptable behaviour" (Traweek, 1988, p. 10). How did the group—the 'normal'—maintain itself? How are the discourses of the 'normal' "lived and fashioned" (Britzman, 2000, p. 31) and how are the boundaries of the 'normal' challenged and maintained in the early childhood classroom. Observing the details of conversations, and the social interactions of the children and their teachers, offers the observer a sense of what discourses are available and sanctioned, as well as those that are resisted or unavailable. Being among the children over time is considered an ethical way of coming to know children as 'building a rapport' is deemed to be a responsible approach (Christensen & James, 2008; Sumsion, 2003).

Troubling the Idea of 'Building Rapport'

O'Kane (2008), and others suggests, that by establishing a degree of rapport, children become positioned as subjects in the research, rather than 'objects' of research. While these ideas are widely promoted in researching with children, as they are thought to promote mutual respect in all encounters, they do suggest a special positioning of children. Are children created as 'needy', or as 'less' capable than adults, if we approach researching with them in a different or special way? After all, adults do not usually require rapport building foundations in adult-adult research. The question asked is, "if children are competent social actors, why are special 'child-friendly' methods needed to communicate with them?" (Punch, 2002, p. 321).

In this project, I began to question the rapport building approach, as I encountered the children in the classrooms. In my experience, children in educational contexts are quite familiar with adults, who continually ask them questions, and spend time observing them. They are conversant in their interactions with different adults; alternative or casual educators, parents, professionals and other visitors, they regularly encounter in the classroom. Some of the children in this project were curious about my presence as someone unfamiliar, and others showed little interest.

> As I sat in the sandpit several children approached me asking, "Who are you?" I replied that my name was Karen and that I was a researcher. I asked them if they had seen a letter at home about a researcher visiting the classroom. Some of the children recalled the letter. Matilda joined the group on her arrival and announced that she had seen my photo on a letter that her dad had read to her. She said, "Ok, I'm ready to get talking to you right now, what do you want to know?" (Field Notes, 16/10/12, S3, p. 2)

Matilda positioned herself as a research participant on her arrival that day. She was informed. She had read (her father had read it to her) the 'Participant Information Statement' that had been handed to caregivers in the hope that they would explain it to their children. I had prepared a picture version of the information statement to explain who I was. Matilda reported her informed consent and positioned me as a researcher. It seemed there was no ambiguity for her about who I was or what she needed to do. The children were positioned throughout as the gatekeepers of their participation and therefore consent (Danby & Farrell, 2005; Warming, 2011). Consent remained open at all times for negotiation and renegotiation. Rapport or relationship building did not seem necessary for Matilda at that time.

The Position and Power of the Researcher

Childhood researchers advocate a variety of possible ways that a researcher could perform when researching with children. Christensen (2004) maintains that the researcher could position themselves as an 'unusual type of adult', who displays a different and deeper level of interest in the children's social world and their perspectives. Whereas, Corsaro (1985) and Mayall (2008), promote the notion of the 'least-adult role', where the researcher makes an effort to get involved in the children's everyday lives while renouncing any adult privilege and authority (Warming, 2005). These positionings assume the researcher has a choice. Ailwood (2010a) in her research encounters, proposed that the children positioned her as a "visiting adult of obscure status" (p. 24). These various positionings present unclear power relations.

Mayall (2008) suggests trying to downplay the hierarchical power in adult-child interactions. In this project positioning myself as a researcher, and not a teacher, achieved this to some degree, as the teacher in the early childhood classroom is positioned as the "boss" (Field Notes, S3). As a consequence there were many times when power relations varied, as the children positioned me as 'less than a teacher'.

> As Amelia arrived at preschool she walked up to me sitting on a platform in the middle of the yard. I was taking notes at the time.
> Amelia: "You're really getting to be a teacher now" (she said as she patted me on the back).
> Me: "Why do you say that?"
> Amelia: "Because you write stuff and take pictures." (Field Notes, 15/8/12, S2, p. 134)

Amelia seems to be praising my efforts in trying to 'become' a teacher. In patting me on the back, she expressed her authority over me, showing me that she positioned me as not quite the same as other adults in the classroom. I had told the children on many occasions that I was not a teacher in their classroom, but Amelia had observed that I had been performing some teacher-like tasks, such as writing stuff and taking photographs, and so she positioned me as a practicing teacher: "You're really getting to be a teacher now".

Spending an extended time *among* the children allowed for an 'informality' to develop and as my 'less than a teacher' positioning evolved, the children became more 'cheeky' towards me, burying me in the sandpit, or allowing me to hear them use 'naughty' words. Initially the children would wait to gauge my reaction, thinking that as a teacher/adult I might make a corrective comment about their words or actions, but when no comment was forthcoming, they perhaps started to think of me as different to a teacher.

Corsaro (1985) suggests that the researcher should let the children define and shape the ethnographer's role. How to go about this, changed all the time for me. I think often I had no choice, as the children continually 'played' with my ambiguous status:

During morning indoor activity time Fleur and Frances asked me to record their song. They were playing with taping sticks and creating the song as they went along.
Frances: (singing) "Star tastic is some fun, makes me happy, makes me laugh."
Fleur: "And the sea and you swim in the sea with lights."
Frances: "Makes me happy if I catch a fish."
Fleur: (giggling) "And her hair looks like wee."
Me: "And the hair looks like wee, that sounds funny."
Fleur: (more giggling) "I want to do a funny bit."
Frances: "Star tastic is a poo haircut." (both giggling loudly now)
Fleur: "And your eyeball looks like paint." (looking at me)
Frances: "Your eyeballs fall out of the paint."
Fleur: "And your nostrils look like a pig." (giggling but directing this at me)
Frances: "Star star tastic I do a wee." (laughing loudly)
Fleur: "Sea sea tastic if you poo in the sea."
Frances: "Sea sea sea, if you do a poo in the sea."
Fleur: (talking not singing) "I always wee in the pool and I wee in swimming class."
Frances: (singing) "If you swim in a class you do a poo in your pants and go to the toilet and ask your dad."
Me: "This song is not getting any better."
Fleur: "Ok star star tastic if you vomit out your nose and poo comes out of your bottom."
Me: "I think I'll turn off my recorder now, it's getting too rude."
Fleur: "No, no, we need it to be rude." (Field Notes, 8/6/12, S1, pp. 146–147)

I do not think the children positioned me as a teacher, or as an authority, in this classroom. They created the song as they went along perhaps to test my position. I felt like they were trying to see if I would stop them or correct them or ask them to sing another song. As I took a less authoritative position they positioned me as someone they could 'play around with'. I had been in the centre two days a week for about five weeks, so Fleur and Frances had become familiar with my presence, and had come to think of me as different to the teachers. Fleur sums it up at the end when she says "we need it to be rude". Their words exercised their power as these words might be considered, in this discursive context, 'forbidden' or at least not said in front of adults. I was positioned by them, as less than a teacher, and able to exercise less authority. The way the children positioned me was not fixed but constantly changing. Similarly, the way that I positioned them was fluid, as our engagements remained open-ended and always uncertain.

Ethnography among children, and among research participants more widely, exposes the researcher to new understandings of everyday practices and flows of the classroom. It cannot provide a reality, or any certainty, but it does give the researcher a somewhat unique view, positioning the researcher, as in this case, as potentially vulnerable. One's vulnerability within the classroom discourses and practices can be, to some extent, appreciated using reflexivity.

Using Reflexivity in Research

Reflexivity exposes and interrupts representations and positionings of the Other (Villenas, 1996). On many occasions reflexivity exposed my inability to think outside the normative discourse, even though I was the one interrogating it. Using this methodological tool it was possible to interrupt categories and common practices in the classroom. However, discarding long held discursive understandings of others presented a challenge.

In societal and classroom discourses the child with a diagnosis, is produced and positioned as a 'tragic' subject, "failing, incomplete and inferior" (Shildrick, 2005, p. 756). This subject invokes sympathy, and in educators, a sense of empathy. Lather (2008) warns against the appeal to 'empathy' as a solution to these issues, suggesting that empathy actually solidifies the structures of discrimination and/or subjugation. Empathy is not helpful in unfixing categories, rather, it works to maintains them. Nevertheless, empathy was entrenched in my previous teaching experience and practice in early intervention. It reinforced and legitimised categories, and the knowledge that being positioned outside the 'normal' was a tragedy. Elsworth (1997) speaks against empathy, advocating counter practices of queering, de-familiarising and denaturalising, which she argues produce an appreciation of differences rather than of sameness and homogeneity. Reflexivity offered a way of recognising and interrupting my own sense of empathy as a teacher and researcher. At times I found myself expressing empathetic attitudes toward all children with and without a diagnosis, and was inadvertently complicit in hegemonic positionings of children (Choi, 2006).

Reflexive notes throughout the chapters, disclose my complicity in contextually framing other people's lives, as this framing conceals my position of power and privilege (Pillow, 2003). The reflexive notes attempt to deconstruct my own subject formation and my practices as a researcher, and previously as a teacher. Reflexivity provides practices that interrogate the truth of the narrative created, providing multiple possibilities, enabling the researcher to tell more unfamiliar and perhaps more uncomfortable tales (Trinh, 1991). The reflexive notes expose and voice my discomfort as a researcher, as I trouble my unmistakable familiarity with the observations and analysis. I am mindful of remaining "reflexive, careful and humble" (Ailwood, 2010b, p. 211) about what I create and my own claims to 'truth'. As a consequence, my "reflexivity of discomfort" (Pillow, 2003, p. 192) is messy and offers no certainty, but nevertheless allows me to engage more critically, examining my part in producing, sustaining and disrupting my position within the discourses.

Reflexivity shows an awareness of some of the problems or limitations of research (Pillow, 2003) and the researcher's position. It affords a personal critical consciousness, a continuing self-analysis and political awareness (Callaway, 1992). More than just a reflection on oneself or recognition of self, it demands some consideration of the Other, as well as a self-conscious awareness of the process of self-scrutiny (Pillow, 2003, p. 177). As the lives of young children are always under scrutiny and surveillance (Foucault, 1977; Laws, 2004), I found the idea of putting their lives under further interrogation somewhat problematic and awkward. Even though I had observed children for many years, making comparisons and judgements about them via developmental profiles, I now felt a fervent sense of discomfort. A poststructural lens had removed a previous sense of certainty and security around my practices. The familiar became less familiar and at times the familiar became strange.

For the most part I tried to deconstruct my authority in the classroom among the children by "hearing, listening and equalizing the research relationship" (Pillow, 2003, p. 179) and by being reflexive of my positionality through self-disclosure (Macbeth, 2001). I endeavoured to continually question the politics of my performance as a researcher, and with it, my representations of the lives of others. I often thought of myself as engaging in an "obscene prying into the lives of others in the name of science" (Lather, 1993, p. 678) and being part of the "the commodification of one set of human beings for the consumption of another" (Quinby, 1991, pp. 104–105). Reflexivity afforded some space for these discussions with myself.

Employing the tool of reflexivity, to deconstruct and examine positioning in power relations, opens up a critique and questioning of my unmediated access into people's lives in my representation. I am mindful that the lives of children are already over scrutinised, already dissected by the workings of dominant medical and psychological discourses. This project adds to this constant inspection of children, diagnosed and undiagnosed. But, possibly inspection is inescapable in the pursuit of new understandings. I would hope that it is "through the act of writing that lives are given space to emerge" (Davies, 2008, p. 197). As Laws (2004) explains further, by making the constitutive force of discourse visible, it might be possible to think about, and work with children in different ways, where uncertainty and flow create possibilities, and new ways of being are given space to emerge.

Creating the Data

In creating the data, close attention was paid to the unmarked children's encounters with and around each other, and the marked child/children. Although not the focus of this research, the child with a diagnosis became conceptualised and viewed as a catalyst, allowing for the examination of the 'normal' and its constitution. I used photographs I had taken of the children, to start conversations about their encounters with each other and their daily activities. These conversations were sometimes audio-taped. The marked children were often in the photographs. I found however that the children liked to see themselves and talk about what they were doing, rather than talk about the marked child. In fact, I felt that they often found discussions about the marked child in the photographs uncomfortable, and I would often need to change the topic of the conversation as they expressed their views. I created hundreds of observations during my classroom visits. These observations of how the children positioned themselves, and each other, in the marked child's presence, made visible inclusionary and exclusionary practices in the classroom. Looking reflexively at this strategy, I do acknowledge that I was also complicit in re/producing the classroom's limiting binaries and recognise the regrettable, but possibly unavoidable contribution that I made to the marked child's positioning.

Inside the classroom, I often asked questions about the marked child, their actions and their relations in the classroom. The way the marked child was viewed and positioned by the unmarked children, was central to understanding the inclusionary and exclusionary work of the unmarked children, in their efforts to maintain the 'borderlands' of the 'normal'. Foucault (1982) argues that in order to find out what a society means by 'sanity' we need to investigate what is going on in the field of 'insanity'. It would be difficult to investigate inclusion without investigating exclusions (Hedegaard Hansen, 2012). In exploring the mechanisms that produce and reproduce the 'normal', there was an imperative to look at the 'not normal' or at least in their vicinity. Looking and asking about the marked child instigated a need to think more about how a researcher effects the research space, the data they create and the way this positions the participants.

Representing the Lives of Those Inside the Classroom

There could potentially be multiple other readings of the data created in this project. In the chapters that follow an effort had been made to be mindful that representation is a privileged space from which to work (Pillow, 2003, p. 185).

The researcher and author, are "not the final arbiter of meaning" (Davies, 2004, p. 6). Working from a poststructural perspective, the use and development of ideas can make up a set of possibilities, but no conclusions can be drawn. In my writing and meaning making "I do not presume to represent their lives as if my words could" (Davies, 2008, p. 197). In representing the lives of others, my ethnographic account is not about the 'real' (Britzman, 2000). In writing about the children's lived experiences I have not wanted to individualise or psychologise them, but have wanted to move beyond the 'real story' (Britzman, 2000) of how 'inclusive' classrooms operate, and grasp at how the children are produced as discursive subjects. In other words, to track how the children came to be particular kinds of beings.

My own 'telling' is similarly limited and regulated within, and by, the discourses of my time and place. The use of the notion of positionality or standpoint epistemology (Lincoln, 1995) recognises the poststructural argument that texts are always partial and incomplete and socially, culturally and historically contingent, and can never represent any absolute truth. In researching, there is the 'inescapability of representation' (Derrida, 1978) but in poststructural knowledge, sharing the shift of responsibility moves from representing 'things' in themselves, to presenting a web of structures, signs and the play of social relations (Lather, 1993). My representation, I hope, shapes a narrative that expresses a concern with experience as a discourse (Britzman, 2000). The children and their teachers, are not individualised, they are presented as being part of a web of social relations, produced and reproduced in words and actions and the place they move within.

References

Ailwood, J. (2010a). It's about power: Researching play, pedagogy and participation in the early years of school. In S. Rogers (Ed.), *Rethinking play and pedagogy in early childhood education* (pp. 19–31). New York, NY: Routledge.

Ailwood, J. (2010b). Playing with some tensions: Poststructuralism, Foucault and early childhood education In L. Brooker & S. Edwards (Eds.), *Engaging play* (pp. 210–222). Berkshire: McGraw-Hill Education.

Alderson, P. (2008). Children as researchers: Participation rights and research methods. In P. Christensen & A. James (Eds.), *Research with children: Perspectives and practices* (2nd ed., pp. 276–290). New York, NY: Routledge.

Britzman, D. (2000). 'The question of belief' writing poststructural ethnography. In E. A. St. Pierre & W. S. Pillow (Eds.), *Working the ruins: Feminist poststructural theory and methods in education* (pp. 27–40). London: Routledge.

Callaway, H. (1992). Ethnography and experience: Gender implications in fieldwork and texts. In J. Okely & H. Callaway (Eds.), *Anthropology and autobiography* (pp. 29–49). New York, NY: Routledge.

Choi, J. (2006). Doing poststructural ethnography in the life history of dropouts in South Korea: Methodological ruminations on subjectivity, positionality and reflexivity. *International Journal of Qualitative Studies in Education, 19*(4), 435–453.

Christensen, P. (2004). Children's participation in ethnographic research: Issues of power and representation. *Children and Society, 18*(2), 165–176.

Christensen, P., & James, A. (Ed.). (2008). *Research with children: Perspectives and practices* (2nd ed.). London: Routledge.

Christensen, P., & Prout, A. (2002). Working with ethical symmetry in social research with children. *Childhood, 9*(4), 477–497.

Corsaro, W. A. (1985). *Friendship and peer culture in the early years*. Norwood, NJ: Ablex.

Danby, S., & Farrell, A. (2005). Opening the research conversation. In A. Farrell (Ed.), *Ethical research with children* (pp. 49–67). London: Open University Press.

Davies, B. (2004). Introduction: Poststructuralist lines of flight in Australia. *International Journal of Qualitative Studies in Education, 17*(1), 1–9.

Davies, B. (2008). Life in kings cross: A play of voices. In A. Y. Jackson & L. A. Mazzei (Eds.), *Voice in qualitative inquiry: Challenging conventional interpretive and critical conceptions in qualitative research* (pp. 197–219). Hoboken, NJ: Routledge.

Derrida, J. (1978). Structure, sign and play in the discourse of the human sciences (A. Bass, Trans.). In J. Derrida (Ed.), *Writing and difference*. Chicago, IL: Chicago Press.

Elsworth, E. (1997). *The uses of the sublime in teaching difference*. Paper presented at the American Educational Research Association, Chicago.

Foucault, M. (1977). *Discipline and punish: The birth of the prison*. London: Penguin.

Foucault, M. (1982). The subject and power. *Critical Inquiry, 8*(4), 777–795.

Gallacher, L., & Gallagher, M. (2008). Methodological immaturity in childhood research? Thinking through participatory methods. *Childhood, 15*(4), 499–516.

Geertz, C. (1973). *The interpretation of cultures*. New York, NY: Basic Books.

Hedegaard Hansen, J. (2012). Limits to inclusion. *International Journal of Inclusive Education, 16*(1), 1–10.

Lather, P. (1993). Fertile obsession: Validity after poststructuralism. *The Sociological Quarterly, 34*(4), 673–693.

Lather, P. (2008). Against empathy, voice and authenticity. In A. Y. Jackson & L. A. Mazzei (Eds.), *Voice in qualitative inquiry: Challenging conventional, interpretive, and critical conceptions in qualitative research* (pp. 17–26). Hoboken, NJ: Taylor & Francis.

Laws, C. (2004). Poststructuralist writing at work. *International Journal of Qualitative Studies in Education, 17*(1), 121–134.

Lincoln, Y. S. (1995). Emerging criteria for quality in qualitative and interpretive research. *Qualitative Inquiry, 1*, 275–289.

Macbeth, D. (2001). On 'reflexivity in qualitative research': Two readings and a third. *Qualitative Inquiry, 7*(1), 35–68.

Marcus, G. E. (1995). Ethnography in/of the world system: The emergence of multi-sited ethnography. *Annual Review of Anthropology, 24*, 95–117.

Mayall, B. (2002). *Towards a sociology for childhood: Thinking from children's lives.* Buckingham: Open University Press.

Mayall, B. (2008). Conversations with children: Working with generational issues. In P. Christensen & A. James (Eds.), *Research with children: Perspectives and practices* (2nd ed., pp. 109–123). New York, NY: Routledge.

O'Kane, C. (2008). The development of participatory techniques: Facilitating children's views about decisions that affect them. In P. J. Christensen & A. James (Eds.), *Research with children: Perspectives and practices* (pp. 136–159). London: Falmer Press.

Pillow, W. S. (2003). Confession, catharsis, or cure? Rethinking the uses of reflexivity as a methodological power in qualitative research. *Qualitative Studies in Education, 16*(2), 175–196.

Punch, S. (2002). Research with children: The same or different from research with adults. *Childhood, 9*(3), 321–341.

Quinby, L. (1991). *Freedom, Foucault, and the subject of America.* Boston, MA: Northeastern University Press.

Shildrick, M. (2005). The disabled body, genealogy and undecidability. *Cultural Studies, 19*(6), 755–770.

Sumsion, J. (2003). Researching with children: Lessons in humility, reciprocity and community. *Australian Journal of Early Childhood, 28*(1), 18–23.

Traweek, S. (1988). *Beamtimes and lifetimes—The world of high energy physicists.* London: Harvard University Press.

Trinh, M.-H. (1991). *When the moon waxes red: Representation, gender and cultural politics.* New York, NY: Routledge.

Villenas, S. (1996). The colonizer/colonized Chicana ethnographer: Identity marginalization and co-optation in the field. *Harvard Educational Review, 66*, 711–731.

Warming, H. (2005). Participant observation: A way to learn about children's perspectives. In A. Clark, A. Trine Kjørholt, & P. Moss (Eds.), *Beyond listening: Children's perspectives on early childhood services* (pp. 51–70). Bristol: Policy.

Warming, H. (2011). Getting under their skins? Accessing young children's perspectives through ethnographic fieldwork. *Childhood, 18*(1), 39–53.

3

Exploring the Production, Reproduction and Maintenance of the 'Normal'

Although not all contributing discourses can be explored here, an account is given of the ones identified as the more pervasive; developmental and psychological discourses, special education discourses, medical discourses, regulatory and disciplinary discourses and play and friendship discourses. In this chapter, critical questions are examined; how are these discourses created and how do they constitute the 'normal' in the inclusive classroom? How do the children, in taking up these multiple discourses, produce themselves, others and the 'normal'? Do these prevailing discourses, and the subject positions they provide, produce inclusionary practices or are exclusions visible? And finally what are the effects on subjectivities?

Developmental and Psychological Discourses

Developmental discourses are widely accepted and proliferated in early childhood classrooms (Burman, 2008; Cannella, 1997; Robinson & Jones-Diaz, 2006). These discourses promote a 'universal' child that develops in a 'normalised', prescribed and predictable way. Any deviations in this development are usually described as deficits, as they are compared to the constructed and fixed 'normal'.

In the early childhood classroom, the children use the terms 'big' and 'little' to describe and position themselves and others. These subject positions, made available in child development discourses, are taken up by the unmarked children as they come to understand themselves and others. These discourses actively and powerfully contribute to the production of the category of the 'normal'. The 'normal' position themselves as 'big'. To be 'big' in this context is to be more adult-like, more developed and closer to an imposed norm. In contrast the 'little' are seen to be more incomplete and less mature.

"I am big, he is little"

> As Hugo (a child with a diagnosis) arrives in the morning he moves down into the yard towards the cubby house. Hayley (a child without a diagnosis) follows him, calling him. He appears to ignore her. She corners him at the garden seat and moves her arms around him in a smothering way. The way she encircles her body around his, is as if he was a much smaller child and she the adult. He tries to move away from her. Two teachers then arrive to 'rescue' Hugo from Hayley's attention. They ask Hayley to give him some space. She moves away while they continue to talk to Hugo saying to him how much Hayley likes him. He then moves away from the teachers. I approach Hayley shortly after this and ask, "Why did you cuddle Hugo?" To which she replies, "Cause he's my little best friend, because he's cute, and I'm five and he's three." (Field Notes, 30/10/12, S3, p. 25)

Hayley moves in on Hugo as soon as he arrives. Hugo appears to ignore her as she calls his name, but she persists and then smothers him, corralling and cuddling him. She positions herself performing an 'adult-like' role, possibly mothering him, or alternatively trying to be the teacher, following him and attempting to keep him close. Formative discourses move around inside the early childhood setting, and it is through these discourses that young children are subjected (Laws & Davies, 2000, p. 207). They shape young children's understanding of the right way to be, and one way of being, is to be 'big'. Child development discourses produce subject positions via numerous stated binaries: big/little, helper/helpless, to know/to not know, already learnt/just learning, rational/irrational, dependent/independent, able/unable, rule follower/rule breaker, play with others/play alone. These binaries are used by the children in their everyday conversations about themselves and others.

How can Hayley's actions be explained? Hayley does not interact with other unmarked children in this way. She positions herself as the 'motherly carer' for Hugo on his arrival and makes comments about Hugo being her best 'little' friend, referring to him as 'cute'. Hayley talks about being five and says that Hugo is three. Being five in the early childhood classroom is significant. To be older in this development-focused environment is produced as more powerful, more desirable and something to be celebrated. Ageism is rampant in the early year's classroom, as age brings privilege and prestige. Age can function as a resource to get what one wants and is used most often to mark out power and social positioning (Löfdahl, 2010). Children will sometimes mention their age as soon as you meet them.

> Chloe: "I'm five and I only have four and a half months till I finish preschool."
> Hunter: "I'm four, nearly five … no not really five." (Field Notes, 18/7/12, S2, p. 22)

Age gives one credibility and legitimacy in the classroom.

> Daniel: "I'm five and a half, five and a half is older than five."
> Noah: "I'm four and half, yeh, four and a half, that's older than four." (Field Notes, 25/7/12, S2, p. 44)

In another conversation the 'battle' to be the 'oldest' transpires amongst the un-marked children.

> Jenna: "I'm 12."
> Elliot: "I'm 4."
> Faith: "I'm 48, 60."
> Me: "You're what?"
> Faith: "48, 60."
> Luke: "I'm 15."
> Jenna: "I'm 13 … no I'm 100." (Field Notes, 28/5/12, S1, p. 87)

Looking back to Hayley's comment about Hugo, she states that he is three. Hugo however is not three, he is five. Hayley remarkably positions herself as older and more capable. The way Hayley moves in to try and hold Hugo might indicate that she positions him as 'little', vulnerable and needy. Her body is much smaller than Hugo's but she positions herself as the bigger and older one. How is Hugo subjected within classroom discourses? Hugo is discursively produced as 'younger', marked by the diagnosis bestowed on him by developmental and psychological knowledge and expertise.

In early childhood education, child development knowledge and understandings for the most part seem to go unquestioned (Cannella, 1997; Soto & Swadener, 2002; Walkerdine, 1993). There has been a century long domination of these perspectives in the field of early childhood (Soto & Swadener, 2002), however more recently, there has been a growing recognition for alternative theoretical and philosophical viewpoints (Bloch, Swadener, & Cannella, 2014; Burman, 2008; Dahlberg, Moss, & Pence, 2013; MacNaughton, 2005). Nevertheless, developmental and psychological discourses are deeply embedded and sanctioned and are readily taken up by the children. Cannella (1997) reminds us that child development has been constructed within a particular social, political, cultural and historical context and has been used to legitimise the surveillance, measurement, control and categorisation of groups of people as normal or deviant (p. 158). In child developmental discourse, performing being 'big', 'older', or more mature is considered more adult-like. The unmarked children recognise what it means to be 'big' and perform this positioning to remain recognisable as 'big'. The adult position in the classroom in relation to the child is typically endowed with power. Cannella (1997) argues that child development "is an imperialist notion that has fostered dominant power ideologies and produced justification for categorising children" (p. 158) rendering children in need of adult support and among children creating categories of those who need help and those who do not. Those who position themselves as being 'big' understand that they are different to those they position as being 'little'.

Developmental and psychological discourses contribute to the 'regimes of truth' (Foucault, 1977) that govern the ways educators think about children and consequently deliver early childhood practice. The 'regimes of truth' (Foucault, 1977) generated in these disciplines produce an authoritative consensus about what needs to be done, and how it should be done (MacNaughton, 2005), what is of value, and what is not of value. The conceptual systems devised within the 'human' sciences, the language of analysis, and the explanations invented, have created ways of speaking about human conduct, and have provided the means whereby human subjectivity, has entered the calculations of the authorities (Rose, 1999, p. 7).

Developmental psychology, as the authoritative discourse, delivers a way for adults to 'speak' about children, while also providing a way for children to 'speak' about themselves and each other. This discourse depends on the constructed knowledge of the 'human' sciences and in particular "the role of psychology, psychiatry and the other 'psy' sciences" (Rose, 1999, p. 7). Available and circulating 'psy' science discourses provide the unmarked children with the sanctioned language to talk about others who are different; the younger child or the child with a diagnosis. The sciences "provide the means for the inscription of the properties, energies and capacities of the human soul" (Rose, 1999, p. 7). Developmental psychology informs the unmarked children of their position as belonging, within the measured 'normal', and the position of others. Big and little, as developmental binaries, are discussed openly, 'naturally' and often, by the unmarked children and their teachers, and are instantly drawn upon to enhance their understandings and explanations of each other. The Other is discussed as younger, deficient and sometimes pathological. This binary thinking is expressed in the following statements made by the children; "He's not a kid, he's a little boy" (Field Notes 21/5/12, S1, p. 57), "We're big kids, when the little kids scream and scream and scream they get a turn on the guitar to keep them down" (Field Notes 21/5/12, S1, p. 60), "What about the big kids in the little room and the little kids in the big room" (Field Notes 21/5/12, S1, p. 62), "No I'm a big girl and I stay inside" (Field Notes 28/5/12, S1, p. 81), "He can't talk and he's little" (Field Notes, 28/5/12, S1, p. 82).

The above statements, made in conversations and noted in observations, show how the 'normal' position themselves as the older. They refer to themselves in one example as 'kids' and not 'little'. They position themselves as mature as they do not show unbridled emotions, such as screaming in the classroom. They 'know' their place and what classroom they belong in. They also position themselves as rational 'rule following', self-disciplined and autonomous subjects who have developmentally appropriate skills. As 'big' kids, they produce themselves as different from, and superior to, the 'little' kids.

I asked one group of children to tell me what 'big' kids can do and they replied, "They can run, they can talk, they can scream, they can climb a tree, they can eat yoghurt and they can play together, they can play nicely." "Little kids don't play nicely" (Field Notes, 28/5/12, S1, p. 83). These statements disclose how they position themselves as competent, with additional social skills that are more developmentally appropriate than their younger counterparts. Children explain how they sit at group time, "He sits at the front because he's little. All the 'big' people sit at the back" (Field Notes, 31/7/12, S2, p. 61). To sit at the front in the group might translate into needing support to stay on task. 'Big' kids don't need that kind of support because they 'know' how to do this. There is a hierarchy, described in this developmental understanding, as Daniel talks about the different class groups in the centre. "The beetle room teaches more than the caterpillar room, they're lower … they're lower and this is higher (he uses his arms to show the levels of the hierarchy). The baby's room is lower, then the beetle room is higher and the caterpillar room is higher" (Field Notes, 8/8/12, S2, pp. 108–109).

The comparisons the children make in their comments establishes the 'normal' and any comparisons to it. The constructed 'normal' provides the guide and judgement about what is desirable, while also extrapolating that it is a goal that should, and needs, to be achieved. The criteria for what is considered 'normal' continues to be "elaborated by experts on the basis of the claims to a scientific knowledge of childhood and its vicissitudes" (Rose, 1999, p. 133). The 'norm' is established via multiple discourses, and provides the 'expertise' and knowledge for understanding the individual, for diagnosing and categorising them, and for providing vocabularies to speak about them as 'normal' or 'not normal'. It also designs the technologies for executing any remediation that is deemed necessary.

Developmental psychology is a formative tool through which children are subjected (Burman, 2008). It is a tool for classification and surveillance, constituting and legitimising subjectivities and power relations (Laws & Davies, 2000). As a science, psychology has produced taken-for-granted practices that have been considered as 'facts' (Walkerdine, 1989), and these substantially contribute to the created conditions and possibilities for the becoming subject, their relational power, and agency. The measurement and categorising achieved by the discipline of psychology, inevitably constitutes "subjects who can have no access to legitimate forms of power or agency" (Laws & Davies, 2000, p. 207). What does this mean for Hugo and Hayley in the classroom? How does Hugo's positioning as 'helpless', and exercising less power, shape his subjectivity? How does the developmental discourse shape Hayley's subjectivity as the helper, with access to legitimised power?

Hayley performs her membership of the 'normal' by drawing on multiple discourses, including developmental. As the more adult-like being, she takes on a caring role, offering to help the 'younger' child. Her positioning marks Hugo as in need of help. Hayley performs her own category boundary work, while at the same time producing Hugo as a marginalised Other. 'Helping' the Other is a performance enacted by many of the children in this classroom, and is mostly supported by the teachers. However, the teachers' actions in this instance show some concern about Hayley's 'over-the-top' greeting and Hugo's rejection of her attention, as he tries to get away from her. The teachers watch Hayley and Hugo, and then act on their understandings of Hugo's discursively constructed needs, rescuing Hugo from Hayley's 'over-caring'. In doing this, however, they reinforce Hugo's marking as not capable of looking after himself, and in need of their help. Hugo appears to reject Hayley's 'helping' attention. He may not wish to be positioned as the 'little' one, in need of her help and 'mothering care'. As the teachers separate Hugo from Hayley, they too engage in category boundary work, reinforcing the 'normal' and the 'not normal'. How does this act of separation by the teachers contribute to the construction of the children's subjectivities?

Using Reflexivity…

I observed and noted the children's persistent statements about being 'big' and being 'little'. I considered how I had positioned myself within this discourse and how my previous ways of knowing had positioned children. Developmental psychology posi-

tions the adult as privileged, and adult ways of 'knowing' and 'doing' as superior, and the child as the binary opposite, immature and deficient. My questioning of my position illuminated for me the children's statements about themselves and others. What once would have been very familiar and acceptable to me now seems undesirable and uncomfortable. As development was always presented to me, as a teacher, as a positive and something to be desired and worked towards, it was 'natural' that 'bigger' was better. Wasn't it? When I thought about the children that I had 'diagnosed' within these discourses, as developing more slowly or differently, I always made the now dubious assumption, that it was important for them to progress and catch up. How does one begin to interrupt these embedded ways of thinking? As I created data, I was challenged in the project every day, to reposition myself within the discourses.

"We're big, we can help"

At packing away time the children are divided into their class groups and sent to separate parts of the yard to put things away. Most of the children seem to do some packing away. However Hugo (a child with a diagnosis) is observed to resist this activity regularly. On this occasion he has spent the morning playing in a 'fire truck' and has been asked repeatedly to pack it away by a teacher. Instead of following these instructions he takes himself up onto the high fort and lies down in the fort. Leah (a child without a diagnosis) follows Hugo up into the fort trying to encourage him to come down and do his share of the packing up. She bends down next to him touching him gently and talking to him softly. "Come on Hugo, you have to pack up the fire engine that you were playing with". He wriggles away from her touch saying "No" several times, each time with increasing volume. She repeats similar words of encouragement. One of the teachers calls to her, "Leah, are you going to get out of packing up?" Leah explains that she is trying to get Hugo to help. After a few minutes she gives up, comes down from the fort and starts to pack away the fire engine. She is told by the teacher to leave some for Hugo to do. Eventually Hugo comes down from the fort, and with the teacher standing over him, he puts one thing away. (Field Notes, 6/11/12, S3, p. 48)

The unmarked children try to ensure that everyone does their share at 'packing away time' as they dutifully follow the routines and rules (Davies, 1993). Drawing on regulatory classroom discourses they seem to have a desire to keep order and maintain the normative way of 'being'. Doing at least some of the packing away work maintains their membership in the 'normal' category. Hiding from doing the packing away, might be viewed as usual for some children, who could be considered naughty. Hugo's hiding on the fort is not the usual or 'normal', due to his pathologised positioning. When I asked a group of children why Hugo did not appear to pack away, Tyler's response was: "Cause he's just learning". When you are 'just learning' you are presumably not expected to do the same as everyone else, the 'normal'. How do the unmarked children then position themselves if they see the 'other' as 'just learning'? How does their knowledge bestow privilege? The statement, 'just learning', is used in addition to, or sometimes in place of, the alternative description of 'little'.

The 'just learning' label, bestowed on the marked child, is authorised as legitimate. Early childhood classrooms, and educational institutions more generally, have established ways of observing children, regulating their conduct, while creating norms that enable them to scrutinise any deviations by charting and measuring them (Rose, 1999). The children within this regime measure themselves against each other. The carefully selected words, 'just learning', infer that they will learn, but at the moment they are not yet there. 'Just learning' however assigns the marked child with deficits, within the network of norms that have infiltrated children's spaces (Rose, 1999). These deficits are identified, labelled and codified, and in this discourse require obligatory remediation. The unmarked children take it upon themselves to become 'remediators' referring to themselves as 'helpers'. 'Helpers' remediate the Other, by guiding and teaching them, and bringing them closer to the more desirable and superior discursively produced 'normal'.

Guidance, or the helping/remediating performances of the unmarked children, are actions that serve as a means of control, keeping order and maintaining category membership. While helping each other is a worthwhile pursuit, it might be important, to also bring to light, the way that this imagined less coercive move to help, is also an exercise and deployment of power (Millei, 2011). Millei (2011) argues, that guidance in the classroom, as an act of helping, is enacted by the children and envisaged by adults as emancipatory. Guidance involves a lessening of sovereign power, as the teacher no longer explicitly instructs or coerces the child about what to do. Contemporary early childhood classrooms are viewed as more democratic places, as children are guided, not disciplined. This discursive practice of guiding/helping each other, is deemed to be a more 'egalitarian' approach. Guidance discourses, not only foster the child to understand themselves as being a considerate (Millei, 2011) and helping individual, but they also fosters an understanding of the Other as one who needs help or guidance.

Leah is positioned as a 'helper'. She has fashioned herself as patient and caring with all the marked children in this setting. Attending preschool on a full time basis she seems very familiar with the routines and rules of the classroom as well as all the children in the centre. She often follows Hugo around the playground and in addition keeps a close watch on Molly, another marked child. She watches them play, shows them how to use equipment and to complete activities, encouraging them with teacher-like phrases, such as "that's right", "well done" and "good work". She positions herself as 'adult-like' and tries to help the marked children to do the 'right' thing. The marked children are usually accompanied by, or closely 'shadowed' by a teacher. Leah enthusiastically adds her support to the teachers and the ongoing process of remediation and guidance.

The unmarked children are often encouraged by the teachers to engage in the practice of helpfulness. MacLure, Jones, Holmes, and MacRae (2012) argue that while this practice might be well intentioned, it positions the marked child in a subordinate position, and perhaps, as "a resource upon which the other children can exercise their developing social and moral competence" (p. 458). Leah, takes up normalising and guiding discourses, in her relentless performance as the 'helper.' In the previous example where Leah wants to conduct Hugo's packing away, she is gentle and caring with him, but nevertheless producing him as subordinate. At the end of the scenario Leah leaves Hugo alone on the fort, as his "No" becomes louder and more resolute. Her reaction to his resistance might be read as her showing an awareness of some potential disruption, and by moving away, avoids this. Hugo's increasing volume informs her that he is becoming more annoyed by her help. Hugo rejects his positioning, at this time, as one who needs help, and the teacher steps in and encourages the separation of the marked child from the unmarked child. Are the teachers positioning themselves as helping Hugo by encouraging Leah to separate from him, or are they also working to avoid any potential disruption?

"We like helping, we can because we're big"

I used a photograph of Leah on the fort with Hugo to instigate a conversation with her and Hayley (child without a diagnosis) about 'helping'.
Me: "Why are you helping Hugo in this photo?"
Leah: "Because I like helping Hugo."
Hayley: "Me too."
Leah: "Oh we help … I help Molly too." (child with a diagnosis)
Hayley: "Me too."
Me: "Why do they need help?"
Leah: "Cause they are liddle … and … and"
Hayley: "They are small."
Leah: "And they need help by the teachers and us and Sarah helps them too."
Me: "Do you need help?"
Both: "No!"
Hayley: "We are big girls."

Me: "Hugo doesn't look little to me."

Leah: "But he still needs help, he always wants to play with fire trucks but he has to do some climbing and some and some things else." (Field Notes, 13/11/12, S3, pp. 65–66)

Leah describes Hugo as 'little' and in need of help. She also states that she likes to help Molly (a child with a diagnosis). 'Helping' it seems, positions Leah as important in the classroom. Hayley (a child without a diagnosis), also identifies herself as a 'helper' and a 'big' girl and they both position themselves alongside the teachers, saying that Hugo and Molly are small and that is why they need help. When I comment that he doesn't look little, referring to his physical size, Leah says that he still needs help and refers to other skill deficits, which need remediating. Performing the 'helping' and remediation, positions Leah and Hayley as grown up, rational, independent and empathetic, which are favoured 'developed' characteristics in this discursive context, and the achievement of these traits, is an expectation that is encouraged, privileged and taken for granted.

Using Reflexivity…

I asked the question, "Why are you helping Hugo?" I wanted to find out what the children thought about Hugo, and in asking this question, I became complicit in also marking him, as I positioned him, and talked about him, as being helped. I positioned myself as not knowing, perhaps in need of help myself, even though I could probably have predicted what the children might say. As an adult I was also positioned as a helper but at times I attempted to redress power relations and presented myself as somewhat vulnerable and in need too. My questioning however wanted the children to speak about Hugo's difference and my questions reinforced that. I constructed the data with my questions and possibly limited the conversation to questions and answers that were acceptable in the discourses. I became more aware of the limiting effect of my questioning, as I spent more time in the field and re-read, and re-wrote my observations. I grappled with trying to 'mix it up a bit', in an attempt to 'do' things differently during my time in the research classrooms.

Helping Is Like Being a Babysitter

Me: "Do you like helping Molly (a child with a diagnosis)?"

Chelsea (a child without a diagnosis): "Sometimes, if I'm not busy I can do that."

Me: "But I haven't seen you do it as much as Leah."

Chelsea: (laughs a little)…" No!! … she's like a babysitter." (Field Notes, 27/11/12, S3, p. 133)

Leah's unswerving performance as a 'helper' has, in Chelsea's view, elevated her to the position of a 'babysitter', possibly someone who does this caring and helping in a more full time and responsible capacity. Chelsea, on the other hand, likes to help sometimes, but concedes that she has other things to do. Leah, while doing all the 'babysitting', has no time for other things. Leah's own positioning as a 'helper' with the marked children is reinforced by how the other children, like Chelsea, position her as well. The 'helper' is the responsible, more adult-like rational way to be. Sometimes the children use developmental comparisons, in a more detailed way, to position the marked child, describing them with multiple deficits and 'needy'.

"We don't need help, we're big"

Me: "Why do you think Molly (a child with a diagnosis) needs help?"

Chelsea: "She needs help to do stuff like sitting over there (she points to Molly sitting at a table with the teacher next to her)

Me: "What else?"

Chelsea: "Like saying different words because she's only young."

Me: "Why does she need that help?"

Chelsea: "Cause you can see how little she is and that's how they know she needs help and stuff."

Me: "What other things might tell you that she needs help?"

Chelsea: "Yeah like cause she can't, she doesn't know a lot of words, she doesn't know how to say different words."

Me: "Anything else?"

Chelsea: "How to play fair?"

Me: "Can you tell me why Molly gets help and you don't?"

Chelsea: "Cause I'm bigger than her." (Field Notes, 27/11/12, S3, pp. 131–132)

"You can see how little she is", Chelsea points out. Molly however is not physically small, as Hugo was not either. How do the unmarked children come to know her as 'little' and in need of help? From within child development discourses there are 'truths' about appropriate physical and cognitive growth and social and emotional maturation. There is an imperative in developmentalism, to closely examine what might be considered 'inappropriate' or 'delayed' growth, when compared to the norm. Historically the study of the child in psychology was made possible by the 'nursery school', as these sites enabled the observation of numbers of children of the same age. Clinical observations "allowed for standardization and normalisation" (Rose, 1999, p. 145). The standards created were based on the ability of the average and performances of children of the same age. The 'normal' created during the child study period of the 1930s "provided new ways of thinking about childhood, new ways of seeing children that spread rapidly to teachers, health workers, and parents through scientific and popular literature" (Rose, 1999, p. 153). The notion of deficits or delays was produced in the gap between what 'real' children actually do, and what they are supposed to do, according to the constructed 'normal'. New expectations and anxieties (Rose, 1999) on the developing child have an intensifying imperative to remediate and 'fix' those who are deemed not to meet the required standard.

Members of the category of the 'normal' are unified as a homogeneous group. Homogeneity works to measure and judge members and non-members, exercising its power to reduce any gaps by correcting difference. The unmarked children in their correction work with the teachers try to 'fix' the difference. Chelsea states that Molly needs help to sit at the table and needs the teacher to contain her there. Molly is positioned as in need of correction and also some degree of containment. Help is produced as a desirable intervention, to maintain social order, to prevent "maladjustments" (Rose, 1999, p. 159) and to correct 'early' what could potentially become "bad habits" (p. 156) that if not corrected, could last a life time. The marked child's difficulty is considered a 'developmental error' (Millei, 2011) and if not put right, he or she runs the risk of becoming a troubled individual, possibly a 'delinquent' child. The image of the deprived child, created in post second world war Europe, was one who was considered to be at risk of a future criminal life and potentially dangerous to the community (Rose, 1999). The imperative to help and 'fix' is shaped by historical discourses of maintaining order and protecting the 'normal' (Foucault, 2006). In early childhood classrooms this imperative is deeply rooted in the long history of the early childhood movement (Gordon & Browne, 2007) and in the foundations of mass schooling.

Molly is described as not knowing lots of words and needing to learn how to play fair. Words and their use create privilege in the classroom. 'Use your words' is a phrase that teachers and children use in conferring appropriate communication, while also identifying it as a strategy for managing conflict resolution (Blank & Schneider, 2011). 'Using your words' promotes an egalitarian approach in disciplining and controlling others (Millei, 2011). This phrase positions the child who can use their words as an autonomous subject who can self-regulate, a desirable and privileged subject position in the early childhood classroom. Conversely those who do not have words or do not use them are created as Other, younger, less able and perhaps undisciplined (or even uncivilised). Molly as an individual in need of help is described by her deficits and her lack of words.

How do children come to see themselves with or without deficits? How do they position themselves? This positioning affects not only what they believe they are capable of, but also what they believe they might deserve, where they might belong in the social hierarchy (Graham & Grieshaber, 2008) and whether they are in a position to help or be helped. Developmental thinking constructs a hierarchy of superior and inferior, and consistent with dominant social ideology, places children on the lowest level (Cannella, 1997). Moreover the deficits identified when comparing one child to another "through statistically derived age-based norms and arbitrary benchmark standard[s]" (Graham & Grieshaber, 2008), leads to educational practices that produce subjectivities through a controlling logic of ableism or the superiority of the 'normal'.

Although limiting and judgemental in its possibilities for children in this context, developmentalism, alternatively, could be viewed as a convenient and useful discourse, as it does provide the children and adults with the words and a way of describing the often indescribable marked children, in an acceptable way. Furthermore, these discourses give authority to the also acceptable notion of 'fixing' or remediating the marked child. In the classroom, developmental discourses work together with special education discourses to sanction the correction of the marked child.

The discourses of special education are examined in the next section and the following questions asked: How do the children position the marked child as they enact practices of assessment, remediation and 'helping', drawing on special education discourse? How do these sanctioned medical and diagnostic ways to speak about the Other contribute to discourses of the 'normal'? And do these discourses contribute to exclusionary practice?

Special Education Discourses

Developmental discourses are reinforced and upheld by the authority of special education discourses, which dominate the 'inclusive' classroom. Inclusion is supported in policy and practice, set down in the *Inclusion and Professional Support Program Guidelines 2013–2016* (Australian Government, 2013), and via an Inclusion Support Subsidy (ISS) which is to "provide eligible ECEC services with practical support that will help services to build their capacity to provide a quality inclusive environment for children with additional needs" (Australian Government, 2013, p. 22). This funding aims to increase educator to child ratios when a child with high needs attends. The supplementary educators/aides employed with this subsidy, closely support and supervise the child. Observed to constantly *shadow* the child with a diagnosis, the support aides use every opportunity to re-mediate the child's skill deficits. Subsidy approval relies on a diagnosis and special education support is expected as part of the 'inclusive' intervention.

In the following scene, the support teacher's interaction with Molly is a re-mediating intervention; it is explicit and visible for all to see. The children, in solidarity with the teacher, draw on special education discourses to help 'fix' the marked child, however, it is also apparent that this remediation further marks and marginalises the child.

"The teacher doesn't help us and we don't need help"

> Molly (a child with a diagnosis) is sitting at the table with a teacher. The table is being used for a craft activity and the children are making binoculars out of cardboard toilet rolls. The teacher is holding Molly's hands around her two rolls. Molly is looking around the yard, not looking at her hands.
>
> The teacher uses short sentences, repeating them when talking to Molly. The teacher's voice is loud so all at the table and nearby can hear what she is saying. "Hold this", "put it there", "scissors down, scissors down, scissors down", "white piece, white piece, white piece", "on the paper, on the paper, on the paper".
>
> When the binoculars are finished being made by the teacher, Molly tries to leave the table but the teacher holds her trying to get her to look through them. Molly reaches across the table and the teacher says: "You have to tell me more, more, say more" and then pointing to pieces of coloured paper says: "This one or this one? Blue? You tell me blue". To which Molly replies: "Blue".
>
> Teacher: "Good girl Molly, tell me, what to do, cut, cut?"
>
> Molly: "Cut."
>
> Teacher: "She's doing very well with the sticky tape" (the teacher comments to a child at the table).
>
> Jonathan (a child without a diagnosis): "She's doing very well at that."
>
> Alexis (a child without a diagnosis): "She's trying hard." (Field Notes, 30/10/12, S3, pp. 30–31)

The unmarked children align themselves with the teacher, positioning themselves in the category of the 'normal', mature and adult-like. They praise Molly for the work she has done with the teacher. They have completed the activity without the teacher's intervention, unlike Molly who is subjected as needing help by the children and the teacher. They are positioned as competent and Molly as the bi-nary opposite. Molly's marking is reinforced by the teacher's actions, holding her hands in place, talking to her loudly, slowly and repetitively. This child-directed and repetitive instruction is considered by speech pathologists to assist in the development of more expressive language and increased vocabulary (Weisleder & Fernald, 2013) in children with delays. Vocabulary acquisition is believed to be an important indicator of later reading and academic success (Biemiller, 2003). Providing endless opportunities for children to develop their language skills through repetition, is viewed as essential for later school achievement. Repetition is seen as an important part of effective intervention (Wasik, Bond, & Hindman, 2006).

Molly's noticeable lack of interest in the activity is perhaps expected in this context due to her diagnosis, and so the intervention is considered essential to improve her concentration, and school readiness skills. Her level of interest would be attributed primarily to her diagnosed delay and deficits; her 'inability' to concentrate and stay on a task, and the 'inadequacy' of her fine motor skills to manipulate the materials independently, and 'correctly'. School readiness discourses promote particular skill requirements (Boivin & Bierman, 2014) in early childhood, and children who fail to measure up to a standard level, are often given tasks to practise and improve these skills. School readiness is seen as central to the work that children 'do' in the early childhood classroom, involving not only pre-numeracy and pre-literacy skills, but also learning how to function in an institutional setting (Ailwood, 2003). These readiness skills are developmentally defined and divided into 'developmental' domains; the cognitive, the social/emotional and the physical. Judgements are made about a child's skills in their early years, using developmental and psychological parameters, and are seen as an indicator and predictor of the child's future academic and school achievements (Boivin & Bierman, 2014).

Special education has been produced, and continually legitimised, by the rise in the authority of the medical and 'psy' sciences (Rose, 1999). The knowledge of physicians, psychologists and psychiatrists is powerful in creating descriptions and judgements of normality and abnormality in the early childhood classroom, with all children undergoing continuing examination, assessment and surveillance (Rose, 1999). The marked child's activities and interactions are often subject to more surveillance and teacher-direction, with a focus on remediation and containment, and the aspiration to reach and maintain prescribed and 'normalised' levels of development.

Mainstream teachers often think about 'inclusive' education as an extra to their classroom practices. They identify, and strongly argue, the need to enlist the help of supplementary teacher aides to achieve 'inclusive' practice, as they see this as separate from their work (Slee, 2011). Supplementary teacher aides, in 'shadowing' the diagnosed child (Field Notes, S1, S2, S3), legitimise the separation of this child from the group. Slee (2011) argues that 'inclusive' education "needs to be decoupled from special education" (p. 155), as the child with a diagnosis in the mainstream classroom is exposed to an almost relentless program of remediation, and as in special education, the assumption of individual defectiveness and need is ever present.

The rise of early intervention programs in recent years is associated with a focus on the importance of the first five years of a child's life and the need to support the education and welfare of children with identifiable disabilities (Odom & Wolery, 2003). Early intervention is considered to be most effective when it is directed, explicit and intensive (Spencer *et al.*, 2012). It prioritises and administers early assessment, individual education programming (IEP) and the documentation of improvements in developmental competencies (Bagnato, 2005). The issue of school readiness is often raised to support the intensive nature of early intervention (Spencer *et al.*, 2012). Much of early intervention requires a collaborative approach among the various experts, with early childhood settings performing a principal role in a marked child's remediation (Talay-Ongan, 2001).

Individual education programs are developmentally goal directed and designed to monitor the child's progress (Dempsey, 2012). Early intervention and special education practitioners recommend that specialised individual instruction is a beneficial practice in the 'inclusive' setting. Just being in an early childhood setting is not enough to address the identified deficits and learning needs of children with disabilities (Odom, Buysse, & Soukakou, 2011). In the previous scenario, the teacher along with the unmarked children, take up the discursive practices of early intervention, as they intensively individualise the focus on Molly's needs and skill development. How does the take up of special education discourse promote inclusionary practices?

A multi-disciplinary team of 'experts' often manage the marked child after diagnosis. These ancillary remediation professionals; speech therapists, occupational therapists, physiotherapists and counsellors provide 'specialist' advice to classroom staff about what needs to be done to support and remediate the marked child's prescribed deficits. Teachers in the classroom often discuss openly the therapies that the marked child needs and they share the advice they have been given by the team of professionals. Special pieces of equipment for remediation and management are shared and discussed. The use of roller boards, 'special' seating, therapy balls, sensory balls/toys, headphones, communication books, Ipads and many other pieces of equipment and techniques, recommended by therapist and specialists, are taken up by teachers and readily applied in the classroom. These special pieces of equipment are discussed further in the following chapter. The various experts 'truth' about the child's diagnosis, and appropriate and necessary therapeutic strategies, are given a high status and priority.

Laws (2011) postulates that dominant 'truth' discourses often constitute children with a diagnosis as "specimens in the scientific laboratory of learning" (p. 59). Molly's remediation was individualised, intensive and separate from the other children, not 'inclusive'. She was positioned as the 'specimen' for others to gaze on. The teacher directed all of her attention to Molly, giving her specific and minimised instructions to complete the activity. It seemed that whatever Molly did, or did not do, it had to be treated and modified. It could not just be left alone, or simply watched, as intervention was the imperative (Laws, 2011). When Molly did not finish the task of binocular making, the teacher did it for her.

The help afforded to Molly isolates her and confines her activities to teacher-rehearsed and controlled pursuits. The children sitting at the table position Molly as 'helpless', as they watch this intensive encounter with the teacher, who tries to force Molly to construct the binoculars. They join in a chorus with the teacher saying "she's doing very well at that" and "she's trying hard". This system of hierarchical observation of Molly, by the children and teacher, was integrated, and functioned "like a piece of machinery" (Foucault, 1977, p. 177), operating to remediate Molly indiscreetly (or maybe not so indiscreetly). The power to discipline her was not just with one individual, but it was everywhere. This mechanism also ensures the constant supervision of the individuals who are entrusted with the task of supervising. "Discipline makes possible the operation of a relational power that sustains itself by its own mechanism" (Foucault, 1977, p. 177). The unmarked children discipline Molly, as she does not perform as a subject in the prescribed way, according to the norm, she cannot sit at the table, she cannot follow the binocular building process, she cannot use the scissors, she cannot communicate appropriately, she cannot do the things that a 'reasonable' being can do. The judgements and comparisons to the 'normal', produce reasonability and rationality, as a goal in the management of subjectivities (Rose, 1999). The unmarked children are unified with the teachers, in constructing their own and Molly's subjectivities, in accordance with the creation of a being, who can 'be' and act, in a prescribed and constrained way.

Using Reflexivity…

In interrogating the discursive practices of special education, I question my years of endorsing and imposing such knowledge in my teaching experiences. Watching this scene with an altered perspective I felt very uncomfortable. As a teacher I had worked to make children more 'normal'. The teacher is positioned as supporting the child and 'armed' with the legitimised power and knowledge of special education tries to 'fix' them. What does the teacher become when they position themselves with the task of 'fixing'? Fixing something that is broken? Repairing? Mending? Who does the teacher become in this mutual co-constitution with Molly? The interactions between Molly and the teacher felt very familiar to me, and they reflected unambiguously, my previous practices with children. In the context of the 'inclusive' classroom, I would have viewed this scene as an appropriate pedagogical interaction, a teacher working one-on-one with a child to remediate deficits. This would have been an intervention that I would have encouraged, consulted on and guided. I continue to grapple with these ideas but I am excited by the possibilities of applying post-positivist ontology and epistemology in the classroom, by declaring that there is no absolute or objective truth. The possibility that the practices of special education create difference in the classroom as negative, needs to be regarded as problematic. What is it about difference that creates this need to 'fix' and 'normalise? How could other possibilities be presented and accepted in the classroom? Is it possible to disrupt and rethink the ways we view the child? What might that mean for the teacher's position of power in the classroom?

'Deficit' based constructions of the child continue to govern how children are viewed, how classrooms are organised, and how assessment, instruction and re-mediation are implemented (Paugh & Dudley-Marling, 2011, p. 819). Teachers in the early childhood classroom create themselves, and are positioned as good and caring people, who value the knowledge of special education, and its power to 'fix', or at least remediate, some of the diagnosed characteristics of the marked child. Teachers are good and caring people who have been misinformed. They position themselves as helping to make the child 'normal' without questioning the effects. However, in their actions and words, they 'speak' ways of being into existence that differentiate and categorise individuals, by consulting a common referent (Graham & Slee, 2008). This has been achieved through the human psy-sciences and the construction of the 'normal' (Foucault, 1972). The children, and teachers in the classroom, readily take up the 'truth' of the 'normal' in their pursuit of special education, and those who are judged to need it.

Medical Discourses

Along with developmental and special education discourse, medical knowledge and language is sanctioned and privileged with authority in the classroom.

"He has something wrong with him"

Me: "In this photo I have taken a picture of Leah helping Hugo. Why does Hugo need help?"

Hamish: "Because he can't walk properly and he has different stuff to us."

Me: "Like what?"

Hamish: "He still has something that's wrong with him and he can walk but something's wrong with him."

Me: "What do you think that might be?"

Hamish: "I don't know maybe … maybe like Coda, the one that you and me (talking to Tyler who is participating also in this conversation) went to their birthday, it was a hot wheel one, what was that one … and he still had a cord in his tummy." (Field Notes, 20/11/12, S3, p. 102)

Hamish portrays Hugo as physically disabled. He describes him as not "walking properly" and compares him to a child who has "had a cord in his tummy", perhaps referring to a feeding tube. Hamish draws on medical discourses to position Hugo as different and bestows on him physical characteristics that are not observed. He uses the word "wrong" twice in one sentence and declares that Hugo can't walk but then corrects himself when it is quite obvious that Hugo can walk. Hamish positions himself and his friends (us) as not like Hugo. He positions Hugo as not able-bodied. Medical discourses privilege a 'correct' and 'able' body while pathologising a body that does not meet the created 'normal' criteria (Shildrick, 2005). Medical models of disability maintain an advantaged and authoritative place in 'inclusive' education (Kearney & Kane, 2006) while privileging the desirable able-bodied. Medical discourses that validate able-bodiedness are taken up by the unmarked children to differentiate themselves from the Other.

Able-bodiedness however only provides the limited binary positions of abled/disabled. The abled/disabled binary is produced, reproduced and vigorously maintained by medical, special education, psychological and developmental discourses. Able-bodiedness is a normative but un-interrogated position which serves to shape the margins and define the 'not able' (Smith, 2004). Discourses that provide a diagnosis for the marked child interrogate the characteristics of 'disabled' in the binary, leaving the 'abled' intact and unscrutinised. In the classroom, the children are limited within the sanctioned contextual discourses, and have only the available deficit descriptions and the language of pathology to describe the marked child. As they draw on the accepted and privileged medical and psychiatric discourses that circulate, they have no other words to describe difference.

In historical and contemporary discourses, when one's physical body is seen to be outside the prevailing 'normal', the difference is fabricated as a failing, incomplete and inferior. The disabled body is seen as diminished and marked not for what it is, but for what it is not (Shildrick, 2005). Hamish might be unsure about what is "wrong" with Hugo but he nevertheless positions Hugo as 'failing to be right' and having "different stuff to us". The "us" is produced by the normative discourses that hold in place the binary power of normal/not normal. The Otherness of the created 'not normal', Shildrick (2005) contends, "can be contained only by the strict imposition of normative categories that separate out and hold apart the supposedly oppositional groups" (p. 757).

Another reading of Hamish's description of Hugo as 'having something wrong', could reveal him drawing on discourses, that position Hugo's discursively created subjectivity as conceivably, an issue of morality (Laws, 2011). Being wrong and needing to be made right. Hamish in drawing on right and wrong moral discourses, positions Hugo as possibly having multiple needs that require attention. He also might be expressing a degree of compassion and tolerance toward Hugo (Brown, 2006).

Using Reflexivity...

I was struck by Hamish's use of the word 'wrong' and his idea that Hugo has "different stuff to us". Within the discourses Hamish uses appropriate ways of describing Hugo. I felt very uncomfortable that Hamish understood Hugo in this way and I thought about my discursive position as a teacher and how my actions would have positioned children like Hamish with a diagnosis in the same way. To be 'right' was to be 'normal'. Hugo was subjected as the opposite. In my attempt to create data about in/exclusionary practices and the children's positioning of each other, I became complicit in a conversation that further marked Hugo. I said nothing and did not challenge Hamish's words. This was the kind of data I wanted (wasn't it) as Hamish 'spoke' via exclusionary discourses. Looking reflexively however by remaining silent I became entwined in the maintenance of the 'right' and the 'normal' along with the children. My silence among the unmarked children might have signalled to them that I perhaps agreed with them or at least positioned myself in their category. Again I was asking the 'wrong' questions. My desire to represent and make sense of the classroom practices remained unchallenged and very uncomfortable when I think about this scene in this way.

Up to this point in the chapter, I have focused my analysis and discussion on child development, psychological and medical discourses that are interwoven with multiple other discourses including special education. These discourses as discussed focus the gaze on the child with the diagnosis, showing how the child is produced as Other and different from the taken-for-granted and unscrutinised 'norm'. The unmarked children repeatedly take up developmental discourses to position themselves and others using comparisons of age, abilities, needs, occupations and physical appearance to name but a few. By performing 'helping' activities they locate themselves as the more capable 'normal'. Children who see themselves as big, a helper, a player or able-bodied, position themselves, and those like them, as 'normal'. They are amenable to separating themselves from the marked child and they recognise the boundary. This separation augments their category boundary work, reinforcing the homogeneity of the 'normal'. Developmental and associated discourses produce available ways of describing and labelling children in the classroom, these are the acceptable ways to talk about each other. These same discourses also sanction including and excluding words and actions. These discourses, along with the regulatory discourses to follow, maintain and reinforce who is 'in' and who is 'out'.

Regulatory and Disciplinary Discourses

The unmarked children often maintain that the marked child does not know the rules, and that the teacher needs to help them to learn and follow them. In the classroom, regulatory and disciplinary discourses are taken up by the children as they position themselves as rule followers. Knowing the rules, and following them, makes one a recognisable (Butler, 1997) member of the 'normal' category. In the following scenario, Jasmine (a child with a diagnosis) is described as not knowing the rules, and this 'not knowing' is explained by Jasmine's deficits and differences. The following conversation, with three unmarked children, began after Jasmine is observed to be loudly protesting against a teacher's instructions.

"We know the rules"

> Me: "Why does Jasmine have to do what the teacher wants?"
> Chelsea: "Cause she has to do what the teacher tells her to do."
> Me: "Do they tell you what to do?"
> Chelsea: "No, but we do it … yeah we just do it."
> Me: "Why do you do it?"
> Chelsea: "Cause we know we will get in trouble."
> Me: "And Jasmine doesn't know that?"
> Tyler: "No, cause she's little."
> Chelsea: "And she's just learning."
> Tyler: "She's just learning, she's five, she's a big girl."

Me: "She is just learning and five ...Why?"

Chelsea: "I don't know ... she doesn't know a lot of things ... cause she's talking really young and she's talking funny."

Tyler: "Yeah ... she's talkin funny ... yeah but she can say hello good, like bye, bye."

Chelsea: "She can say my name."

Me: "Why are you different?"

Chelsea: "Cause my name's Chelsea and I'm a girl and his name is Tyler and he's a boy."

Jackson: "I know why we're different because ... we can talk ... ummm ... like this and she doesn't talk ... mm ... mm ... mm (making a sound to imitate). We talk normal but she talks like different." (Field Notes, 20/11/12, S3, pp. 94–95)

The unmarked children 'know' that they have to do what the teacher wants. They understand the power relationships, between adult/teacher and child, that govern in this context and they position Jasmine as not having this understanding. The unmarked children engage here in a discussion about classroom discipline and self-discipline. Discipline, as a form of control in the early childhood classroom, is dominantly based in behaviourist ideals (Millei, 2005). Any disruption to the social order of the classroom by those deemed to be a 'problem' often leads to stimulus-response conditioning where rewards and punishments are the consequences. Chelsea's comments reflect her understanding that in the classroom, children have to execute the teacher's orders, follow the rules and act in a certain way (Millei, 2005). She understands that by doing what teachers' ask, and staying out of trouble, she avoids punishment. It is the 'right' way to be. Classroom discipline, self-discipline and the control of the undisciplined, all play a part in the constitution of the 'normal'. Chelsea's response: "We just do it" clearly states her self-disciplined position.

Classroom discourses of control and discipline contribute to understandings of the Other. They focus on the control of disruption or the threat of a disruption. Chelsea says that Jasmine has to do what the teacher tells her and avoid any disruption that might be caused. Jasmine, it seems, needs more management and discipline to control her in the classroom, as she does not always do what the teacher says. Discourses of regulation and control constitute particular ways of being as the 'normal' and 'right', and the desirable way to be (Davies, 1993).

Classroom discipline is enacted on all young children in multiple ways; through timetables, architectural and spatial design, rules, routines and expectations. Children are disciplined or 'civilised' (Leavitt & Power, 1997) in the early childhood classroom to act in particular ways. The children are not passive in the construction of the order of the classroom, and they actively cooperate in the establishing and maintaining of order (Davies, 1983). The control of the classroom thus involves collaboration with the teachers and the children.

Disciplinary techniques identified in education institutions, and examined by Foucault (1977), in *Discipline and Punish: The Birth of the Prison* are observed in operation here as the unmarked children discipline Jasmine, using normalisation techniques. Foucault argues that the chief function of disciplinary power is to train:

> Instead of bending all its subjects into a single uniform mass, it separates, analyses and differentiates … Discipline makes individuals: it is the specific technique of power that regards individuals as both objects and as instruments of its own exercise. (Foucault, 1977, p. 170)

The unmarked children are simultaneously made objects under the disciplinary gaze of the norm and their teachers, but they also work to exercise discipline on themselves and each other as part of this system. The unmarked children use "normalising judgements" (Foucault, 1977) as an instrument of power to coerce and correct themselves and each other. The children discipline Jasmine, via their normalising judgements of her, identifying her inability to understand, follow and maintain the rules.

Jasmine's actions are again elucidated via deficit discourses, as the unmarked children measure and compare her to the constructed 'normal'. Jasmine is described in the conversation as "little", "just learning", "she doesn't know a lot of things" and "she talk's funny". Jackson's final comment completes this appraisal when he says, "We talk normal but she talks like different." These normalising judgements discipline the Other, while again highlighting the need for correction. The judgements reinforce the coercive power of the 'normal' and its disciplinary training in the "minute arts of self-scrutiny, self-evaluation and self-regulation" (Rose, 1999, p. 226). These disciplinary techniques exercised by the children echo the classroom discipline, producing the unmarked children as self-disciplined, self-regulating and 'able' to follow the discipline of the classroom. These same discourses however constitute Jasmine as the opposite, and as such, a disruption and problematic for the order of the group.

The unmarked children draw on multiple discourses to create Jasmine's subject position as being 'little' and 'just learning'. They discuss and debate her age on numerous occasions. Chelsea's comment about why she was different to Jasmine, using gender discourses, illustrates how she has only certain ways to speak about Jasmine, and her difference. Is she unsure about Jasmine's gender? Possibly her use of gender discourses shows how the unmarked children draw on sanctioned discourses that identify accepted differences. There is a shared understanding about the importance of doing as the teacher tells you, acting in a certain way, showing a level of maturity. Jasmine's position as the Other, produces her as a subject who is of concern, and in need of discipline from the classroom, and from the 'normal'.

He Does Not Follow the Rules

> Me: "I have noticed that Sam (a child with a diagnosis) doesn't eat his morning tea with all the children. What do you think about this?"
>
> Luke (a child without a diagnosis): "He wants to go outside and run."
>
> Faith (a child without a diagnosis): "He wants to have a nappy change."
>
> Frances (a child without a diagnosis): "He doesn't."
>
> Jenna (a child without a diagnosis): "And he wants to run out, have morning tea and get his nappy changed."
>
> Me: "Why doesn't he have morning tea with all the children, Frances?"
>
> Frances: "He likes to run. He likes to steal people's food."
>
> Fleur (a child without a diagnosis): "And he doesn't talk really."
>
> Me: "He doesn't talk?"
>
> Fleur: "No."
>
> Frances: "He's very quiet, he only cries."
>
> Me: "Why do you think he doesn't talk?"
>
> Fleur: "Cause … people who don't talk … umm …"
>
> Tahlia (a child without a diagnosis): "Sam whinge." (her face is wrinkled and mouth turned downwards at sides)
>
> Me: "Why does he whinge?"
>
> Tahlia: "Cause he wants his lunch."
>
> Fleur: "He wants his mum to stay but parents aren't allowed to stay at school, only teachers."
>
> Me: "If you are hungry can you eat when you want to eat?"
>
> All: "No."
>
> Fleur: "You have to eat at morning tea time but he can eat anytime he wants."
>
> Me: "Why?"
>
> Fleur: "Because … he … doesn't … talk." (she says this slowly and precisely)
>
> Jenna: "Because … it's … not … the … time." (she emphasises each word)
>
> Me: "What about you Frances, would you like to eat when you feel hungry? Why can't you?"
>
> Frances: "Cause it's not the time." (Field Notes, 21/5/12, S1, p. 53)

When the children are asked why Sam does not have his morning tea with the group, they draw on the acceptable and authoritative regulatory and developmental discourses to explain his position. In this discussion, there is the hint of a potential 'threat' and the need for some risk management (Rose, 1999) around Sam, as he likes to run outside, break the rules, and "steal people's food". Running outside, at the 'wrong' time, presents a disruption to the timetable and ultimately the social order. Regulatory discourses are strongly entrenched and coercive in this context. The unmarked children only go outside when it is the 'correct' time, and those who deviate from this, are positioned as younger, not knowing, naughty or 'just learning'. Moreover, there is the idea expressed that there is something morally 'deviant' about Sam, as Frances states that he steals food. The unmarked children avow that Sam does not eat with the other children as perhaps he is 'dangerous', a thief. Dangerousness is often described as an internal quality of a pathological individual (Rose, 1999). Is Sam produced in this way? Regulatory and moral discourses position someone who 'steals' as immoral and threatening.

Furthermore, Sam is subjected as 'baby-like', described as wearing a nappy, not really talking, and only crying. These are not the actions of a preschool child, viewed using a 'normal' developmental profile. They are the actions of someone who might be failing to make the necessary 'progress' (Cannella, 1997) towards a rational and more adult-like being. Fleur says "he wants his mum to stay", which contributes to his baby positioning, as wanting your mum characterises you as a less autonomous being. Tahlia, is two and half years old, and has only attended the preschool for a month, but has readily taken up the circulating discourses as she declares "Sam whinge". She positions herself as not like Sam and the tone of her voice expresses some animosity towards him, positioning him as a younger 'deviant' individual, and somewhat annoying. Her understanding of Sam's difference is clearly voiced here.

The children in their responses seem to grow impatient with my questioning or possibly they think I am not listening to their responses. They talk slowly to get their ideas across about Sam, maintaining their own position, which they make clear are recognisably different to Sam's. The children definitely argue here that Sam is not like them, the 'normal', but they do not use this particular language. They draw on the legitimate discourses of development, rules, regulation and 'time' to describe his deviations. In this conversation, it seems that they are quite overwhelmed by all his differences, and they position him as an enigma.

The unmarked children seem to know things about Sam, they have scrutinised him and his actions, but interestingly, they rarely, if ever, engage with him. They have come to know him via the discourses that subject him and their observations of him from a distance. They maintain a separateness from him, as his actions position him as a 'threat' to them, as members of the 'normal', and guardians of the social order. Their comments illuminate their shared understanding of Sam and his actions.

Using Reflexivity…

During this conversation, or should I say my relentless questioning, I think I wanted the children to say the things that they said. I asked lots of why questions to provoke particular answers. Positioning myself as a researcher with an agenda "in the process of seeking to know" (Schneider, 2002, p. 461). I reflect on how I limited the possibilities as I tried to obtain certain knowledge. Again by asking different questions I may have disrupted these positionings. Researching in the field I did try to be aware of the power of my questions but in these more spontaneous conversations I often became complicit in drawing on the 'normal' and positioning myself as part of the 'normal', I think without even realising it. The 'normal' has the power to do this.

Both scenarios in this section reveal, how regulatory and disciplinary discourses in the early childhood classroom, produce limited subject positions and create subjectivities around being a rule breaker, one who disrupts, or a rule follower, one who conforms. Classroom disciplines work to control and manage the children in the classroom and the unmarked children position themselves as compliant within the regulations. Disciplinary techniques, using 'normalising judgements' (Foucault, 1977), as mentioned previously, are reinforced by the unmarked children's performance of their 'normal' status, in the vicinity of the marked child. Drawing on these available and authorised discourses the unmarked children create Sam and Jasmine as unreasonable and rule breakers. Rule followers are constructed as the 'normal'. Not understanding the rules and acting erratically is constructed as 'not normal' and the unmarked children position the 'not normal' as out of step with the way they see themselves.

Play and Friendship Discourses

Discourses of play and friendship are ensconced in early childhood education, constructing play as a pleasurable and beneficial activity, however, as they are taken up by the children in the classroom, they can and do produce exclusionary practices. Virtually all early childhood educators (and many others) espouse play as a sacred right of childhood. It is seen as the way in which young human beings learn and a major avenue through which children learn to be happy, mentally healthy human beings (Cannella, 1997, p. 124). But what might be the effects of this pervasive discourse of play and its authoritative position in the 'inclusive' early childhood classroom in the construction and maintenance of the 'normal'?

How do the unmarked children draw on play discourses in their category boundary work and what are the effects? This analysis ruminates on the idea that play functions to manage and organise relationships between children and groups of children (Ailwood, 2003)

"I play with others"

> Me: "I've noticed that Ethan (a child with a diagnosis) plays a lot on his own. Have you noticed that?"
> Chloe (a child without a diagnosis): "Max (a child without a diagnosis) plays on his own too."
> Me: "Why do they play on their own?"
> Chloe: "Maybe...?" (voice rises as if thinking)
> Daniel (a child without a diagnosis): "I never play on my own."
> Chloe: "Me neither."
> Daniel: "If I stay at home I can play with my sister and sometimes if my dad stays home, I can play with my dad."
> Chloe: "Sometimes my big sister only likes sporty games so I don't offer her other games I only offer her sporty games."
> Me: "Do you think children like to play on their own or with others?"
> Daniel: "I just think some people play on their own, and most people play with some other people." (Field Notes, 8/8/12, S2, pp. 105–106)

'Playing on your own' Daniel says, is something that "some people" do, but he also says that "most people play with some other people". Daniel's statement positions him in the 'normal' category, a member of the "most people" group, the homogenous body. Daniel recognises that 'some' people, those outside this discursive category, play on their own. Daniel is quite certain about play, saying: "I never play on my own" and Chloe joins him to show her solidarity with Daniel by saying: "Me neither." They make a clear statement that they do not like to play on their own.

Play has become an essential constituent in policy frameworks (Australian Government, Department of Education, Employment and Workplace Relations, 2009). The notion that children learn through play is accepted in play-based pedagogy and practice (Nolan & Kilderry, 2010). Play is thought to underpin learning, and observations and documentation of play are deemed to provide evidence of learning, progress and achievement (Wood, 2010). Play is assumed to promote a democratic society and to respond to the 'natural' development of children (Cannella, 1997). As a deep-rooted discourse, play has been shaped by developmental understandings, where play is individualised, and ages and stages have been created to explain how it progresses (Macintyre, 2012). Playing alone is labelled as solitary or parallel play, and associated with younger children. Co-operative play, or playing with others, is viewed as an important milestone (McDevitt & Ormrod, 2007) and regarded as 'typical' or 'natural' for children in the early childhood classroom (Grieshaber & McArdle, 2010). Play with peers is viewed as developmental advancement. Daniel and Chloe draw on these discourses as they come to understand that solitary play is 'not normal', perhaps for younger children only, and they want to avoid being positioned in that way. What might be the effect of these discursive statements, made by Daniel and Chloe, for children who play alone?

The effects of these established understandings of play, where play is constructed as an almost compulsory and 'natural' activity for children, produce Ethan as different from the unmarked children. His way of being, in playing alone, is not recognisable (Butler, 1997) as the 'normal' way to be. Playing alone, as a form of 'social withdrawal', is similarly pathologised in psychological discourse. Coplan and Armer (2007) speculate about long standing concerns for children who refrain from social interaction in the presence of their peers. They make the claim that it is widely accepted, that children who do not interact with their peers are "at risk of social and emotional difficulties later in their lives" (p. 26).

Play as a sanctioned discourse is regarded as a central feature in a young child's life and a child's right (UNICEF, 1989; Wood, 2010). Play has emerged from the hegemonic discourses of developmental psychology. The historical influence and widespread uptake in early childhood education of Developmental Appropriate Practice (Bredekamp & Copple, 1997), has turned the focus onto play, as a primary vehicle for a child's cognitive growth, as "play enables children to progress along the developmental sequence" (p. 3). Play is described as a 'leading activity' and a driving force in children's development (Siraj-Blatchford, 2009). Without play, could development be compromised? Play has continued to be discursively produced uninterrupted, as a childhood essential, 'natural' and 'innocent' (Grieshaber & McArdle, 2010) until recently.

Cannella (1997) argues that "constructions of play assume linearity, universal human behaviour, unidirectional progress, and standards of normalcy" (p. 124). Play is now often questioned as a taken-for-granted and discursively constructed 'norm' in childhood. It has now been problematised and interrogated in research (Ailwood, 2003; Grieshaber & McArdle, 2010). Research in the area of gender and play (Ailwood, 2003; Blaise, 2005; Davies, 1989) has found that, when scrutinised, children's play can produce oppressive gender relations (Walkerdine, 1981). As children position themselves and others, within and through the available discourses, they engage in invoking a set of rules about what might be possible to think, feel, say and do as a subject (Campbell, 2005). This set of rules produces recognisable categories that the children work to maintain. "Children's play perpetuates the status quo" (Grieshaber & McArdle, 2010, p. 77) reinforcing social and cultural divisions, strengthening those who are already in powerful positions.

Alternatively, it has been argued that play is not developmental, but contextually and discursively produced and it is not always 'natural', fun and fair (Grieshaber & McArdle, 2010). Play "reproduces what exists in society in terms of relations of power about 'race; gender; social, economic and cultural capital; ethnicity; heteronormativity and proficiency with English" (p. 75). Ability could also be added to this list, as children through play, marginalise and isolate for any, or all of these reasons (Grieshaber & McArdle, 2010).

"I do not play alone"

> I am sitting at a small round table with several children, about to open my computer to look at some of the photos I had taken at the preschool the previous day. Some more children arrive wanting to join in, but I asked them if they could come back in a while, as we could not all see the photos at once.
> Ethan (a child with a diagnosis) approached the table but hearing my words turned around saying: "I will come back in a while" repeating these words several times as he walked away.
> Amelia: (a child without a diagnosis) "He's a funny."
> Me: "Why do you say that?"
> Amelia: "Cause he doesn't play with anyone."
> Me: "Why is that?"
> Grace: (a child without a diagnosis) "Maybe because he's shy."
> Me: "Ok."
> Grace: "Maybe he will when he grows up." (Field Notes, 21/8/12, S2, p. 151)

Grace suggests that Ethan could be shy. Shyness, as already mentioned is produced, within psychological discourses. It is described as a level of wariness or an anxiety in the face of some social novelty, which can create particular behavioural inhibitions (Coplan & Armer, 2007). However within these discourses, shyness is an acceptable way to describe and mark Ethan and his actions, as the word also has links to personality traits, that are not pathologised (Coplan & Armer, 2007) and are part of the 'normal' discourse. Shyness traits are considered "biologically based" (p. 27), potentially decreasing with maturity. Grace continues in her conversation clarifying her positioning of Ethan as younger, while positioning herself as older. She says that maybe he is going to play with others when he grows up. Ethan is a similar age but positioned as immature. She already plays with others and so positions herself as already grown up. His actions position him as undeveloped, with shyness being one way to reasonably discuss his pathologised status.

"We can do stuff, he does nothing"

> Amelia, Grace and Penny (children without a diagnosis) look at a photo of the volcano-making in the sandpit and the following conversation transpires.
> Me: "Do you think Ethan (a child with a diagnosis) was building the volcano?"
> Penny: "Nah."
> Grace: "No."
> Me: "Why not?"
> Penny: "Because he can't build much stuff ... he doesn't do much stuff."
> Me: "Is he little?"
> All: "Nah."
> Amelia: "He's five."
> Me: "So why doesn't he do the stuff that others do?"
> Penny: "I don't know."
> Amelia: "I don't know either."
> Me: "What does he do?"
> Grace: "He walks around and does nothing."
> Penny: "He just talks to his self."
> Me: "Do you ever talk to yourself?"
> All: "No."
> Grace: "Er ... well ... sometimes at home I do." (Field Notes, 21/8/12, S2, p. 156)

There are expectations that young children engage in both independent and social activities, as they learn by doing and 'playing' (Grieshaber & McArdle, 2010). The early childhood classroom is constructed as a place where children 'do stuff'. The unmarked children here position Ethan as not doing stuff, they say he "can't build" and he walks around doing nothing. Playing is contextually produced as a 'natural' thing to do and young children are created as being 'naturally' interested in doing things at preschool (Grieshaber & McArdle, 2010). Doing nothing positions Ethan as outside the 'normal' and the 'natural' discourses.

The unmarked children discuss how Ethan talks to himself. Drawing on normative discourses, where talking to yourself is not particularly acceptable (just like playing alone), they chorus "no" when asked if they talk to themselves. Grace finishes the conversation admitting she does sometimes talk alone, but with the qualification that she does it only at home, or perhaps home alone when no one hears. With this statement she might be inferring that this is not an 'appropriate' thing to be doing at preschool. The early childhood classroom is discursively produced as a place for socialisation (Epstein, 2009) where the norm expects children to be developing their social and emotional competency in their interactions with each other. Ethan's actions, or what is recognised as his lack of actions, position him outside the 'normal' category of how to 'be' and what to 'do' as the 'right' kind of pre-schooler. Ethan is subjected as someone whose performance sets him apart, as he does not operate within the boundaries of the discursively produced 'normal'.

Throughout history those who have been positioned as 'normal' have endeavoured to disassociate and separate themselves from the behaviour of talking to oneself (Foucault, 2006), as it has been conceived to exhibit 'madness'. 'Talking to yourself' in psychological and psychiatric discourses characterises the performance of someone who is without reason (Birchwood, Spencer, & McGovern, 2000). Talking to oneself is described by child development theorist Piaget (1959) as 'egocentric speech', regarded as an indicator of a child's early level of development. Vygotsky (1986) regards this behaviour as 'private speech' arguing that children talk to themselves before they internalise thinking (Verenikina, Vialle, & Lysaght, 2011). Nevertheless, Ethan's actions position him here as immature and unreasonable, and the children drawing on normative discourses, categorise him as different to them. His actions bring into question his position as a rational being.

"We play games with friends"

Jack and Noah (children without a diagnosis) are in the sandpit. Each has a large plastic tip truck which they fill and empty. I move toward the sandpit and sit down on the edge. Ethan (a child with a diagnosis) has been following me for several minutes. He dances in circles, dancing away from me and then back again. He is singing as well as telling a story with melody. He returns and stands in front of me each time and waits for me to say something. This goes on for many minutes.

Jack and Noah look up each time Ethan returns. Their faces show surprise and bemusement. They look at me for a reaction.

Me: "Why does he keep dancing?"

Noah: "Probably cause he likes it?"

Me: "Do you like to do that?"

Noah: "Nah."

Me: "Why not?"

Noah: "Cause I like playing with my friends."

Me: "What about Ethan? Does he like playing with friends?"

Noah: "No." (Field Notes, 29/8/12, S2, pp. 195–196)

As Jack and Noah 'do' their kind of play in the sandpit they take note of Ethan's play.

Children playing in a sandpit with trucks, is a 'typical' preschool activity, and normative in the early childhood centre. Ethan does not join the normative sandpit play but dances around in circles, moving toward and away from the sandpit while singing 'a story song'. Jack and Noah look at him and then look at me somewhat perplexed. Ethan is not observed to play in the sandpit at all. He does not appear to want to play with the others or with the sand.

When asked why Ethan dances, Noah states that he probably likes it. In the child-centred pedagogy of the early childhood classroom, there are prevailing notions about autonomy and democracy (Burman, 2008; Walkerdine, 1988), where children are thought to be able to, and encouraged to, make choices and self-regulate. A desirable level of self-direction in play, as an innocent and enjoyable enterprise, shapes pedagogical practices (Grieshaber & McArdle, 2010). Yet this ignores the possibility, that play and its interactions are sometimes coercive, cruel and dangerous (Burman, 2008). Play is discursively produced with some degree of 'free choice' and self-initiation, but as Cannella (1997) argues, "choice for children is an illusion" (p. 121) and adults control the choices that surround children. The unmarked children take up the notion that they have choices and can make decisions about what they can do.

Historically and within western European culture, children's play has been socially constructed as a self-initiated, spontaneous activity, an act of 'freedom' (Grieshaber & McArdle, 2010), where children can do what they want, and can follow their interests in an uninhibited way. This concept of play emanated from the philosophers and educators of the 18th and 19th century, including Rousseau and Froebel, where understandings about childhood constructed it as a romantic, natural and boundless time (Grieshaber & McArdle, 2010). The image of the young child as 'innocent', playing happily and harmoniously with others, has been produced and reproduced in historical discourses and permeates present-day approaches to child-centred early childhood education (James, Jenks, & Prout, 1998). Contemporary pedagogical discourses encourage children to show self-initiative and follow their interests. Even though choice might be limited by adults and environments, the idea of deciding what, and where to play, is seen as both a privilege and an obligation. Playing is regarded as an imperative for the young child; it is thus expected and normalised.

Noah states that Ethan was probably doing what he likes to do. Early childhood classrooms are produced as places where options are presented, and children are positioned as "autonomous choosers" and "decision makers" (Millei, 2011,

p. 89). They are trusted to direct themselves (Porter, 2008). Classroom discourses of adult control and discipline have been replaced in recent years with more egalitarian and democratic designs for managing children and their behaviours. This more moderate 'guidance approach', as discussed previously, is thought to empower students (Millei, 2011). The prevailing humanistic discourses offer the appeal of democratic relationships, where teachers offer choices and children are 'free' to make them (Millei, 2011). This discursive move in the early year's classroom, from adult control to more 'guiding' practices, has shifted the regulation that adults once performed, to the children, who now regulate their own conduct and the conduct of others (Millei, 2011). Ethan is positioned by Noah as a choice-maker, but makes it clear that Ethan's choice is not one that he would make.

The obligation to 'do' something and not be 'idle' is tacit. To be 'idle' is viewed as unconstructive and possibly suspicious. Children are often reminded in the early childhood classroom that they should find something to do. The notion of play has been created as "the work of childhood" (Ailwood, 2003, p. 293) and being idle, it could be suggested, is like being 'out of work' and unproductive to society. Idleness has an historical connection with the irrational in psychological and psychiatric discourses identified by Foucault (2006). Being occupied therefore is regarded as necessary and essential for being rational. Being idle is undesirable. Noah positions himself as someone who plays with friends constructively and appropriately, while Ethan's actions are unproductive and irrational. Dancing around alone, and being idle, positions Ethan outside the membership of the 'normal'.

Play discourses create category binaries and subject children in particular ways while excluding those children who do things differently. The discourses of play and playing with friends that circulate, and are repeatedly taken up by the children in classrooms, provide only limited possible ways of being. They provide no leeway in this discursive context for difference.

"We are all friends"

This piece of data came from a longer conversation about friends. When talking about Hugo (a child with a diagnosis), the children (without a diagnosis) make these comments.
Jon: "He doesn't do anythink."
Jake: "We don't play wiff him."
Me: "Is there any reason why you don't?"
Jon: "Yeah … you have to be friends but you don't have to play with them." (Field Notes, 21/11/12, S3, p. 116)

For Jon and Jake, being friends with everyone is compulsory, and it is one of the rules that children know they must follow in the classroom. The distinction made here by Jon is between 'being friends' and 'playing with friends'. Jon describes Hugo as not doing anything and Jake explains that they don't play with him. In what ways does Jon imagine that Hugo does nothing? Hugo is similarly positioned as somewhat 'idle', as Ethan was, in the earlier scenario. Jon may consider that Hugo doesn't do the kinds of things that other unmarked children do, and as he doesn't do what is recognised as the 'normal' things to do at preschool. What Hugo does do is regarded by Jon as nothing, or of no value, from his viewpoint, as a member of the 'normal' category. Hugo's idleness positions him outside the rational 'normal' membership.

The unmarked children refer to Hugo as a friend but they do not play with him. Nevertheless, regulatory discourses around friendship, legitimised in the classroom, inform them that they must label him a friend. Playing with friends is the taken for granted norm and as the boys don't play with Hugo, merely calling him a friend does not position him as a member of the norm. Co-operative play with friends is developmentally appropriate and progressive (Siraj-Blatchford, 2009). Friendships however are dynamic and sometimes volatile (Grieshaber & McArdle, 2010) but having friends, knowing who your friends are, and performing friendship by playing together, is central to category production, maintenance and recognisable membership.

"We are all friends here" is a testimony voiced regularly in the classroom, by both the teachers and children. Social competency is in part judged on ones' ability to play cooperatively with others. In addition, the development of a capacity to understand the emotions and thoughts of others, is deemed 'natural' during the preschool years (Gifford-Smith & Brownell, 2003), along with the development of theory of mind (Robson, 2012). The 'we are all friends' imperative and instruction in the classroom, shepherds children to become cooperative peers (Wohlwend, 2007), who can conceivably, with guidance (Millei, 2011), develop perspective taking and moral reasoning (Piaget, 1965). How do children position themselves and others in this discursive context where everyone is a friend? What work does this statement do? What are its effects? These words, used by children and teachers, have a particular meaning but what is observed in actions suggests that the statement 'we are all friends' has multiple meanings and modes of practice in the classroom. 'We are all friends' is not taken to mean that friends necessarily 'play' together. The words are created to promote 'inclusive' practice, but the children's actions are not always 'inclusive'.

Jon's comment: "You have to be friends but you don't have to play with them", could be understood to mean that you have to include but at the same time you can also exclude. It is the 'act' of 'playing', or participating in play that produces the 'normal' subject and category membership. It is in the performativity (Butler, 1997) of playing, where friends become recognisable members of the category, and from that position 'do' their maintenance work. Friendship, in this sense, is a performance that "must be understood not as a singular or deliberate act but rather as the reiterative and citational practice by which discourse produces the effects that it names" (Butler, 1993, p. 2). In many ways friendship comes from the 'act' of 'doing' friends. The act is political and the subject is discursively produced, not just in utterances but also in recurring bodily performances of friend play.

"They are 'friends' but we don't play with them"

> Jonathan (a child without a diagnosis) is standing next to the see-saw as Joseph and Angus (children without a diagnosis) are having their turn. Jonathan is waiting for his turn. Abbey (a child without a diagnosis) approaches the trio asking for a turn on the see-saw. She asks. "Who's in charge?" No one answers her. Jonathan seems to notice Abbey's unhappy face as she turns to move away and he calls to her: "Ok you can have a go." Abbey waits. Jasmine (a child with a diagnosis) approaches the see-saw and she places a hat from the dress ups on Angus's head. He immediately throws it away a little annoyed. Angus and Joseph then get off the see-saw and move away and Jonathan gets on. Jasmine quickly gets onto the other side and Jonathan says to Abbey: "You missed out." He shrugs his shoulders. After a quick turn Jonathan gets off and moves away. Abbey gets on the see-saw hesitantly opposite Jasmine. Jasmine enthusiastically starts up the see-saw. Abbey: "Stop … Stop … I don't want to do it with you I want … Jasmine … Stop."
> Abbey calls out to Angus nearby saying: "I don't want Jasmine on here with me." Her face contorted with anger, her checks flushed and her eyes narrowed.
> As noise levels rise a teacher arrives and says: "No one else is here waiting. She's your friend too. Jasmine is a great friend to everyone here."
> Abbey: "I don't want her! Jasmine go and get someone." Jasmine is not listening to Abbey, she is enjoying the see-saw going more quickly up and down and laughing. The teacher says: "Just gentle Jasmine, it will hurt you if you go down too hard."
> Abbey then says to the teacher: "Can you count to ten so she can get off."
> After the count, Jasmine gets off and Henry joins Abbey on the see-saw. Soon after the incident I asked Abbey why she did not want to ride on the see-saw with Jasmine and she replied: "She's not my friend." (Field Notes, 30/10/12, S3. pp. 33–34)

Sometimes the compulsory 'we are all friends' discourse is resisted and disrupted. As the see-saw scenario unfolded different subject positionings became visible. When Abbey moves to the see-saw and waits her turn, asking who might be in charge, she draws on regulatory discourses around the socially expected norms of turn taking and sharing at preschool (Dunn, 1988). She seems to understand that she is entitled to have her turn, but must wait for it. Jonathan, also drawing on this discourse, reassures Abbey that she can have a turn.

However, when Jasmine moves to the area and jumps onto the see-saw ahead of Abbey, the sanctioned social practice of turn taking is interrupted. Turn taking is considered developmentally appropriate, and those who do not engage in turn taking practices are routinely pathologised, and measured as socially incompetent and immature (Burman, 2008). Jasmine's action, in not waiting for a turn, is not disciplined or challenged by Jonathan, even though the children were observed on many occasions to negotiate and challenge for a turn on the see-saw. Jasmine's 'unruly', rule breaking behaviour is not confronted or reprimanded by Jonathan, as he positions her as Other, socially immature and incompetent. Directly addressing Jasmine's unreasonable action is avoided by Jonathan.

Abbey and Jonathan seem to share this understanding of Jasmine and tolerate her actions at this time. Keeping quiet about her transgressions maintains the social order of the classroom. Jonathan comments to Abbey: "You missed out." Jonathan's statement of resignation communicates to Abbey that she should just endure Jasmine's action. By waiting for her turn Abbey takes up the position of the recognisable 'normal'. Subsequently, when Abbey finally gets a turn on the see-saw, she does not want to ride the see-saw with Jasmine, saying that Jasmine is not her friend. The 'friend' discourse taken up here permits a level of exclusion, even though the statement 'we are all friends' seems to be a cultural mantra. Normative 'friend' discourses produce all children as friendly, good humoured, and getting along together (Grieshaber & McArdle, 2010). However, as mentioned before, it is in the playing and interacting and the performance of friends that the belonging and the category membership is created and recognised.

Jasmine is produced here as what Butler (1993) refers to as 'abject'; "those who are not yet 'subjects' but who form the constitutive outside of the domain of the subject" (p. xiii). The 'abject' is produced in the category boundary work; the 'abject' represents what it is not possible to be. The abjecting of another is thought to be a way of establishing an "I". Kristeva (1982) contends that in order to establish an "I", or one's own subjectivity, there is a separation of a part of oneself that is considered the "not-I". The endorsed discourses provide the ways of being the "I" and also ways of being that are the "not-I". "This expulsion is thought of as an expulsion of some aspect of the self" (Davies, 2004, p. 74). Jasmine's way of being, rushing in and not waiting her turn is rebuffed by the unmarked children as not a part of them.

The teacher steps in and attempts to guide Abbey, saying that Jasmine is a friend. But this does not change Abbey's desire to ride the see-saw with someone else, conceivably anyone else. Abbey's actions do not position her as a 'cooperative peer', and the teacher acts as a neutral guide providing support (Wohlwend, 2007) for Abbey in learning cooperation and possibly tolerance. This does not appear to work at this time. Abbey's rejection of and response to Jasmine is very loud and visceral, her actions and forceful words, created Jasmine as the 'abject' (Butler, 1993). The 'we are all friends' discourse is openly challenged and resisted by Abbey, and Jasmine is loudly excluded. Jasmine is positioned by Abbey as undesirable and best avoided and she moves to separate herself from Jasmine. Abbey is not constrained by the prevailing discourse on this occasion, and by her actions, may have been positioned as unsocial or immature in the classroom. Abbey, in her abjection of Jasmine, unsettled and challenged the boundary of the 'normal', and her membership in it. Instead of giving in, or moving on silently, she resisted her positioning by this performance. Although Abbey resisted her positioning, Jasmine's position remained as Other.

Using Reflexivity…

There were very few times in the field work where an unmarked child expressed so loudly and vehemently that they did not wish to 'play' with a child with a diagnosis. Did Abbey exclude Jasmine or was she just upholding the rules of the classroom? Viewing the classroom via 'inclusive' discourses, the exclusion of Jasmine seems very obvious, as I myself positioned Jasmine as Other. However reflecting on my position and viewing the encounter differently via the 'rule' discourses, Jasmine had broken the rules, and Abbey's role in loudly reminding everyone, could be viewed as possibly 'inclusive' as the rules apply to everyone. Thinking within other discourses I may have viewed Abbey's actions as immature or perhaps cruel towards Jasmine who is positioned as the marked child. Both girls could alternatively be presented as exercising power and struggling to represent themselves by resisting the positionings bestowed on them. When thinking otherwise, Abbey's claim to ride the see-saw with a partner of her choice might be viewed as acceptable and Jasmine's spontaneous desire to ride the see-saw understandable. My construction of this note however illustrates the multiple possibilities for interrogating what seemed 'immediately' and 'naturally' like an exclusionary act. I was drawn to this encounter as I think I saw it this way. Multiple ways of viewing and making meaning are not explored by educators(or by researchers) in the early childhood classroom, as only the familiar tales are told, as they work to re/legitimise the authority of the 'normal'.

Play and friendship discourses are actively re/produced in the early childhood classroom. They constitute cooperative play as developmentally appropriate and do not challenge the power relations that include and exclude. They constitute certain subject positions, such as 'playing with friends' as the norm, and 'playing alone' as the 'not normal'. Interplaying with this norm is the expectation to play in ways that are predictable, acceptable and in line with rules. Rules mark the boundaries of this category and establishes the criteria for category membership. Those who fall outside the boundaries are produced as not yet subjects (Butler, 1993) and assigned other positions. The position of the Other is described by the unmarked children as substantially different from them, the Other is 'not normal' and somewhat curious, 'unruly', and lacking reason. The Other, is created in friend discourses as undeveloped as a friend, without the skills needed to be a friend, a loner in play or pathologised as 'shy'. Unpredictable and unruly in their actions the Other is best avoided, as they are not a 'play' friend, since their unreasonable actions set them outside the domain of the rational subject. The limited understandings of each other, offered via friend discourses in the classroom, marginalise difference, and reinforce the power of the 'normal'.

Competitive Hegemonic Discourse

"I can make a better eel than you"

> Ben (a child without a diagnosis) has built, from a construction toy, what he calls an electric eel. The other boys make comments about how good it is, and then try to make one the same. James (a child with a diagnosis) approaches the table and standing next it, waits silently. The boys tell me that there is a rule that only four people can play at a table activity at one time. As I am sitting at the table I stand up so that James can sit down in my place. He sits down next to Ben. Ben's immediate response is: "I don't want to sit next to James!" (his face wrinkled and eyes narrowed). He gets up off the seat and stands at the end of the table, now standing and building. Ben continues to move his electric eel in front of the others. James now tries to make an eel like the one Ben has made. Charlie (a child without a diagnosis) now starts to stare at James, narrowing his eyes and wrinkling his face. Charlie stands and moves away from the table saying that he doesn't want to play this anymore and that he wants to play Zombies. (Field Notes, 10/7/12, S2, pp. 3–4)

Being able to create a recognisable object, to skilfully make things with your hands, using the equipment available, and then confidently label your creation, using interesting and 'mature' language, confirms Ben's membership in the 'normal' category. The early childhood classroom is a competitive place where being

capable and competent is desirable. When the other children admire Ben's creation and try to copy it, his membership is powerfully reinforced and their aspiration to show themselves as similar members is made visible. By their words and
actions they wish to be recognised in the same group as Ben. Access to the friendship group created around this table, involves positioning oneself as accomplished
within these competitive hegemonic discourses. Validating these positionings is
important and occurs through repeated performances (Butler, 1990) in the preschool day.

Hegemonic discourses are taken up by the unmarked children as they show
their own groups' domination over another group. As Blaise (2005) explains, "Hegemony is a process that perpetuates the status quo" (p. 57) and is a characteristic
in the social construction of gender, class, race, ability and so on. The domination
of one group over another, the 'able' over the 'not so able' and the maintenance
of this domination, governs and subordinates other ways of being (Blaise, 2005).
'Whiteness', as identified in critical race theory exercises power over other 'racial'
groups. In the same way as able-bodiedness is privileged over the non-ablebodied,
perpetuating the status quo and superiority of the 'normal'. The hegemony of
'ablebodiedness' is visible in the previous and following scenario. This discourse
prevails in the classroom, coercing and competing "to attain this type of 'normal'
and a desirable way of being" (Blaise, 2005, p. 58).

When James arrives at the table and stands next to it silently, the unmarked
children quickly draw on acceptable and sanctioned regulatory discourses, to prevent James from joining the table game. They discuss the particular rules about
the number of children allowed at any one time at an activity. These rules inadvertently countenance exclusionary practices. The unmarked children recite and
promote the rules to display and maintain their category membership. By telling
me, as the closest adult, the rules about the number of play participants, the unmarked children draw on the ubiquitous regulatory discourses, performing their
rule-following selves, while revealing the authority of their 'normal' group membership. It seems here, that the rules take priority, and are more powerful at this
table, than the notion of including James.

The power in this relation is in the knowledge of the rules, and how they
can be exercised. James is excluded using promoted and sanctioned regulations.
When I offer James my place at the table, Ben expresses loudly, verbally and non-
verbally: "I don't want to sit next to James". Ben moves to regain his category
membership by standing up at the end of the table away from James who is now
seated. Ben's move from sitting to standing leaves one seat vacant. His actions
show his desire to almost disassociate himself from James, produced here as the

'abject' (Butler, 1993), as Jasmine was in an earlier scene. By moving his electric eel in front of everyone at the table Ben reminds them of his eel building ability, and his continuing presence at the table. He maintains his membership credibility by not sitting next to James, who is considered outside this group.

Remarkably, James acts to ignore the exclusionary moves of the other children. He constructs his own eel, in an attempt to become recognisable as a member of the group. However, another child at the table, Charlie, joins Ben and protests against James' presence at the table. He gets up and moves away expressing his disconnection with James, by way of his facial expressions and actions, while at the same time demonstrating his association with Ben and the category of the 'normal'. Charlie and Ben's association and separation from James is made clear in this bodily shift. The effect of their association is the obvious exclusion of James. Being able to perform your category membership, and have everyone recognise it, by displaying your hegemonic positioning in the classroom, creates exclusionary effects for those positioned as Other.

Charlie and Ben's actions could also be read as an act of 'bullying'. Bullying as suggested by Davies (2011) reflects an overly fervent maintenance of the dominant moral order. Bullying from this perspective, is not considered as an individual characteristic but as a social process (Søndergaard, 2012) and is produced as a result of the negotiation and struggle for positioning in the social hierarchy of the peer culture. The unmarked children's recognisability (Butler, 1997) depends on their actions and performance of being a member of the 'normal'. However, by critiquing the accepted thinking around bullying as an individualising and pathologising act, Davies (2011) offers an alternative view as she considers bullying to be discursively constructed via the normative order. The bully acts to uphold the 'normal'. It is the power of the hegemonic 'normal' that is put under the spotlight here and not the individuals.

Using Reflexivity…

I felt repeatedly concerned about James and the relentless rejection he received from the children. They were just upholding the 'normal' weren't they? I felt empathy for James, I felt sorry for him as he was continually rejected and no one seemed to disrupt this. The children positioned him as not worthy of playing with. The adults in the setting seemed to consider that the boys had the right to make decisions about who they played with. They did, didn't they? They were not asked to play with James and their unkind words and actions were mostly not spoken about. Keeping the 'normal' intact meant that sometimes James had to be excluded. My feelings of empathy merely rein-

forced the hegemony of the 'normal'. I wondered if I had created the data this way, as I was so constrained within this empathetic discourse.

"I'm the king of the castle"

> Ben (child without a diagnosis) and Jack (child without a diagnosis) are in the sandpit digging and piling sand. They are covering up 'treasure'.
>
> Jack: "If the baddies come we keep still … stay still so they can't see us. Stay still … go. Stay still … go" (they are still in-between the digging and heaping)
>
> Ben: "Stay still … go dig … stay still … go."
>
> This interaction continues for several minutes.
>
> James (child with a diagnosis) approaches the sandpit to join in the play. He looks for a large spade like the ones Ben and Jack are using but can only find a smaller one as Ben and Jack have buried the rest during the game. He begins to help cover the toys with his small spade.
>
> Natalie (a teacher and James' mother) moves toward the sandpit and corrects the way that James is using the spade. She comments: "Use both hands James … yes that's better." James follows his mother's/teacher's directions. Natalie then moves away.
>
> This spade work continues for less than a minute more.
>
> Jack then stands on the top of the mound of toys covered in sand, raising his spade triumphantly above his head saying:
>
> "I'm the king of the castle … I'm the king of the castle."
>
> Ben quickly joins him on the top of the pile and he says:
>
> "I'm the king of the castle … and James is the dirty rascal."
>
> Ben and Jack repeat this several times with James standing next to the sand pile.
>
> James stands there very still looking at them. He waits and they stop the chant. He waits again for only about 30 seconds and then he leaves the sandpit. His eyes cast downward and his shoulder slumped. Ben and Jack keep playing as they had been before. (Field Notes, 25/7/12, S2, pp. 47–48)

Ben and Jack play together often. In this scenario they are burying treasure and drawing on their knowledge of baddies, who they understand are capable of stealing their treasure. To avoid the baddies they try to keep their bodies still, as they imagine the baddies are watching. This play scenario of 'baddies' and 'goodies' is built on culturally produced stories of good versus evil. In these types of play, "children use dominant cultural storylines such as goodies and baddies as a vehicle to produce their own identities" (Giugni, 2006, p. 97). The children perform their identity as 'goodies', hiding treasure from the 'baddies', in order to consolidate and maintain their relationship with each other. They seem to understand each other, and the game they are playing, and their friendship is built on these mutual understandings. This shared experience illustrates their shared membership, and their actions illuminate their boundary work to maintain their positioning in the category. Giugni (2006) contends that the performance of one's identity is enriched by the amount of 'cultural capital' one has, knows about, recites and can access (p. 99). Power is linked and woven through these performances and here the performances of gender and masculinity, are linked to what is culturally and socially acceptable.

When James approaches the sandpit he takes the available smaller spade and starts to dig. Ben and Jack make no comment. A teacher nearby, comments on the way James is holding his spade. Her comments are aligned with developmental and pedagogical discourses that produce knowledge about how children should perform particular activities, alongside the responsibility of the teacher to teach. James is marked and under surveillance and in need of remediation at all times. Curiously, the teacher makes no comment to the other children about their spade-holding technique.

The unmarked children stand *on top* of the mound of sand and reinforce their hierarchical positioning in taking up accepted hegemonic discourses. No challenge is made against them. These discourses support a knowledge and culture of dominance, and have the effects of exclusion and silence, on those who are not constituted as the same (Alloway & Gilbert, 1997). The unmarked bodies are raised up to be taller than James. They show their power, using the space available, to give them superiority over James, and mark a boundary between them and him. Higher and taller are enhanced positions, and more powerful, in this developmentally focused hegemonic context. The king stands *above* his subjects and *looks down* from his castle. Here Ben and Jack use their imagination, something encouraged in the early childhood classroom, however as Davies (1997) cautions "the power of imagination is not just to shape what is real, but to lend power differentially to real players, with very real effects" (p. 123). Jack and then Ben start to chant a traditional, centuries old rhyme, "The King of the Castle".

Ben and Jack use the rhyme to position themselves powerfully; they reinforce their domination and the protection of this territory, just as a king would do. They "take up these subjectivities within the discursively produced, patriarchal spaces available to them" (Alloway & Gilbert, 1997, p. 56). When they personalise the rhyme by including James' name, they emphasise his subordinate position as the 'rascal'. They repeat it several times staring *down* from their castle at James.

A spatial boundary for the 'normal' is demarcated. There is power invested in the children's boundary work of the territory around the sandcastle. The boy's spatial positioning or spatial tactics are techniques of discipline (Foucault, 1977) and these tactics are productive of particular subject positionings (Pike, 2008). The spatial terms illustrate how Jack and Ben use the area as a part of a battle for power, via the surveillance of James. The spaces, taken up and occupied both productively and negatively, produce subject positions for the children. As the unmarked children at the *top* of the sand pile *look down* on the marked child, they can discipline, keeping this site of surveillance. By employing these tactics they can maintain their position in the social hierarchy.

The use of traditional rhymes by children has been explored by Opie and Opie (1959) and they write, "The scraps of lore which children learn from each other are at once more real, more immediately serviceable, and more vastly entertaining to them than anything which they learn from grown-ups" (p. 1). Children use these rhymes, which pass from generation to generation, to both regulate their games and their relationships with each other, while in addition contributing to their 'cultural capital'. Rhymes are more than playthings to children and are a means of communication with each other (Opie & Opie, 1959). They recognise that traditional rhymes can have particular effects. Some are described as 'just for fun', others provide 'parody and impropriety', and yet others produce jeers, torment and guile. These particular rhymes are distinct from the 'nursery' rhyme recited to young children, and approved by adults. The more traditional rhymes were not particularly intended for adult ears and were not encouraged (Opie & Opie, 1959), or approved of, even though they are often associated with the traditional 'innocence' of childhood. A child's understanding of the words and their meaning, is underscored by the inherent value of knowing a rhyme, using the language, and reciting the words. The rhyme is considered a 'harmless' recitation, and a part of tradition and folklore, and as such, becomes active in the approved discourses of the classroom.

Following up on the recitation and performance of the rhyme, I asked some of the children about it and the other rhymes they frequently use in the classroom. I asked Jack about what the rhyme meant and he replied that he did not know and he appeared uncomfortable with my questioning (Field Notes, 1/8/12, S2, p. 75). Jack however seemed to understand the effects of the rhyme during the chanting of it. When I asked Ben about it he said that his brother sometimes says it. When I asked who his brother says it to, he said: "He says it to the ground" (Field Notes, 1/8/12, S2, p. 78). In another conversation when I asked Ruby about what the rhyme meant she said: "I tell you … umm … because it's not a nice word, I forgot but ummm…, that's not a good thing to … um … the teacher might saw it when they were goin' um … when we were there we won't steppin' on it (the mound of sand), they're not appropriam (appropriate?) to do it" (Field Notes, 1/8/12, S2, p. 79–80). Other children in other conversations shared this sentiment. There was a shared feeling that this rhyme was something that was allowed but also not allowed. Rhymes regularly heard among the children included; "Eeeny meany, miney, mow" which was used to remove unwanted players or extras from a group activity (Field Notes S2, 1/8/12), "Inky pinky ponky" used to make a choices about the inclusion and exclusion of others, and a group game called "Duck, duck, goose" was popular and played in all classrooms. In this game some of the children remained forever 'ducks', as they were never chosen to be the 'goose', the one who could get up, run and chase around the circle. At times a teacher would intervene to ensure that all were included (Field Notes, S2, 21/8/12). The effect of the rhymes seemed to be understood by all the children, but to talk about these effects, and the exclusion produced, generated a silence among them.

In reciting the rhyme and performing their hegemony on top of the sand pile, can Ben and Jack's actions be read as anything but 'bullying' and exclusion? Could it be imagined as innocent banter? Davies (2011) contends that within any moral and normative order, categorical difference and relations of power can become fixed. When they are fixed by the normative, the relations of power "instead of being mobile, allowing the participants to adopt strategies modifying them, remain blocked, frozen" (Foucault, 1997, p. 283). This 'fixedness' in the relations of power was observed many times in James' encounters with the unmarked children; he was often excluded on arrival, particularly if the other boys had arrived first and were already playing. He was often left out of competitive games, and on several occasions called a 'loser', as they said he couldn't play a game as well as them (Field Notes, S2, 22/8/12). Davies (2011) identifies that the bully is supported by the normative order, creating a fixed "state of domination" (p. 283). Power in this discursive context, is produced by the hegemonic discourses, taken up by the unmarked children. This enacted power remains unchallenged as it excludes and subordinates those positioned as not belonging.

Productive and Exclusive Normative Discourses

In the analysis within this chapter, developmental and psychological discourses are viewed to produce a pathologisation of the Other. As these understandings are taken up by the unmarked children, they regulate and position themselves as the 'normal'; bigger, older and mature, knowing the rules and how the preschool day operates. They position themselves as 'able' to have friends, performing friendship and playing with friends and sharing an understanding about how they are the same. These discourses also produce another subject position that is in opposition to the 'normal', as the available categories produce binary positionings. The classroom discourses position the 'not normal' as a concern, and in need of remediation and intervention.

As the 'normal' engages in this "coercive assignment", a disciplining (Foucault, 1977, p. 199) is imposed on the 'not normal'. Some of the disciplinary effects on the excluded, bring into focus the constructed notion of the potential threat of the 'not normal', characterised as unruly, unpredictable and possibly even dangerous, at the very least, to the social order. Foucault (1977) argues that the mechanisms of power that uphold the 'normal' produce a constant division between the normal and the abnormal to which every individual is subjected. The effect of the maintenance of the 'normal' shapes an avoidance of those individuals positioned as 'unreasonable' or 'irrational', because of their discursively created unruliness and unpredictability.

In the following chapter, the analysis of the 'inclusive' classroom turns to the non-human constituents of the 'normal'. During my time inside the classroom many questions emerged about the role of non-human actors, and their contribution to the re/production of subject positions. One example is a plastic 'wrist band' worn by teachers to signify their responsibility in caring for a marked child. This seemingly innocuous non-human actor, seized my attention as its presence on a teacher's wrist, made a statement about the teacher and the marked child that for me needed further interrogation. What discourse informed the wearing of it? How did they contribute to the 'normal'? How did this small non-human actor affect the children's subjectivities? The performance and meaning of the wristband, and other non-human actors in the classroom became all too obvious, and so the inclusion of the ensuing discussion became unavoidable.

References

Ailwood, J. (2003). Governing early childhood education through play. *Contemporary Issues in Early Childhood, 4*(3), 286–299.

Alloway, N., & Gilbert, P. (1997). Poststructural theory and classroom talk. In B. Davies & D. Corson (Eds.), *Encyclopedia of language and education—Volume 3: Oral discourse and education* (Vol. 3). Dordrecht: Kluwer Academic Publishers.

Australian Government Department of Education, Employment and Workplace Relations (AGDEEWR). (2009). *Belonging, being and becoming: The early years learning framework for Australia.* Retrieved June 6, 2010 from http://docs.education.gov.au/system/files/doc/other/belonging_being_and_becoming_the_early_years_learning_framework_for_australia.pdf

Australian Government Department of Education, Employment and Workplace Relations. (2013). *Inclusion and Professional Support Program Guidelines 2013–2016*. Retrieved October 7, 2014 from https://education.gov.au/inclusion-and-professional-support-program

Bagnato, S. J. (2005). The authentic alternative for assessment in early intervention: An emerging evidence based practice. *Journal of Early Intervention, 28*(1), 17–22.

Biemiller, A. (2003). Vocabulary: Needed if more children are to read well. *Reading Psychology, 24*(3), 323–335.

Birchwood, M., Spencer, E., & McGovern, D. (2000). Schizophrenia: Early warning signs. *Advances in Psychiatric Treatment, 6*(2), 93–101.

Blaise, M. (2005). *Playing it straight; Uncovering gender discourses in the early childhood classroom*. New York, NY: Routledge.

Blank, J., & Schneider, J. J. (2011). 'Use your words': Reconsidering the language of conflict in the early years. *Contemporary Issues in Early Childhood, 12*(3), 198–211.

Bloch, M. N., Swadener, B. B., & Cannella, G. S. (Eds.). (2014). *Reconceptualising early childhood care and education: Critical questions, new imaginaries and social activism*. New York, NY: Peter Lang.

Boivin, M., & Bierman, K. L. (Eds.). (2014). *Promoting school readiness and early learning: Implications of developmental research for practice*. New York, NY: The Guilford Press.

Bredekamp, S., & Copple, C. (1997). *Developmentally appropriate practice in early childhood programs serving children from birth through to age 8*. Washington, DC: National Association for the Education of Young Children.

Brown, W. (2006). *Regulating aversion: Tolerance in the age of identity and empire*. Princeton, NJ: Princeton University Press.

Burman, E. (2008). *Deconstructing developmental psychology*. East Sussex: Routledge.

Butler, J. (1990). *Gender trouble: Feminism and the subversion of identity*. New York, NY: Routledge.

Butler, J. (1993). *Bodies that matter: On the discursive limits of 'sex.'* New York, NY: Routledge.

Butler, J. (1997). *Excitable speech. A politics of the performative*. New York, NY: Routledge.

Campbell, S. (2005). Secret children's business: Resisting and redefining access to learning in the early childhood classroom. In N. Yelland (Ed.), *Critical issues in early childhood education* (pp. 146–163). Maidenhead: Open University Press.

Cannella, G. S. (1997). *Deconstructing early childhood education: Social justice & revolution*. New York, NY: Peter Lang.

Coplan, R. J., & Armer, M. (2007). A 'multitude' of solitude: A closer look at social withdrawal and nonsocial play in early childhood. *Child Development Perspectives, 1*(1), 26–32.

Dahlberg, G., Moss, P., & Pence, A. (2013). *Beyond quality in early childhood education and care: Languages of evaluation*. London: Routledge.

Davies, B. (1983). The role pupils play in the social construction of classroom order. *British Journal of Sociology of Education, 4*(1), 55–69.

Davies, B. (1989). *Frogs and snails and feminist tales: Preschool children and gender*. Sydney, NSW: Allen & Unwin.

Davies, B. (1993). *Shards of glass: Children reading and writing beyond gendered identities*. Sydney, NSW: Allen & Unwin.

Davies, B. (1997). The construction of gendered identity through play. In B. Davies & D. Corson (Eds.), *Encyclopaedia of language and education—Volume 3: Oral discourse and education* (Vol. 3). Dordrecht: Kluwer Academic Publishers.

Davies, B. (2004). Introduction: Poststructuralist lines of flight in Australia. *International Journal of Qualitative Studies in Education, 17*(1), 1–9.

Davies, B. (2011). Bullies as guardians of the moral order or an ethic of truths? *Children & Society, 25*, 278–286.

Dempsey, I. (2012). The use of individual education programs for children in Australian schools. *Australasian Journal of Special Education, 36*(1), 21–31.

Dunn, J. (1988). *The beginnings of social understandings.* Oxford: Blackwell.

Epstein, A. S. (2009). *Me, you, us: Social-emotional learning in preschool.* Ypsilanti, MI: High/Scope Press.

Foucault, M. (1972). *The archaeology of knowledge and the discourse on language.* New York, NY: Pantheon.

Foucault, M. (1977). *Discipline and punish: The birth of the prison.* London: Penguin.

Foucault, M. (1997). The ethics of the concern for self as a practice of freedom. In P. Rabinow (Ed.), *Michel Foucault: Ethics, subjectivity and truth* (pp. 281–302). New York, NY: The New Press.

Foucault, M. (2006). *History of madness.* Oxon: Routledge.

Gifford-Smith, M. A., & Brownell, C. (2003). Childhood peer relationships: Social acceptance, friendships and peer networks. *Journal of Social Psychology, 41*, 235–284.

Giugni, M. (2006). Conceptualising goodies and baddies through the narratives of Jesus and Superman. *Contemporary Issues in Early Childhood, 7*(2), 97–108.

Gordon, A. M., & Browne, K. W. (2007). *Beginning essentials in early childhood education.* Canada: Thomson Delmar Learning.

Graham, L. J., & Grieshaber, S. (2008). Reading dis/ability: Interrogating paradigms in a prism of power. *Disability & Society, 23*(6), 557–570.

Graham, L. J., & Slee, R. (2008). An illusory interiority: Interrogating the discourse/s of inclusion. *Educational Philosophy and Theory, 40*(2), 277–293.

Grieshaber, S., & McArdle, F. (2010). *The trouble with play.* New York, NY: Open University Press.

James, A., Jenks, C., & Prout, A. (1998). *Theorizing childhood.* Cambridge, UK: Polity Press.

Kearney, A., & Kane, R. (2006). Inclusive education policy in New Zealand: Reality or ruse? *International Journal of Inclusive Education, 10*(2–3), 201–219.

Kristeva, J. (1982). *Powers of horror: An essay on abjection.* New York, NY: Columbia University Press.

Laws, C. (2011). *Poststructuralism at work with marginalised children.* Sharjah: Bentham Science Publishers.

Laws, C., & Davies, B. (2000). Poststructuralist theory in practice: Working with 'behaviourally disturbed' children. *International Journal of Qualitative Studies in Education, 13*(3), 205–221.

Leavitt, R. L., & Power, M. B. (1997). Civilising bodies: Children in day care. In J. Tobin (Ed.), *Making a place for pleasure in early childhood education.* Michigan: Edward Brothers.

Löfdahl, A. (2010). Who gets to play? Peer groups, power and play in early childhood settings. In L. Brooker & S. Edwards (Eds.), *Engaging play* (pp. 122–135). Berkshire: Open University Press.

Macintyre, C. (2012). *Enhancing learning through play: A developmental perspective for early years settings* (2nd ed.). Oxon: Routledge.

MacLure, M., Jones, L., Holmes, R., & MacRae, C. (2012). Becoming a problem: Behaviour and reputation in the early years classroom. *British Education Research Journal, 38*(3), 447–471.

MacNaughton, G. (2005). *Doing Foucault in early childhood studies: Applying poststructural ideas.* Abingdon, Oxon: Routledge.

McDevitt, T. M., & Ormrod, J. E. (2007). *Child development and education* (3rd ed.). Upper Saddle River, NJ: Pearson.

Millei, Z. (2005). The discourse of control: Disruption and Foucault in an early childhood classroom. *Contemporary Issues in Early Childhood, 6*(2), 128–139.

Millei, Z. (2011). Thinking differently about guidance: Power, children's autonomy and democratic environments. *Journal of Early Childhood Research, 10*(1), 88–99.

Nolan, A., & Kilderry, A. (2010). Postdevelopmentalism and professional learning: Implications for understanding the relationship between play and pedagogy. In L. Brooker & S. Edwards (Eds.), *Engaging play* (pp. 108–121). Berkshire: Open University Press.Odom, S. L., Buysse, V., & Soukakou, E. (2011). Inclusion for young children with disabilities: A quarter century of research perspectives. *Journal of Early Intervention, 33*(4), 344–356.

Odom, S. L., & Wolery, M. (2003). A unified theory of practice in early intervention/early childhood special education: Evidence-based practices. *The Journal of Special Education, 37*(3), 164–173.

Opie, I., & Opie, P. (1959). *The lore and language of school children.* London: Oxford University Press.

Paugh, P. C., & Dudley-Marling, C. (2011). Speaking deficit into (or out of) existence: How language constrains classroom teacher's knowledge about instructing diverse learners. *International Journal of Inclusive Education, 15*(8), 819–833.

Piaget, J. (1959). *The language and thought of the child* (3rd ed.). London: Routledge & Kegan Paul.

Piaget, J. (1965). *The moral judgment of the child.* New York, NY: The Free Press.

Pike, J. (2008). Foucault, space and primary school dining rooms. *Children's Geographies, 6*(4), 413–422.

Porter, L. (2008). *Young children's behaviour: Practical approaches for caregivers and teachers* (3rd ed.). Marrickville, NSW: Elsevier Australia.

Robinson, K. H., & Jones-Diaz, C. (2006). *Diversity and difference in early childhood education: Issues for theory and practice.* New York, NY: Open University Press.

Robson, S. (2012). *Developing thinking and understanding in young children: An introduction for students.* Oxon: Routledge.

Rose, N. (1999). *Governing the soul: The shaping of the private self* (2nd ed.). London: Free Association Books.

Schneider, J. (2002). Reflexive/diffractive ethnography. *Cultural Studies <=> Critical Methodologies, 2*(4), 460–482.

Shildrick, M. (2005). The disabled body, genealogy and undecidability. *Cultural Studies, 19*(6), 755–770.

Siraj-Blatchford, I. (2009). Early childhood education (ECE). In T. Maynard & N. Thomas (Eds.), *An introduction to childhood studies* (pp. 172–184). London: Sage.

Slee, R. (2011). *The irregular school: Exclusion, schooling and inclusive education.* Oxon: Routledge.

Smith, P. (2004). Whiteness, normal theory and disability studies. *Disability Studies Quarterly, 24*(2). http://dsq-sds.org/article/view/491/668

Søndergaard, D. M. (2012). Bullying and social exclusion anxiety in schools. *British Journal of Sociology of Education, 33*(3), 355–372.

Soto, L. D., & Swadener, B. B. (2002). Toward liberatory early childhood theory, research and praxis: Decolonizing a field. *Contemporary Issues in Early Childhood, 3*(1), 38–66.

Spencer, E. J., Goldstein, H., Sherman, A., Noe, S., Tabbah, R., Ziolkowski, R., & Schneider, N. (2012). Effects of an automated vocabulary and comprehension intervention: An early efficacy study. *Journal of Early Intervention, 34*(4), 195–221.

Talay-Ongan, A. (2001). Early intervention: Critical roles of early childhood service providers. *International Journal of Early Years Education, 9*(3), 221–228.

UNICEF. (1989). *Convention on the rights of the child.* New York, NY: UNICEF.

Verenikina, I., Vialle, W., & Lysaght, P. (2011). *Understanding learning and development.* Macksville, NSW: David Barlow Publishing.

Vygotsky, L. S. (1986). *Thought and language* (A. Kozulin, Trans.). Cambridge: MIT Press.

Walkerdine, V. (1981). Sex, power and pedagogy. *Screen Education, 38,* 14–24.

Walkerdine, V. (1988). *The mastery of reason: Cognitive development and the production of rationality.* London: Routledge.

Walkerdine, V. & the Girls and Mathematics Unit, Institute of Education. (1989). *Counting girls out.* London: Virago Press.

Walkerdine, V. (1993). Beyond Developmentalism? *Theory & Psychology, 3*(4), 451–469.

Wasik, B. A., Bond, M. A., & Hindman, A. (2006). The effects of a language and literacy intervention on head start children and teachers. *Journal of Educational Psychology, 98*(1), 63–74.

Weisleder, A., & Fernald, A. (2013). Talking to children matters: Early language experience strengthens processing and builds vocabulary. *Psychological Science, 24*(11), 2143–2152.

Wohlwend, K. E. (2007). Friendship meeting or blocking circle? Identities in the laminated spaces of a playground conflict. *Contemporary Issues in Early Childhood, 8*(1), 73–88.

Wood, E. (2010). Reconceptualizing the play-pedagogy relationship: From control to complexity. In L. B. S. Edwards (Ed.), *Engaging play* (pp. 11–24). Berkshire: Open University Press.

4

Exploring the Role of Non-Human Actors in the Production and Maintenance of the 'Normal'

Attention to non-human actors, and how they contribute to the construction of the 'normal', while at the same time further marking the diagnosed child in the 'inclusive' classroom, is the focus of this chapter. Foucault's (1977) exploration of the effects and disciplinary power of architecture and other created physical spaces, provides the stimulus for this section of work. It brings into focus the material and non-human world and the power relations with the human world. From this perspective, physical things and actions take on meaning and become objects of knowledge within discourse and context (Hook, 2001). As Foucault (1972) argues, nothing exists outside discourse where meaning and meaningful practice is constructed. Continuing with this postulating, Foucault appreciates that we can only have knowledge of 'things' if they have meaning which is constructed in discourse, as it is not the 'things' themselves that produce the knowledge. Discursive formations produce the objects about which they speak (Dreyfus & Rabinow, 1982, p. 61). Objects and 'things' are discussed here, as they produce meanings within the 'inclusive' early childhood classroom. "Attention to non-human others—the physical world, the materials—that mingle in early childhood practices is the key" (Pacini-Ketchabaw, 2012, p. 155) to this chapter. Non-human actors produce meaning about human subjects, creating a network that actively and powerfully shape subject positionings.

The work of Latour (2005) and the ideas underpinning Actor Network Theory (ANT) provide a starting point for this analysis. The ideas of 'ANT' are used as a 'toolkit', or a 'sensibility' (Laws, 2004, p. 157) but there is no intention to present a complex theoretical consideration of this field. This analysis merely draws on some of the concepts of ANT. The objective is to shift understandings of the classroom, thus making it thinkable to "open up the possibility of seeing, hearing, sensing and then analysing the social life of things—and thus of caring about, rather than neglecting them" (Mol, 2010, p. 255). Mol (2010) critiques ANT, arguing that it is not a theory in the true sense as it makes no "attempt to hunt for causes: the aim is rather to trace effects" (p. 261). Yet its adaptability lends itself to the tracing of effects by examining both human and non-human actors, as they act in the world, their associations with other actors, and their acquired meaning through the relations in the networks in which they are engrained. As Mol (2010) suggests researchers involved in 'ANT' are amateurs of reality, who in their theoretical repertoire, allow themselves to be attuned to the world and learn to be affected by it. 'ANT' helps to train "researcher's perceptions and perceptiveness, senses and sensitivity" (Mol, 2010, pp. 261–262). Actors act, they can make a difference, they do things. They join with other actors to form networks acquiring meaning through associations and relations. They are afforded the ability to act by what is around them in the network, and if they are not being enacted by others, they will stop working (Mol, 2010).

In addition, Barad's (2007) understandings of the "intra-activity of the material-discursive relations that encompass early childhood education" (Pacini-Ketchabaw, 2012, p. 155) offers an approach for further exploration. In early childhood education, the work of Lenz-Taguchi in considering the human and material world (Hultman & Lenz-Taguchi, 2010; Lenz-Taguchi, 2010) borrows Barad's theorising about the intra-activity of human and non-human relations and the formed assemblages that intermingle between "all living organisms and the material environment such as things and artefacts, spaces and places that we occupy and use in our daily practices" (p. xiv). Lenz-Taguchi (2010) maintains that it is not only humans that have agency. Objects and materials can also be appreciated as being a part of the "a performative production of power and change in an intertwined relationship of intra-activity with other matter and humans" (p. xiv). Materials and the non-human become important players in any examination of the social world, as they are active agents, constructed in discourse, and as such, contribute to the construction of discourse and reality.

Deleuze and Guattari (1987) stress that bodies, both human and non-human, work concurrently to form assemblages, which are an arrangement of bodies in constant relation (Pacini-Ketchabaw, 2012). Using the concept of intra-action (Barad, 2007) we see that these bodies form assemblages in relation to each other and the "elements of the assemblage do not necessarily precede the assemblage; they emerge through it" (Pacini-Ketchabaw, 2012, p. 156). Barad (2007) theorises that in intra-action there is a mutual entanglement.

Non-human actors, as they form assemblages, produce relations of power, making connections in the classroom. As they do this, they perform some of the category boundary work around the 'normal'. Without the lens of poststructuralism, the constitutive power of actors and their networks could be passed over as unremarkable. Non-human actors are most often taken for granted as 'just things' that have no effect. But as Latour (2005) and others argue, studies in social sciences need to see objects and things as "interesting, variegated, uncertain, complicated, far-reaching, heterogeneous, risky, historical, local, material and networky" (p. 158). The non-human actors examined here, are only some of the actors in these networks. It is not feasible to consider all the possible non-human actors in their relations in the complex setting of a classroom. Therefore, I make visible by noting just a small number of non-human actors and the effects of their mutual entanglement within this space.

'Everyday' non-human actors produce and are produced by discourses within the classroom that uphold the 'normal'. Material things are seen here as performative, intra-acting with other things and humans, emerging as an assemblage to 'do' things, to include and to exclude, and to regulate participation. These material things in assemblages compel and constrain activity.

'Everyday' Non-Human Actors

The Timetable as a Non-Human Actor

The 'timetable' compels and denies activity at particular times in the classroom day. Foucault (1977) describes this organisation of the child's institutional life as 'disciplinary time'. The timetable, as a non-human actor, performs disciplinary work by establishing rhythms, imposing particular activities and regulating with cycles of repetition. The timetable allows and controls the activity of subjects in the classroom. The discipline of time requires both the correct use of time alongside the correct use of the body (Foucault, 1977). The teachers' task is to 'civilise' children and their bodies, as the child's body is considered unruly, disruptive, in need of direction (Leavitt & Power, 1997) according to developmental perspectives. Time can be used to 'normalise' the child, move them as individuals in a group, and create a desired homogeneity in the classroom.

The classroom's daily practices are dictated by the timetable and revolve around routines. Leavitt and Power (1997) argue that routinised control of children's bodies "is crucial to the order and efficiency of the classroom" (p. 44). As well as monitoring and restraining a child's body, the timetable enforces that children must learn to defer gratification, as the timetable tells the children that they cannot always do what they want. The timetable teaches rules of management and codes of conduct that contribute to the social order (Leavitt & Power, 1997). Time to arrive, time for toileting and washing one's hands, time to eat, time to play outside/inside, time to nap: "Children must adapt their bodies to the temporal order of the day" (Leavitt & Power, 1997, p. 46). The timetable as a non-human agent produces and regulates how to act 'normal'. The clock-educator-child assemblages are coupled with the operation of practice. The practice moments of the timetable, observed in the classrooms, create assemblages of ideas, genetic material, things and matter (Pacini-Ketchabaw, 2012) and they connect in their intra-action and are transformed by it as a "mutual constitution of entangled agencies" (Barad, 2007, p. 33).

Bodies are not always 'civilised' in the same way or at the same time, and the timetable is not always appreciated by all the children in the same way. Pacini-Ketchabaw (2012) examined how the clock structures the classroom day and both produces and enables certain kinds of practices. Timetables produce a 'norm' by regulating actions. The assemblages of human and non-human emerge, as connections are made in an "ongoing materialisation" (Barad, 2007, p. 151). The timetable, and its emergence with human actors, produces the becoming subjectivities of those who follow time, and also those who deviate and do not follow time. Those who deviate emerge in this intra-action as outside the 'normal'. In the early childhood classroom, children whose bodies are subjected as 'uncivilised' by the disciplinary power of the timetable, are often under the surveillance of teachers, who aim to remediate and normalise them. This is made possible via the enactment and re-enactment of the timetable and its routines.

Time informs everyone in the classroom about what they should be doing and where they should be doing it. The unmarked children often refer to the 'right time' to do things. The right time to play, to pack away, to have story, to listen, to wash hands, to toilet, to eat and so on. The marked child is often talked about as not knowing or adhering to the 'right time'. Time is central to how the classroom is understood, structured and enacted (Pacini-Ketchabaw, 2012). These understandings appeared to be shared in the classroom. The subject who can follow the time is produced as the 'normal'. There are times when some members of the 'normal' disregard the time, but they are quickly disciplined by fellow members of the category. This disciplinary act involves tapping into the authority of the teacher and telling the teacher about the transgressions of this 'naughty' child, who does not follow the clock. In this way, order can be re-established, and the 'normal' maintained.

The child with a diagnosis conversely is not regulated by the group in this way. The 'rule of time' is enacted differently for the marked child. As the timetable intra-acts with the marked child, it "emerges as something different and it affords the conditions for the emergence of certain bodies and not others" (Pacini-Ketchabaw, 2012, p. 158). The timetable affords different rules for the marked child, and in this intra-action different subjectivities materialise, creating exclusions. Sam, a child with a diagnosis, has time outside when others cannot, and he eats at times when others do not. Michael, a child with a diagnosis, can have more time to prepare for pack away time, he is given timed warnings about when it will occur (Field Notes, S1). Ethan, a child with a diagnosis, can have time in the morning inside while others must play outside (Field Notes, S2). The time to pack away is often not adhered to by Hugo, a child with a diagnosis, but this is not disciplined in the same way as the unmarked children discipline each other, and his emergence with the timetable produces him as Other (Field Notes, S3). The timetable produces practices that enable and constrain and its ongoing materialisation with other bodies, human and non-human, is a process creating differential effects on different bodies in the classroom (Pacini-Ketchabaw, 2012).

Morning Tea Time

Sam (a child with a diagnosis) is created as following a different timetable.

Me: "If you are hungry can you eat when you want to eat?"

All: "No."

Fleur (a child without a diagnosis): "You have to eat at morning tea time but he [Sam] can eat anytime he wants."

Me: "Why?"

Fleur: "Because … he … doesn't … talk." (says this slowly and precisely).

Jenna (a child without a diagnosis): "Because … it's … not … the … time." (emphasises each word)

Me: "What about you Frances? Would you like to eat when you feel hungry? Why can't you?"

Frances (a child without a diagnosis): (shakes her head) "Cause it's *not* the time." (Field Notes, 21/5/12, S1, p. 56)

The unmarked children, prompted by my questioning, discuss Sam's deviation from the routine of the timetable. They talk about morning tea time and how it has nothing to do with being hungry. The timetable, as a disciplinary practice, is taken up by the unmarked children as they position themselves as knowing that you cannot eat when you are hungry, you must wait for the 'right' time, 'You have to eat at morning tea time'. The timetable, as a non-human constituent, intra-acts with Sam, differently positioning him as Other, because 'he can eat anytime he wants'. As a non-human actor, the time/clock while regulating the 'normal', also marks the 'not normal'. The tyranny of time has been debated for centuries (Rose & Whitty, 2010). Foucault (1984) discussed the "governance of time and its perpetuation of normalised subjectivities" (Rose & Whitty, 2010, p. 260). Time has been judged to be "an invasive standardisation of people" (Rose & Whitty, 2010, p. 260). Early childhood classrooms, along with school systems, where a modern industrial conception of time (Rose & Whitty, 2010) prevails, employ timetables to keep people and things ordered, regulated and normalised. Time and keeping time, are discursive cultural orientations that produce particular subjectivities, which are individualised and disciplined.

Sam as a subject, emerges in an intra-action with the timetable, as disruptive and resistant to business as usual. As the timetable contributes to meanings in the discursive context, it "is involved in making and remaking boundaries" (Pacini-Ketchabaw, 2012, p. 158), Sam is positioned by the unmarked children as not conforming to the 'tyranny of the timetable'. He is not disciplined by it, in the same way they are. The 'normal' are identified when the timetable is taken up as a fundamental element of appropriate classroom practice; the timetable is a marker of belonging (Pacini-Ketchabaw, 2012). Those who do not follow the timetable emerge in the process as not belonging. Belonging and/or not belonging are concerns for 'inclusive' education policy and practice.

Packing Away Time

Packing away time is an authoritative time of the preschool day. Time governs actions and forms assemblages with the human actors, positioning them as a certain kind of being.

> Me: "Can you tell me what is happening in the photo?"
> Patrick: (a child without a diagnosis)" I know … well it's time to pack, it's time to pack up and Michael (a child with a diagnosis) likes playing with his computer and he won't pack it away and Gail's (teacher) getting him to pack it away and he's sad." (Michael is crying).

Me: "Why doesn't he like packing away?"

Patrick: "Well he doesn't like packing away his note book, he doesn't like packing away the computer, he doesn't like packing away his trains. He doesn't like packing up every, anything."

Me: "Do you cry if you don't like to pack up?"

Patrick: "No."

Me: "So why do you think Michael cries?"

Patrick: "Cause he doesn't want to get his stuff packed up. One time he cried when he wasn't using his shop and he went 'Oh no where's my shop?' (using a whining voice) and the teachers told him that Anne (teacher) had packed it away."

Me: "Do you think all children are sad at packing away time?"

Patrick: "Well some are … (thinking) … well no … no only Michael." (Field Notes, 18/5/12, S1, pp. 72–73)

Patrick positions himself as being able to perform the pack away routine. In contrast he has experienced firsthand Michael's distress when he is asked to pack away. He says that Michael is the only one who has trouble with this time of the day, "well no, no only Michael". The prevailing discourses, about time and timetables that are taken up by Patrick at pack away time, have the effect of subjecting Michael as different and unnecessarily emotional. Patrick is interested in Michael's response to pack away time, as he can give many examples of the things that Michael does not like to pack away. Michael's response to pack away time positions him as Other, not following the timetable, and being over-emotional and unreasonable at the same time. Patrick, as the member of the 'normal', considers that being 'sad' is unwarranted, as no one else responds this way in this situation, and this positions Michael as developmentally immature and unruly. The timetable, as a time/people regulating non-human actor, along with its associated discursive practices, forms an assemblage with the children, and in this intra-action, become mutually entangled and transformed in the process. Michael and Patrick's subjectivities are materialised and constituted by the timetable, as it shapes certain bodies, meanings and boundaries (Pacini-Ketchabaw, 2012). As the timetable forms an assemblage and intra-acts with Patrick, he emerges as the 'normal', a disciplined body, a body who can pack away. However, in its assemblage with Michael, he emerges as the unreasonable and in need of correction.

The Physical Space as a Non-Human Actor

The early childhood classroom is an institutional space, and an architectural structure, that is designed with the education, surveillance, control and regulation of the young child in mind. Young children are deemed to be in need of civilising and disciplining. Foucault's consideration of physical spaces and regulatory practices in *Discipline and Punish* (1977) provides significant insight. The 'civilising' work done in the classroom imitates what Foucault (1977) refers to as "the means of correct training" (p. 170) where disciplinary techniques such as hierarchical observation, normalisation and examination are employed. The preschool classroom is a mechanism for training, authorising surveillance at all times, in order to maintain the 'civilising' and 'normalising' work. Disciplinary techniques require enclosure, a place "closed in upon itself" so it can produce uniform individuals within its bounded space (Foucault, 1977, p. 141). The preschool is enclosed, surrounded by high fences and the classroom designed to contain its occupants within its walls and closed doors if needed. The physical space is a non-human actor as it plays its part in the disciplinary machine, using enclosure, partitioning and surveillance (Foucault, 1997), as a place where occupants are on view, to be gazed upon and regulated.

Preschool classrooms are divided into various activity areas, which are claimed to encourage individual or small group encounters. Areas are partitioned with low shelves to allow for supervision and surveillance. This partitioning controls the movement of bodies around the room and also allows for the individual to sometimes be on their own so that they can be analysed, assessed and compared. These areas also assign ways to act, and to be, as "teachers unceasingly use the power of the gaze to ensure that children are doing *what* they should be doing and *when* they should be doing it" (Leavitt & Power, 1997, p. 67, author's emphasis). This also includes *where* they should be doing it. Leavitt and Power (1997) refer to the teacher's panoptic urge to control everything that goes on in the classroom. The disciplinary power of the architectural space of the preschool supports this control, as it 'makes' individuals and works to 'train' individuals (Foucault, 1977, p. 170) who can be compared, normalised and corrected if and when necessary.

Spatial practices in the classroom are regarded as disciplinary techniques that are underpinned and legitimised by specific rationalities (Pike, 2008). What are the rationalities that legitimise the spaces and their use? Classroom spaces are produced by, and produce social meanings derived from rational 'norms' (Goodfellow, 2012). The space, and the physical equipment in the space, assign particular ways of being and doing that are sanctioned in child development and pedagogical early childhood discourses; so toys are age appropriate, furniture is size specific, spaces are designed for smaller bodies and movement is monitored by barriers, doors and gates. Rationalities of safety, child development and child-centeredness prevail and inform the social construction and reconstruction of the space. But how do these rationalities affect the children's subjectivities, and how are those who 'resist', or do not conform, positioned?

The organisation of space, shapes and interacts with the conduct of the children and the teachers (Pike, 2008). The space of the preschool, including the fences, the walls, the doors and the partitions, as non-human actors, are discursively produced and act to discipline and control. Each space is created with its own and multiple meanings, and there are no neat and single or fixed narratives about space as "spaces are encountered in and through embodiment, in and through practices, in and through particularly located everyday lives" (Horton & Kraftl, 2006, p. 85). There are discursively produced ways to be and act in the spaces in the early childhood setting; inside, outside, on the story mat, in the bathroom, at the activity tables, in the block corner, in the home corner, in the sandpit, up the tree, on the climbing frame. It is in the intra-action of the human and the multiple non-human spaces of the classroom that subjectivities emerge.

As children intra-act with the space they build relationships with the material and the social spaces in which they live (Millei & Cliff, 2014). The space provides for a host of animate and inanimate things and is both a producer and enabler of certain ways of being and practice. In these spaces, bodies are transformed as they become entangled agencies (Barad, 2007). The spaces are enacted by the actors and are not pre-existing, they emerge as they create meaning and subjectivities. The classroom 'story mat' emerges as a place of quiet attention, and the children who form an assemblage with this non-human actor, emerge from the process as attentive story listeners. The physical space of the preschool as "an actor does things" (Mol, 2010, p. 255) producing ways of being in that space. Spaces both enable and inhibit action by de/mobilising particular discourses and prescribing certain actions.

The role and function of space, in the production and reproduction of difference in the classroom, became significant when examining inclusionary discourses. Spaces are not neutral places, as they are closely associated with the governing values and norms of the classroom and society (Armstrong, 2003). Space works to sustain ruling discourses by reinforcing the "spatialisation of otherness" (Masschelein & Verstraete, 2012, p. 1194). This space, created for the Other, has been observed in the history of the West where "intentionally designed spaces were created for people who were considered refractory, special or abnormal" (Masschelein & Verstraete, 2012, p. 1194). These spaces work to legitimise the circulating discourses of the 'normal', while confirming the difference of the Other. They are not impartial spaces.

The timetable, as well as the physical spaces, work together to produce and discipline the 'normal' in the classroom. The unmarked children take up the discourses that produce and are produced by the timetable and spatial ordering. They maintain the rules and try to regulate others who may deviate from the timetable routines and temporal spatial arrangements (Davies, 1983). However, as discussed with the timetable, the unmarked children rarely try to regulate the marked child and their use of classroom spaces. The unmarked children seldom enact an explicit 'disciplining' on the marked child, as they do with members of the 'normal'. Instead membership of the 'normal' is maintained by separating from or avoiding the marked child. The marked child is out of place in this space, and out of time/rhythm in this timetable. Their intra-action with the non-human actors creates them outside the material-discursive apparatus (Pacini-Ketchabaw, 2012) of the timetable and the organised spaces that constitute certain boundaries of ways to 'be'. The spaces and the timetable are not considered external forces that operate on the children's bodies from the outside, rather, they are components of the material-discursive practices that are "inextricable from the bodies that are produced and through which power works its productive effects" (Barad, 2007, p. 230). The child with a diagnosis emerges in this process, subjected and positioned as Other, in and through their encounter with the spaces of the classroom and the practices regulated through the timetable.

Category boundaries are maintained by the children as they talk about the *when, what* and *where* things happen in the preschool day. These are important things to 'know' and if you 'don't know', or don't follow, you are subjected as different either as younger, 'little' or less experienced or perhaps seen as 'new' to the preschool. The timetable and spaces for activity provide the children with meaning about themselves as the 'normal' and Others, about inclusion and exclusion. Some subjectivities that emerge, in the human and non-human intra-action, know when and where to do things, and become the attentive, quiet, agreeable and docile subjects (Foucault, 1977) with minimal resistance. But other subjectivities, are not produced, or are produced differently, and as they materialise in this intra-action, they are Othered.

'Special' Non-Human Actors

'Special' non-human actors are so named, as they operate in the classroom, as objects specific for the child with a diagnosis and are part of the special education mechanism that functions in this space. These 'special' actors vigorously produce knowledge about the children and about how to be a 'right' or 'not so right' subject. They construct the conditions of possibilities, structuring the arrangements in the classroom, giving meaning to how humans in the setting are understood, organised and how they are expected to act. How these objects produce, enable and maintain certain positions within the discourse is underscored in the data to follow. My interest lies not in the objects themselves, by themselves, but in their performative aspects (Pacini-Ketchabaw, 2012). What do these objects do, what is their function in this context, how do they form assemblages and relationships with other non-human and human bodies?

The Wrist Band

> It is indoor activity time and I move into the room. Sam (a child with a diagnosis) is crying loudly and moving restlessly around the room. He moves to the door banging on it and trying to open it. The teacher picks him up and moves him back into the room. The director informs me that Sam needs to have a teacher with him always as he has tried to escape. The teacher responsible for him must wear a wrist band to show that they are 'with' Sam at that time. The band is transferred from teacher to teacher every half an hour. (Field Notes, 30/4/12, S1, p. 3) (Watson, Millei, & Petersen, 2015)

Sam's loud crying and restiveness positions him as 'disruptive', concerning and different in this classroom. Loud noises and lots of uncontrolled movements are discouraged in the early childhood classroom. Settled work and focused activity play are fostered and promoted as practices that inspire learning. Sam appears to be attempting to leave the classroom, to go outside, when he should be inside. The unmarked children know they should be inside.

The centre director describes Sam as a 'flight risk' and an 'escapologist' (Field Notes) and, informed by safety discourses, enlists the support of teaching staff to act as protectors or guards for Sam (Watson *et al.*, 2015). They wear a plastic coloured wrist band to signify this position. The wrist band has a legitimised authority, as it protects Sam from his potential erratic actions and protects the teachers from the risk of losing him. The teachers engage in a hand-over of the wrist band and the associated responsibility, every half an hour during the preschool day. The teachers more than once expressed their reluctance to take up this position as Sam's guard.

> Edith: "I have had him for half an hour."
> Chris: "I had him just before you."
> And later another teacher comments after being given the wrist band:

Anne: "Odette, how come every time you hand him over to me he has a dirty nappy. Don't you have a sense of smell?" (Field Notes, 11/5/12, S1, p. 35)

Sam is positioned as a responsibility that the teachers do not wish to have. They resist being positioned as his guard and seem to want to avoid other responsibilities like changing his nappy. Sam is produced as an 'abject' object, unhappily passed around from one teacher to another.

The wrist band represents Sam's dangerous status as a 'flight risk' (Watson *et al.*, 2015). As mentioned before, dangerousness has been historically constructed as an internal quality of the pathological individual (Rose, 1999). Rose (1998) proposes however that more recently the notion of dangerousness has been replaced by the discourse of risk, as risk is thought to not harbour derogatory connotations. Risk assessment is thought to avoid or minimise the danger. The wrist band has been introduced to reduce the risks associated with Sam, as he has been assessed as a risk to himself and to others. The wrist band manages the risk as "risk thinking tames chance, fate and uncertainty" (Rose, 1998, p. 180). But does this risk management of Sam keep everyone safer? Rose (1998) argues that the discourse around risk "not only generates but exacerbates the very fears it claims to secure against: a population suffused with fears about 'the risk of risk'" (p. 181).

Sam does not appear to follow the routines and timetables. In the classroom context teachers are informed by discourses that promote the importance of program planning and schedule following. These are regarded as crucial for children's learning (Leavitt & Power, 1997). Children must be encouraged to follow the timetables and teachers position themselves as responsible for assisting all children to consistently follow the routines. Sam's resistance to inside time/space and outside time/space is observed regularly. The inside space, the walls and the locked door, provide a space to contain Sam. His actions need to be contained, as he needs to learn to follow the timetable, like the 'normal', and the 'inside' space performs this role. He needs to remain on time, and in place, for inclusion to work. The space of the classroom, the space outside, and the wrist band worn by the teacher, create a composition of bodies (Pacini-Ketchabaw, 2012), human and non-human, that act to restrict, contain and separate Sam. In this intra-action, Sam emerges as the unpredictable and unreasonable, a risk to the classroom, to the children and to the teachers.

It is not just Sam's actions that position him in need of correction and containment but also his diagnosis. The wearing of the wrist band is enabled by the diagnosis and his stated escaping behaviours. The wrist band contributes to Sam's management, as characteristics of his diagnosis judge him to have behaviour problems, making him difficult to control (Maskey, Warnell, Parr, Le Couteur, & McConachie, 2013). The wrist band signifies the careful containment of Sam, 'for his own safety', while at the same time suggesting his unruly, unreasonable and irrational positioning. As an actor, it communicates the risk posed by Sam to the social order of the classroom; the risk of disrupting the routine, the teaching and learning day, and the safety of others. The teachers and the wrist band work together to keep Sam in check, while also powerfully contributing to his positioning as Other.

The need for order and predictability is shaped by developmental discourses, and as already mentioned, the need for civilising (Tobin, 1997). Sam's 'disruption' in the classroom, his loud crying and banging on the door and the 'threat' of his escape, are read as a 'control' problem, a problem resulting from Sam's immaturity. Sam's 'behaviour problems' require the teachers "to develop practical competencies to better 'manage' disruptive behaviours" (Millei, 2005, p. 129). The wrist band wearing could be seen as a practical way to manage Sam, but what are the effects?

While the wrist band provides powerful validation of the teacher's position as a 'guard'; responsible adult or safety custodian, the teacher responsible for 'watching' Sam is positioned as different from the other teachers, with different responsibilities. The mutual entanglement of the human and the non-human transforms bodies, and gives them meaning. The wrist band is legitimised as the authority and exercises power in disciplining and correcting Sam. Foucault's (1977) consideration of the disciplining work of prisons, extends into educational institutions, as he regards them as similar establishments of training and correction where surveillance and supervision are hierarchical, continuous and techniques of control.

> A relation of surveillance, defined and regulated, is inscribed at the heart of the practice of teaching, not as an additional or adjacent part, but as a mechanism that is inherent to it and which increases its efficiency. (Foucault, 1977, p. 176)

The teachers' gaze of surveillance rests heavily on the individual who needs training, as their deviation from the norm must be corrected as "the power of normalization imposes homogeneity" (Foucault, 1977, p. 184). The wrist band, along with the teacher, does some of this surveillance work. Sam is disciplined, isolated, and judged and his remediation and reformation individualised. He is to be taught new habits and new ways, while being under the constant surveillance and judgement of his 'guards' (Foucault, 1977).

The wrist band and the assemblage it forms with the responsible teacher and Sam, provides for a potential and genuine re-education of the delinquent (Foucault, 1977). However Sam is confined, feasibly imprisoned, by the entanglement created in the intra-action of the human and non-human, as he is separated from the 'normal', and under constant scrutiny. Sam is made subject to the 'truth' and the power of psychopathology (Harwood, 2006). Foucault (1977) challenges us to think not only about the 'truth' of these pathologising discourses, but importantly the effects of them. The wrist band might provide for Sam's safety, but in the assemblages it forms, it also contains and separates, and contributes to his and others' subjectivities. The wrist band, creates a very visual and fixed reminder to all, that Sam is categorised outside the 'normal', while at the same time, shoring up the authority and power of the knowledge that produces him in this way.

The Wrist Band and Separation

> Sam (a child with a diagnosis) is on one end of the see-saw. The teacher Anne (wearing the wrist band) is at the other end. Dylan (a child without a diagnosis) moves toward the see-saw indicating his interest in having a turn and the teacher offers him the place opposite Sam. Momentarily both seem to be enjoying themselves, smiling as the see-saw goes up and down. Sam makes a move abruptly getting off the see-saw and runs off across the yard. The teacher follows without a word to Dylan. He is left on the see-saw his end now on the ground. (Field Notes, 7/5/12, S1, p. 28)

Dylan (a child without a diagnosis) is observed to be closely following the teacher Anne, as he is a new enrolment in the centre. As he follows Anne to the see-saw, he climbs onto the opposite end to Sam. When Sam abruptly gets off and moves away Dylan is left on the ground alone. Anne, wearing the wrist band, must assume sole responsibility for Sam and so follows him. In her haste to fulfil the obligations of the wrist band, she abruptly leaves Dylan without a word. The wrist band in its assemblage with Anne, creates an exclusion zone for Sam, while also creating effects for the unmarked children and the teacher (Watson *et al.*, 2105).

The band marks the teacher who wears it and the unmarked children easily recognise this marked position. The unmarked children know that when a teacher wears the wrist band they must remain with Sam. Some of the children, like Dylan, find this difficult when a teacher they like to be with, cannot be with them. They are separated from the teacher by the power of the wrist band. They are also constrained by it, even though the band is not needed for the 'normal' subject. The wrist band has power in its relations in this discursive context controlling the 'disruptions' of Sam, and disciplining his 'problem behaviours', via the discourse of control (Millei, 2005). The band's assemblage with human bodies disciplines the teachers and the unmarked children who are controlled, managed and separated by it.

The wrist band, as a mechanism of control, upholds individualising and disciplinary practices to manage Sam. These practices are imposed on the excluded. Foucault (1977) argues that all authorities exercising individual control do so

> according to a double mode; that of binary division and branding (mad/sane; dangerous/harmless; normal/abnormal) and that of coercive assignment of differential distribution (who he is; where he must be; how he is to be characterised; how he is to be recognised; how a constant surveillance is to be exercised over him in an individual way, etc.). (Foucault, 1977, p. 199)

The wrist band contributes to, and is a visual reminder to everyone, of the constant division between the 'normal' and the 'not normal', to which every individual is subjected. The wrist band as a mechanism of power is "disposed around the abnormal individual, to brand him and to alter him" (Foucault, 1977, p. 199). As a mechanism for individualising, it communicates to all who Sam is, where he must be, how he must be and how he can be recognised and at the same time tells the story about the 'normal'. The wrist band actively articulates the importance of the constant surveillance of Sam.

In the following conversation with some unmarked children, I question them about why the teachers need to wear the wrist band. How do the unmarked children talk about the wrist band? What are the effects of the 'truths' made visible through the non-human actors?

In this conversation I show the children a photo of one of the teachers wearing the wrist band:

Me: "I have noticed that the teachers wear a band like this one."
Jenna: (a child without a diagnosis) "Cause they have to look after Sam (a child with a diagnosis).
Fleur: (a child without a diagnosis) "Cause he's naughty and he might hurt someone but he doesn't."
Me: "Why do you think they wear the band?"
Faith: (a child without a diagnosis) "Because they have to, because that just because."
Frances: (a child without a diagnosis) "Cause he just … That's why a teacher…
Fleur: "Cause he will hurt himself inside."
Me: "Do the teacher's wear one like this for you?"
Frances: "Nooo."
Jenna: "No."
Me: "Why not?"

Frances: "Because we're kids."
Fleur: "And we have to be older."
Me: "So is Sam not a kid?"
Frances: "Arh … no?"
Fleur: "No, he's a little boy … he's … I'll tell you how old he is … he's two."
Jenna: "No … not two year old … he looks bigger … umm…"
Me: "How old is Sam?"
Jenna: "He's three … he's really three, he's really three."
Michaela: (a child without a diagnosis) "He's one … no he's three." (Field Notes, 21/5/12, S1, p. 57) (Watson *et al.*, 2015)

Children often came and went during this recording possibly due to a level of disinterest, or a level of discomfort with the line of questioning. There were many pauses in the children's responses as they looked for possible answers to my questions. The children's explanation of the wrist band shows how robustly this non-human actor interacts to produce Sam as a certain kind of subject. The wrist band informs the unmarked children that Sam 'has to be looked after', 'he is naughty' and 'he might hurt someone' and 'he will hurt himself inside' (Watson *et al.*, 2015). Fleur's reference to 'inside' could reflect her experiences of Sam being confined in this space; his crying and restlessness, loud and visceral, noticeably inappropriate within the walls of the classroom. Her understandings of Sam have come from her encounters within the spaces of the classroom and Sam's intra-action and becoming within them.

Fleur positions herself and Sam, by drawing on available and speakable discourses, explaining that he is younger, and they are older, and not like him. Ways of speaking about the marked child are limited by these discourses. Sam is not especially younger than Fleur, but they have no other way to speak of him. The limited and 'normalising' sanctioned discourses produce Sam as somewhat 'unspeakable' as he can only be described in certain terms or sometimes not at all. The unmarked children comment "we're kids". They position Sam as a much younger child, a baby, not a "kid". Fleur comments that he is a little boy, as identifying his gender is a speakable discourse in the early childhood classroom, as remarked on previously. The unmarked children here, may want to place him, to some extent, within an available 'normal' category which gender provides. The children have a debate about how old Sam might be, again drawing on the speakable discourses. They seem to try to fit Sam into an age group, using his size as a guide, saying "he looks bigger" and negotiate a number, coming to some agreement over this. In this conversation they wish to establish that they are older than Sam, "we have to be older". The children see themselves as older, and different to Sam, and work to ensure that they demonstrate and maintain themselves as the 'normal'.

Attention to non-human actors creates the possibilities of who Sam is in this classroom. Pacini-Ketchabaw (2012) explains that "What emerges, then, is constituted; it is not a static relationality, it is a doing" (p. 157). The plastic wrist band as a signifier of the need to 'guard' Sam, did not exist before the assemblage came together, and materialised in the take up of these discourses and associated practices. The wrist band, as a material-discursive device, constitutes bodies and conveys meaning.

The Wrist Band Transforms

> Anne (a teacher) is sitting on the verandah and Sam (a child with a diagnosis) is sitting on her lap. Fleur (a child without a diagnosis) gets up from a nearby craft table and moves toward the pair. Fleur comments on the wrist band that Anne is wearing saying that she had owned one like it. I am sitting nearby and the teacher is aware of my presence. She starts a conversation with Fleur.
>
> Anne: "Why do we wear it?"
> Fleur: "I don't know."
> Anne: "We wear it when we are looking after Sam so he doesn't hurt himself."
> Fleur: "You need to look after him so he doesn't knock them over."
> Me: "Does Anne need to look after you?"
> Fleur: (shakes her head) "Because we are older than him and we don't hurt anyone."
> Me: "Does Sam hurt people?"
> Fleur: "Sam hasn't hurt anyone yet."
> Me: "Do you think he might?"
> Fleur: "He doesn't usually." (Field Notes, 11/5/12, S1, p. 41)

This conversation about the wrist band begins with Fleur remarking that she has one like it at home. The teacher Anne asks the children if they know why she is wearing it. At first Fleur says that she does not know. This could be because she is not sure what to say or she is trying to think about her band at home. She may prefer to position herself as 'unknowing' and 'innocent', as children are often positioned this way, in the adult-child power relations in this discursive context (MacNaughton, 2005). Fleur, in an earlier conversation with me, seemed to have some knowledge about the wrist band, but interestingly did not at first, want to divulge this to her teacher. The teacher's explanation of the wrist band connected her with her responsibility for Sam and his safety. Fleur asserts that the teacher wears the band to watch over Sam as he might "knock them over". Sam is again produced as dangerous and a violent threat to others. Fleur, when asked if the teacher needs to look after her, she again refers to herself as older, adding that she does not hurt anyone. Fleur's category boundary work here draws on developmental discourses, as well as psychological discourses, that render the child with a diagnosis as unpredictable and risky for others. Sam sits on his teacher's lap throughout most of this conversation looking around for a while and then wriggling and moving away. What is he thinking?

Using Reflexivity…

The wrist band wearing by the teachers challenged me. I tried to understand the director's position and safety concerns, but I could not see that these concerns outweighed all others. The director's position was clear as her knowledge of Sam's diagnosis rendered him a 'risk'. How did safety concerns come to be privileged in this way over all else? I had used many non-human actors like the wrist band in my work as a teacher. In special education specialised equipment for the diagnosed child abounds. Various physical and sensory aids, as well as visual communications devices and strategies, are used by experts in remedial therapy. These non-human actors had authority within the discourses of remediation and as an intervention teacher my legitimacy was reinforced in my assemblage with various non-human actors. I saw my work at the time as crucial in changing and 'improving' the children I worked with. The non-human actors in their intra-action with me powerfully legitimised me, as an 'expert'. 'Experts' are often subjected as more 'expert' if they have extra special equipment that they can perform with. In this context I was not sure if the wrist band created the teachers as 'experts' or merely produced them as everyday 'guards' for Sam, a role they did not usually want or appreciate.

In this understanding, matter, discourse and subjectivity are brought together (Højgaard & Søndergaard, 2011). Human, as well as non-human phenomena, are consequently seen as simultaneously enacted and enacting. The consequence of this is not only to conceptualise the subject as enacting along with objects, but also to conceptualise objects as enacted along with subjects. In the case of the wrist band, it is not seen in this context, as just a plastic band worn on the wrist, but as an "enacting material technological force" (Højgaard & Søndergaard, 2011, p. 349). The materiality of the wrist band is seen as a constitutive force in its intra-action with other discursive forces, and is not an added effect but mutually constitutive (Højgaard & Søndergaard, 2011). The non-human intra-activity with the human, has the effect of identifying and demarcating a subject of exclusion, the marked child, and simultaneously re-demarcating the subject/category of the 'normal'.

The Lock

The door of the preschool classroom opens to the garden and has to be closed when Sam (a child with a diagnosis) attends. The door is fitted with a large lock for the purpose of keeping Sam in. It is white and 25 centimetres in length and approximately 10 centimetres wide. The lock as a 'special' non-human actor is loudly visible and oversized to emphasise (as a special education visual communication strategy) that the door is locked and is meant to be locked.

> Sam (a child with a diagnosis) was crying loudly and trying to wriggle away from the teacher who was holding him. A large group of children was sitting at a nearby table playing with play dough. They looked up momentarily at Sam and then went back to what they were doing. Sam then got up and moved towards the door. He was confronted by the large white lock. He knocked hard on the door. It appeared that he wanted to get out. He was not allowed to go outside at this time. (Field Notes, 30/4/12, S1, pp. 3–4) (Watson *et al.*, 2015)

Sam is observed on many occasions to struggle with teachers and to resist the constraints of the inside space and inside time. The space and the timetable do some of the disciplinary work, and as discussed previously, the space is not passive in this relationship (Lenz-Taguchi, 2011). It has meaning and provides understanding about one's subjectivity. The space has intentionality. Windows and doors are locked, separating Sam from the outside. As Lenz-Taguchi (2011) maintains, there is a relationship between the material and a child's subjectivity, or their becoming, which occurs organically in the multiple encounters and inter-relations they have with the non-human. Humans form assemblages with the non-human actors, transforming them after each new encounter (Lenz-Taguchi, 2011).

The large group of children who are playing play dough at the table look to Sam briefly, as he cries out and tries to get away from the teacher's hold. Sam is contained and marked by the large white lock on the door to the verandah and the outside. Sam's loud struggle to get away and move outside, did not hold the unmarked children's attention for long (Watson *et al.*, 2015). His noises and actions are ignored for the most part, as the unmarked children enacted their category boundary work, maintaining the 'normal' by sustaining their self-regulated, and self-disciplined focus on their work, keeping themselves separate from Sam. Their desire for order, is observable in the way they turned away from Sam, and back to their activity.

The inside space informs the children of the right way to be and we see the children here 'becoming with' (Haraway, 2008) the world/space around them.

This 'becoming with' is performed over and over again by the children. Classroom discourses circulate that 'normalise' the child who can play independently, be autonomous, and show a developing social competence (Burman, 2008). The children repeatedly take up these discourses during morning inside activities, sitting nicely at the table, while working independently, and quietly.

The agency of the lock is enacted and authorised when it is put on the door when Sam attends. It is not used at other times. The lock, is an active co-constituent of the classroom's social order and as an 'artefact', it communicates a message and 'acts' upon the human actors in the setting (Preda, 2000, p. 269). Like the wrist band, the lock is considered as an object to keep Sam safe, but it has other effects as well. Sam's discursive constitution in this classroom renders him risky. The non-human lock forms an assemblage with the human actors, transforming the space into a prison-like space, the teachers into prison-like guards and Sam into a prisoner-like subject. In this intra-action understandings are produced. Sam is created as the 'abject' being (Butler, 1993) and the 'normal' is further legitimised.

> I used a photograph that I had taken of the white lock to begin the conversation with the children and began by asking them what they could see in the photo.
> Michaela: (a child without a diagnosis) "Sam … It's Sam opening the door." (quick to identify Sam)
> Me: "Is he able to open the door?"
> Faith: (a child without a diagnosis) "No, no, not if that's on." (pointing to the padlock)
> Me: 'And what is that?"
> Michaela: "It's a lock a door."
> Me: "Why do we need to have a lock on the door?"
> Faith: "So he doesn't open it and run outside."
> Rachel: (a child without a diagnosis) "Excuse … umm … excuse me … I have that at grandmas."
> Me: "Do you have one at your place?"
> Faith: "I do at my house in my cupboard so my little brother doesn't get in."
> Me: "Does this padlock keep you inside when you want to go outside?"
> Michaela: "No I am a big girl and I stay inside. I go outside after morning tea." (Field Notes, 28/5/12, S1, p. 80) (Watson *et al.*, 2015)

Michaela starts the conversation about Sam even before I ask her a question. She says: "It's Sam opening the door". There is some alarm in her reaction as she performs her 'normal' category work. She assumes that Sam is trying to get out at this time. Sam is not in the photograph. Even though she can see the lock is in place she still thinks of him as 'escaping'. Faith says that the lock on the door means that Sam cannot escape but recognises that if the lock were not there Sam would open the door and run outside. The children take up and create meaning in the established safety and risk discourses. Rachel says that she has one at Grandmas. This may have been an attempt by Rachel to somehow 'normalise' the lock, or perhaps she was just wanting to show her understanding of what locks were for, and in doing this reinforcing her 'normal' status, performing her knowledge and superiority. Faith talks about the locks on the cupboards in her home that keep her little brother from opening cupboard doors. Safety discourses and safety practices; staying inside, not running outside, not climbing the fences and keeping out of cupboards and so on, are universal in early childhood classrooms and these regulations are endorsed and closely monitored by the children.

Safety discourses highlight potential risks positioning Sam as the risky one. These principle discourses in early childhood settings, sit alongside "the moral panic over the 'riskiness' of our modern society" (Kernan & Devine, 2010, p. 373) and set constraints on children's action, through the regulation of their time and space in institutionalised settings. These discourses have led to an ever increasing confinement of children in separate, 'safe' spaces (Kernan & Devine, 2010). Michaela says that she doesn't need the lock to keep her inside, as she knows that she can go outside after morning tea. She draws on discourses of safety but also ideas about confinement of space and time. The unmarked children position Sam as not knowing the rules of safety and so he needs the lock to tell him to stay inside. The lock compellingly marks the space. It sits 'loudly' across the doorway, its presence is evocative. It marks a territory to contain Sam. Its size and visibility reinforce to all, including Sam that he must remain inside. The lock communicates a narrative about Sam and how practices inscribe him (Watson *et al.*, 2015). The unmarked children understand that the lock has meaning, as a signifier for Sam, as it differentiates them from Sam, and re/produces the category boundary. It creates a boundary between the unmarked children and Sam, and produces a sense of who Sam is, as the Other.

Time and space work together to give the lock meaning. The lock alone does nothing, but in its intra-action with the space, time and with Sam it becomes an assemblage, creating new meanings. The lock, the wrist band, the space and the timetable, as discursive practices of the classroom, powerfully produces Sam as outside the domain of the 'normal' subject and a risky deviant. As a risk to the 'normal', the lock and the wrist band as mentioned, produce the marked child Sam, as separate and contained in his own space, alongside the 'guarding' teacher. Harwood (2010) makes the argument that the psycho-pathologisation of the individual creates the effect of a 'mobile asylum', a separate space, a confined space. Non-human actors in this situation contribute to this 'mobile asylum' effect, as the wrist band and the lock form assemblages with human actors. In the assemblage there is an enclosing around and isolation that emerges, locating Sam in his 'mobile asylum'.

The Scooter Board

A scooter board is a piece of equipment used in special education, by occupational therapists and physiotherapists for therapeutic objectives, for children diagnosed with sensory and physical impairments. Regular use is thought to improve upper body strength and develop balance and equilibrium. Sensory integration therapy (Ayres, 1972) is thought to effect the "neurological process that organizes sensation from one's own body and from the environment and makes it possible to use the body effectively within the environment" (p. 11). Techniques and pieces of equipment like the scooter board, are widely used in educational and intervention settings. The director at one preschool made a point of saying that they did not 'do' therapy with the diagnosed children (Field Notes). However while observing in the classrooms, I documented many therapeutic practices. In this classroom the scooter board is often used as a distraction, or as a 'soother' for Sam, particularly when he wants to go outside and cannot. The scooter board is used exclusively with Sam and the other children are discouraged from using it.

> The children are told that it is pack away time. While some begin the task others move to the mat where Sam (a child with a diagnosis) is using a scooter board (a rectangular board, approximately 50cm by 30cm, on four small wheels) with a teacher. The children watch Sam being rolled forward and backward by the teacher while he lies on the board. The teacher rolls him, rubbing and massaging his back. Sam moves off the board and another child tries to lie on the roller board. The teacher comments, "Don't use it that way you might hurt yourself". The children who have been watching then move away leaving Sam and the teacher to continue the rolling. (Field Notes, 30/4/12, S1, p. 7) (Watson *et al.*, 2015)

While most of the group is busy packing away, some of the children show an interest in what Sam and the teacher are doing on the scooter board. The intra-action of the human and the non-human mutually constitutes the teacher and Sam in this assemblage (Barad, 2007). When some children show an interest in having a turn they are told that they might "hurt themselves". This is an unlikely consequence of using the board, but the children are deterred by the teacher's comments. Unlike the 'wrist band' and 'the lock', the unmarked children actually show some interest in this non-human actor (Watson *et al.*, 2015). Still, the teacher using safety as justification, reinforces Sam's marking and his distinct association with this non-human actor. What are the effects of this exclusive use of the scooter board and the frequent take up of safety discourses around Sam?

The unmarked children, more often than not, ignore or stay separate from Sam. Contrastingly, in this observation, they stand and watch him on the scooter board with some interest. As one child makes an attempt to use the scooter board there is the potential to splinter, if only for a short time, the 'normal/not normal' binary created in this classroom. This actor, in contrast to the lock and wrist band, could have produced a change in the storyline at this moment. There was an opportunity for some disruption to the assemblage, however, the teacher's actions and words recreated the non-human actor as 'special' and therefore Sam, in his association with it, as Other.

The Squishy Ball

The squishy ball, like the scooter board, is a tool/'toy' used by educational, psychological and physical therapy specialists to remediate what they have diagnosed as sensory impairments or sensory dysfunction in children (Cook, 1991). The small soft ball, placed in the palm and squeezed, is thought to provide sensory feedback for a child who could be described as tactile defensive (Bundy, Lane, & Murray, 2002). This kind of feedback is considered helpful to improve the registration of sensory input and its integration, by facilitating nervous system organisation and adaptation (Cook, 1991). These soft balls are typically used with children, who are considered to be fidgety, tactile seekers or avoiders (Bundy *et al.*, 2002). Providing the child with a 'fidget' is thought to help the child reach a regulated state by contributing to their "sensory diet" (DeWeerd, 2013, p. 89).

> During group time before morning tea Hugo (a child with a diagnosis) is seated on the mat with the other children towards the back of the group. After a minute or two he starts to move around getting restless. A teacher nearby comments to the director who is speaking to the whole group, "Do you think he should sit in the chair, I'll get it for him." The director replies, saying that she thinks he usually sits quite well. The teacher then stands and disappears into the director's office momentarily and returns with a small soft 'squishy' ball and she hands it to Hugo as he sits on the mat. A child nearby, distracted by the ball, tries to touch it but Hugo expresses his disapproval loudly. Most of the children stay focused on what is happening at the front of the group, Tyler's news. Hugo stays focused on the squishy ball. Another teacher takes a photo of Hugo with the squishy ball. (Field Notes, 27/11/12, S3, p. 128)

Group time is a time to sit and listen in the early childhood classroom. To sit and listen is not only a rule but it is also seen as the 'normal', and "although the norm is sometimes used as synonymous with 'the rule', it is clear that norms are also what gives rules a certain local coherence" (Butler, 2004, p. 49). As a preschool social practice, group time or story time has an implicit standard of normalisation that is shared. The children have to sit in a particular way, cross legged with their hands in their laps and their eyes forward toward the teacher. The rules are displayed on the wall behind the teacher in pictures using boardmaker (Field Notes, Site 3). Boardmaker is an assistive technology, a picture communication strategy and learning tool software that is thought to have "the potential to increase developmental skills and provide solutions to challenges such as behaviour, attention and communication" (Parette & Stoner, 2008, p. 313). However, the pictures also have an effect to communicate to everyone the expected 'normal'. Classrooms "establish norms of conduct and performance that organise behavioural space and enable divergences between children to be charted" (Rose, 1999, p. 140). The unmarked children are those who adjust to the social demands of the classroom, including group time. This adjustment contributes to how they see themselves as a classroom subject and how they see others.

A subject who might be seen to divert, or "fail to learn appropriate body management incorporates this stigma into his or her self-identity" (Leavitt & Power, 1997, p. 43). Hugo, in this observation, does not take up the group time rules and is not regulated by the norm. Nonetheless he is positioned by it. The teachers show their concern about trying to find ways to normalise his presence at group time. At first they think about a chair, but the director says that he does not need the chair, as he usually "sits quite well". The teacher then decides that a squishy therapy ball, designed for 'fidgets', might help to normalise Hugo. This distracts one child for a short time as Hugo lets them know that the ball is meant for him.

In forming an assemblage that transforms actors, the use of the ball, as a practice of special education, for 'taming' the 'overactive' and 'disengaged' child, produces Hugo as a subject in need of discipline, at a time when the 'normal' sit quietly, conform and attend. The unmarked children do not need to hold the squishy ball to help them 'settle'. They do not have a need for it, as they take up the regulatory discourses of time and space and sit attentively at group time. Hugo's body is diagnosed as unsettled and inattentive. In the early childhood classroom, the 'still' body is considered the more attentive, learning body (Leavitt & Power, 1997). As a non-human actor, the squishy ball, forms an assemblage with Hugo's body, it momentarily produces conditions of possibility for everyone in the group. The assemblage is capable of exerting force on a subject's actions, changing and shaping them (Fenwick & Edwards, 2010), as they assemble together and form networks that affect particular subjectivities and ways of being.

As special education and remediation discourses have authority in the classroom, these 'special' non-human actors are infused with authority and certainty, about who can use them and who cannot, who is included and who is not. The unmarked children do not request to have a turn of the ball even though they show some interest. They recognise its association with Hugo, and by not asking for a turn, they maintain their positioning as the 'normal'. They mostly ignore or avoid watching Hugo playing with the ball regulating themselves within the 'normalising' discourse. As Butler (2004) argues, the 'normal' only subsists in and through its actions. The children's actions, in regulating themselves and others, are operating by way of the norm. The unmarked children become subject to the norm, subjected by it and its regulatory power (Butler, 2004, p. 41). The 'normal' disassociates itself from the non-human squishy ball at group time. Its association with Hugo, and its use as a remediating tool, positions it as a signifier of the 'not normal'.

The wrist band, the lock, the scooter board and the squishy ball, are non-human actors that take their influential place in a classroom embedded within special education and therapy discourse. They are positioned as both objects of regulation to settle the 'inattentive' or 'overacting' child, and objects of remediation to 'fix' the identified deficits of the child with a diagnosis. They reinforce category boundary work, separating and creating a divide between the 'normal' and the Other. In their mutual entanglement with the human actors, they create a narrative about the child with a diagnosis that is exclusionary, as the child with a diagnosis is produced as separate, in this association with the non-human. The non-human actors become 'barrier creators' and 'barrier keepers', sustaining the 'normal' and Other as separate. The inattentive, overacting, unreasonable, and the unable, all have particular associations with 'special' non-human actors and, in an assemblage with the humans, teachers and children, act to correct, normalise and separate.

A Festive Holiday Non-Human Actor

The Xmas Decoration

A table was set up in the yard for Xmas craft. A large branch from a tree balanced in a bucket of sand nearby. On the table were Xmas shapes to be decorated with paper and glitter which were to be hung on the branches creating a Christmas tree. The children busied themselves making shapes hanging them on the tree with pipe cleaners.

> At packing away time some of the children were concerned that they had not finished or had not had a chance to make a decoration. Some children hurriedly made a decoration to put on the tree. Jasmine (a child with a diagnosis) was sitting under the tree branch with another child, Hayley (a child without a diagnosis). As packing away became more vigorous, the teachers gave various directions, praising those who were working hard to clean up and stop the latecomers by taking away the craft pieces. Hayley moved away from under the tree to do her share of the clean-up work. Jasmine, still sitting at the table, started to cry and moan loudly. Nancy, a teacher, approached Jasmine asking her why she was crying. Jasmine pointed to the Xmas decoration she had made which was hanging on the tree. Hayley had put it there in her packing up activity. Nancy asked Jasmine if she wanted to take her decoration home (even though the other children were asked to leave their decoration on the tree). Nancy handed Jasmine her decoration. Jasmine stood up, took it and quickly moved away; the crying stopped. Nancy looked at me pityingly and commented, "She wanted to take it home … her lack of words makes it hard for her". Children were working to pack up the table within earshot of Nancy's statement. (Field Notes, 27/11/12, S3, p. 126)

In this relation between the teacher, the children and the Xmas decoration, subjects are brought into being. The 'special' non-human actors discussed earlier acquired their authority from the knowledge created in special education, psychology, and other therapeutic or remedial discourses. However, the above scenario brings to light how objects, not 'special' or even every day, can be nevertheless significant in forming assemblages with human actors in a particular moment in time. These assemblages 'do' things, transforming understandings, as it is in the 'doing' that meaning is produced.

During the morning activity, Xmas decorations were made by the children, which when completed were attached to the branches of the tree set up nearby. As an adult-planned classroom activity, thematic and pertinent as it was December, the unmarked children cooperatively positioned themselves as understanding the meaning of this activity. They follow the directions, drawing on the dominant adult-child discourses that regulate and organise their activities in the classroom (Leavitt & Power, 1997; Millei, 2005). When the packing away starts, some of the unmarked children move to clean up the table, possibly to re-position themselves as 'capable' and 'helpful' to receive some feedback or praise from the teachers. Early childhood teachers frequently use praise, considered a form of reward, to regulate and shape children's behaviours. Teachers in many contexts use behaviourist techniques, handing out rewards, including verbal praise, to encourage appropriate behaviours and discourage the inappropriate (Millei, 2005). As I have deliberated several times already, packing away time is a regulated time of the day when order is restored. Regulation discourses powerfully inform everyone in the early childhood classroom. Children are praised for their efforts and at the same time are regulated. They also regulate themselves and others, to achieve these rewards.

Jasmine does not help to pack away, she does not follow the regulatory discourses of the classroom, and is not disciplined by the same reward and punishment regime. She does not follow the lead of the other children, and sits and cries until she is allowed to take her decoration with her. This display of emotion is possibly recognised as part of her diagnosis, her inability to self-regulate, as the other 'normal' children follow the directions without a fuss. When the decoration is removed from the tree, and handed to Jasmine it forms a new association with her, marking her as different and separate from the other children, and the decoration different from the other ones on the tree. The teacher positions Jasmine within a deficit discourse, explaining to me that her show of emotion is the result of her lack of communication skills, and her inability to understand the requests to leave the decoration on the tree. The teacher, drawing on the dominant deficit discourses, makes the comment, "her lack of words make it hard for her". There is also the hint of tragedy in the teacher's comments. It is "hard for her" the teacher says with a look of pity on her face. The teacher positions Jasmine as in need of sympathy as she cannot understand the rationality of the Xmas tree decorating activity. Jasmine is subjected as 'unable' and in need of soothing, sympathy and tolerance, as well as separate expectations and rules.

Jasmine's Xmas decoration, in its intra-action with human actors, produces Jasmine as marked. The gaze of the teacher and the children is on her and her decoration, and together they tell a story about Jasmine. The unmarked children, informed by normative discourses of development, regulation and rationality do not ask to take their decoration home. The Xmas decoration, at this moment in time, reinforces and maintains the unmarked children category work around the 'normal'. The non-human actor is equally at play here, as a contributing force in the becoming of Jasmine and the production of the 'normal' (Hultman & Lenz-Taguchi, 2010).

Materialities and Subjection

Using Højgaard and Søndergaard (2011) and others including Barad, 2007; Latour, 2005; Lenz-Taguchi, 2010; Pacini-Ketchabaw, 2012, this chapter has examined how materials and discourses are enacted and taken up, constitutively working to create and shape subjectivities. Engaging in poststructural work and examining the processes of subjectification by analysing discourse alone, could have provided "sophisticated and complex analyses" (Højgaard & Søndergaard, 2011, p. 342). However, this would have meant stopping short of thinking about materialities, and their force in creating particular discursive practices, as well as their potential for subjectification. It is through the performances and practices of both human and non-human actors that knowledge is constructed and circulated (Højgaard & Søndergaard, 2011). There are many other non-human actors, intra-acting in the classroom on the subjectivities of the human participants and producing particular understandings, but only the most prominent have been discussed.

In the previous two chapters the discursive nature of the 'normal' in the classroom has been explored. In the following chapters, some of the discernible effects of the 'normal' category boundary work enacted in the classroom will be explored. These effects became overwhelming in the examination of the data collected inside the classroom. What happens inside the classroom when the 'normal' is maintained and protected?

References

Armstrong, F. (2003). *Spaced out: Policy, difference and the challenge of inclusive education.* Dordrecht: Kluwer.

Ayres, A. J. (1972). *Sensory integration and learning disorders.* Los Angeles, CA: Western Psychological Corp.

Barad, K. (2007). *Meeting the universe halfway.* Durham: Durham University Press.

Bundy, A. C., Lane, S., & Murray, E. A. (2002). *Sensory integration: Theory and practice* (pp. 227–240). Philadelphia, PA: FA Davis.

Burman, E. (2008). *Deconstructing developmental psychology.* East Sussex: Routledge.

Butler, J. (1993). *Bodies that matter: On the discursive limits of "sex."* New York, NY: Routledge.

Butler, J. (2004). *Undoing gender.* Hoboken, NJ: Taylor and Francis.

Cook, D. G. (1991). A sensory approach to the treatment and management of children with autism. *Focus Autism and Other Developmental Disabilities, 5*(6), 1–19.

Davies, B. (1983). The role pupils play in the social construction of classroom order. *British Journal of Sociology of Education, 4*(1), 55–69.

Deleuze, G., & Guattari, F. (1987). *A thousand plateaus: Capitalism & schizophrenia.* Minneapolis, MN: University of Minneapolis Press.

DeWeerd, K. A. (2013). Understanding how sensory input affects children and helps them cope. In H. N. Frye Myers (Ed.), *Social skills deficit in students with disabilities: Successful strategies from the disability field.* Maryland: Rowman and Littlefield Publications.

Dreyfus, H. L., & Rabinow, P. (1982). *Michel Foucault: Beyond structuralism and hermeneutics*. Brighton, Sussex: The Harvester Press Limited.

Fenwick, T., & Edwards, R. (2010). *Actor-network theory in education*. New York, NY: Routledge.

Foucault, M. (1972). *The archaeology of knowledge and the discourse on language*. New York, NY: Pantheon.

Foucault, M. (1977). *Discipline and punish: The birth of the prison*. London: Penguin.

Foucault, M. (1984). What is enlightenment? In P. Rabinow (Ed.), *The Foucault reader* (pp. 32–50). New York, NY: Random House.

Foucault, M. (1997). On the genealogy of ethics: An overview of work in progress. In P. Rabinow (Ed.), *Michel Foucault: Ethics, subjectivity and truth, the essential works of Michel Foucault* (Vol. 1). New York, NY: New York Press.

Goodfellow, A. (2012). Looking through the learning disability lens: Inclusive education and the learning disability embodiment. *Children's Geographies, 10*(1), 67–81.

Haraway, D. (2008). *When Species Meet*. Minneapolis, MN: University of Minnesota Press.

Harwood, V. (2006). *Diagnosing 'disorderly' children; A critique of behaviour disorder discourse*. London: Routledge.

Harwood, V. (2010). Mobile asylums: Psychopathologisation as a personal, portable psychiatric prison. *Discourse: Studies in the Cultural Politics of Education, 31*(4), 437–451.

Højgaard, L., & Søndergaard, D. M. (2011). Theorizing the complexities of discursive and material subjectivity: Agential realism and poststructural analyses. *Theory & Psychology, 21*(3), 338–354.

Hook, D. (2001). Discourse, knowledge, materiality, history: Foucault and discourse analysis. *Theory and Psychology, 11*(4), 521–547.

Horton, J., & Kraftl, P. (2006). What else? Some more ways of thinking and doing 'Children's Geographies'. *Children's Geographies, 4*(1), 69–95.

Hultman, K., & Lenz-Taguchi, H. (2010). Challenging anthropocentric analysis of visual data: A relational materialist methodological approach to educational research. *International Journal of Qualitative Studies in Education, 23*(5), 525–542.

Kernan, M., & Devine, D. (2010). Being confined within? Constructions of the good childhood and outdoor play in early childhood education and care settings in Ireland. *Children & Society, 24*(5), 371–385.

Latour, B. (2005). *Reassembling the social: An introduction to actor-network theory*. Oxford: Oxford University Press.

Laws, C. (2004). Poststructuralist writing at work. *International Journal of Qualitative Studies in Education, 17*(1), 121–134.

Leavitt, R. L., & Power, M. B. (1997). Civilising bodies: Children in day care. In J. Tobin (Ed.), *Making a place for pleasure in early childhood education*. Michigan: Edward Brothers.

Lenz-Taguchi, H. L. (2010). *Going beyond the theory/practice divide in early childhood education: Introducing an intra-active pedagogy*. Oxon: Routledge.

Lenz-Taguchi, H. L. (2011). Investigating learning, participation and becoming in early childhood practices with a relational materialist approach. *Global Studies of Childhood, 1*(1), 36–50.

MacNaughton, G. (2005). *Doing Foucault in early childhood studies: Applying poststructural ideas*. Abingdon, Oxon: Routledge.

Maskey, M., Warnell, F., Parr, J. R., Le Couteur, A., & McConachie, H. (2013). Emotional and behavioural problems in children with autism spectrum disorder. *Journal of Autism and Developmental Disorder, 43*(4), 851–859.

Masschelein, J. & Verstraete, P. (2012). Living in the presence of others: Towards a reconfiguration of space, asylum and inclusion. *International Journal of Inclusive Education, 16*(11), 1189–1202.

Millei, Z. (2005). The discourse of control: Disruption and Foucault in an early childhood classroom. *Contemporary Issues in Early Childhood, 6*(2), 128–139.

Millei, Z., & Cliff, K. (2014). The preschool bathroom: Making 'problem bodies' and the limit of the disciplinary regime over children. *British Journal of Sociology of Education, 35*(2), 244–262. doi: 10.1080/01425692.2012.761394

Mol, A. (2010). Actor-network theory: Sensitive terms and enduring tensions. *Kolner Zeitschrift fur Soziologie und Sozialpsychologie, 50*(1), 253–269.

Pacini-Ketchabaw, V. (2012). Acting with the clock: Clocking practices in early childhood. *Contemporary Issues in Early Childhood, 13*(2), 154–160.

Parette, H. P., & Stoner, J. B. (2008). Benefits of assisted technology user groups for early childhood education professionals. *Early Childhood Education Journal, 35*, 313–319.

Pike, J. (2008). Foucault, space and primary school dining rooms. *Children's Geographies, 6*(4), 413–422.

Preda, A. (2000). Order with things: Humans, artifacts and the sociological problem with rule-following. *Journal for the Theory of Social Behaviour, 30*(3), 269–298.

Rose, N. (1998). Governing risky individuals: The role of psychiatry in new regimes of control. *Psychiatry, Psychology and Law, 5*(2), 177–195.

Rose, N. (1999). *Governing the soul: The shaping of the private self* (2nd ed.). London: Free Association Books.

Rose, S., & Whitty, P. (2010). "Where do we find the time to do this?" Struggling against the tyranny of time. *The Alberta Journal of Educational Research, 56*(3), 257–273.

Tobin, J. (Ed.). (1997). *Making a place for pleasure in early childhood education*. London: Yale University Press.

Watson, K., Millei, Z., & Petersen, E. B. (2015). 'Special' non-human actors in the 'inclusive' early childhood classroom: The wrist band, the lock and the scooter board. *Global Studies of Childhood, 5*(3), 266–278.

5

Disrupting Tolerance as a Practice

Many questions arose for me during the classroom project, in particular, questions about the regular performances enacted by the unmarked children as they encountered and interacted with the marked child and each other. Noteworthy, were the countless observations of the unmarked children engaging in 'helping' performances with the marked child. These performances were accompanied by an obvious degree of 'concern' for them and their actions, their inactions, or their indiscretions in the classroom. The 'helping' and 'concern' performances exhibited a shared understanding among the unmarked children. There was a collective understanding that the marked child was someone in need of monitoring, and in need of assistance with their deficits, and their multiple and constant transgressions. I wish to clarify here, that while I am not arguing that the 'act of helping', or 'being helpful', has no public value in producing a caring society, and that people should not help each other (Watson, 2016). I do wish however, to problematise the power of this discourse and practice, and the way it constructs the marked child as Other. There is a need and desire to disrupt the naturalised innocence of the discourses that circulate around 'helping', as these discourses normalise this act of helping, as an act of virtue, without any questioning of the power and subjection involved.

Helping in the Classroom

The children's help at times, was quite direct and often teacher-like, remediating the marked child's difficulties, by telling or showing them what to do. At other times, a more mother-like helping was observed, where the unmarked child took on a gentler and more nurturing role in order to help or change the marked child's behaviours. Sometimes the marked child was helped by the whole class to join in with the group at story time (Watson, 2016). What became of interest was the way the unmarked children helped the marked child, but they did not help other unmarked children who were unsettled, disruptive, or 'naughty', to join the class at group time, or join in other activities.

In contrast to these overt helping performances, some of the unmarked children did not engage in this helping at all. Instead, there were times when the unmarked children observed the marked child's transgression, and they stood back and said nothing, or moved on. This differed to the way the unmarked children were managed by each other. When they got the rules wrong, they disciplined each other. There seemed among the group, to be a mutual understanding, to leave the marked child alone. No matter what the marked child did, the unmarked children shared an acceptance, or at least made an allowance for it, without complaint. There was a degree of resignation around the actions of the marked child. This resignation manifested itself in several ways, such as not interfering, not challenging, putting up with, giving in to, or not telling the teacher about the marked child's indiscretions and transgressions. The shared accord accepted that the marked child had to be endured. Both the helping actions and the performances of resignation are deemed here to be practices of tolerance.

The practice of tolerance is considered a discourse of power, and although typically conceived as an individual virtue, also articulates identity and difference, as well as belonging and marginality (Brown, 2006). Tolerance produces subjectivities of virtue for the bearer of tolerance, and a position of deviance for the tolerated. How does tolerance get taken up as a discursive practice in the classroom? How do the children come to see each other in this way? What are the effects of tolerance on inclusionary and exclusionary practices?

Helping: Performances of 'Concern'

A Community of Tolerance

> The children gradually get settled onto the mat after pack away time. Michael (a child with a diagnosis) is seated at the back of the group holding some trucks in his hands. A teacher, Chris, seated next to Michael, tries to take the trucks away, as there is a 'no toys at story time' rule. Michael protests loudly. Without warning the director, Sue, moves quickly from inside her office where she has been watching through a window calling "Chris, Chris, let him have them, it soothes him". The director hands the trucks back to Michael. Chris remains silent. The director then apologises to Chris for her abrupt entry but reinforces that she did not want to "set Michael off". The whole group watches on. Anne, the teacher at the front of the group asks the children to sit in a circle and asks Michael individually to join them to which he replies "No".
>
> When they are settled Anne asks them to clap their names in turn around the circle. When Anne calls Michael's name the other children join with the teacher calling "Michael, Michael". This was the only time the children called another child's names. (Field Notes, 4/5/12, S1, p. 17) (Watson, 2016)

Michael became the centre of everyone's attention. The teachers, the director and the unmarked children combine as a group to show their concern for Michael (Watson, 2016). They all, in their various ways, help him join the activity. But what else is going on here?

The strategic positioning of the teacher's body next to Michael on the mat, initially marks Michael. Special education discourses commonly inform teachers that a child with a specific diagnosis can potentially be disruptive for the 'normal' whole class group. Michael is created as in need of close supervision at this time, as his diagnosis produces him as inattentive, easily distracted, impulsive and hyperactive (Washbrook, Propper, & Sayal, 2013). Sitting quietly and attentively for any activity is characterised as problematic for anyone with such a diagnosis. When the teacher attempts to take the trucks from Michael, she re-positions herself as a regular, not special teacher, by following the rules for everyone in the classroom. She is possibly trying to position Michael as part of the regular group.

The regular pedagogical rule of not playing with toys at group time is customary in early childhood classrooms. Toys are measured as a possible distraction for children, as at group time they are expected to follow teacher-directed activities like story reading. As Chris the teacher tries to remove the trucks from Michael, the director vehemently interrupts her, as she bursts out of her office and into the classroom to stop the trucks being taken from Michael. With this act, Michael is positioned as Other, and the teacher is re-positioned by the director, as a non-expert in special education practice. This authoritative move by the director, takes everyone by surprise. In her capacity as the special education 'expert' in the centre, she positions herself as 'knowing' Michael, via the characteristics of his diagnosis. Her actions are seen as averting the potential disruption of the class. Michael is diagnostically created as unruly and a potential threat to the group's stability (Watson, 2016). The intensity of the director's intervention however creates a sense of anxiety in the classroom. How does this position Michael? How does this position the teacher and the director? How scary could his disruption be?

Using Reflexivity…

As this scene unfolded I came to think that my presence in the classroom may have been a provocation for the director's actions. As I was a researcher examining 'inclusive' practices, I often felt that I was positioned as an 'expert' and some of the teachers I encountered also wished to be positioned as 'experts' and so often enacted special education strategies to show their knowledge of the discipline. I noted my discomfort at the time with the awkward power relations and positionings produced, possibly by my presence at this time. I wondered whether this would have happened if I had not been there and what role did I play at this moment in further marking Michael. My presence possibly strengthened the power exercised by special education knowledge, and the 'truth' about the 'normal', and about Michael. As a researcher my positioning was unavoidable, but I have to grapple with the idea that the effect of my presence in the classroom was not neutral.

Special education knowledge, in its power relations with regular educational knowledge, robustly positions the director in this classroom as the 'expert'. Special education trumps regular education every time in the 'inclusive' classroom (Watson, 2016), because special education has the knowledge of the special child, and this knowledge has become particularly valued in the move toward 'inclusive' practice and education. Slee (2011) argues, as mentioned already, that the field needs to be reframed and freed from previous underlying assumptions. 'Inclusive' education is informed and framed by what we think we know about the special child. By showing more concern for them, and their diagnosis, and by improving our professional knowledge of the diagnosis and its characteristics, special education proponents believe they can better 'include' the child, helping them to assimilate through remediation (Diamond, Hestenes, Carpenter, & Innes, 1997; Odom, 2000). Special education identifies that the diagnosed child has needs that are extra to other children's needs. The use of the word 'needs' powerfully fashions a picture based on concern. To have extra needs positions one as more dependent, less autonomous, and less rational, which are values of substance and privilege, in a Western liberal 'civilised' society (Brown, 2006).

Special education discourses confer special conditions on the marked child. The unmarked children in the group sit silently, watching this interaction between the director and the teacher, understanding that special concessions are to be made for Michael because he needs to have toys at story time. The unmarked children at story time position themselves as good students, sitting still, listening intently, performing the 'normal'. What do they draw on to understand Michael and his actions and the actions of the teachers? How do they position themselves, as they are not afforded the concession of having a toy?

As the scene continues Michael is asked to join the group and he replies with a definite and loud "No". The whole group then attempts to 'bring him into line', to 'normalise' him. The unmarked children clap their own names, each child having their turn, as the teacher moves around the group. This activity/game is often used as a transitioning technique in early childhood classrooms to settle the group and gain their attention. However, when it comes to Michael's turn he says "No". The group then encourages him and try to regulate him by calling and clapping his name. They actively take up and reinforce Michael's marked position as a subject in need of extra support and remediation. The children show their 'normal' category solidarity and membership, communicating an understanding of themselves and Michael, as they all join in to regulate and treat him. They try to create social order by imposing the 'normal' on Michael who is created as 'not normal'.

Michael is produced as a risk or a potential threat to the order and routine of the story time activity. The unmarked children join with the teachers to try to manage Michael, to avoid "setting him off". Interestingly, the unmarked children appear to tolerate Michael's indiscretions in not following the rules. He is not positioned as being 'naughty' for holding the trucks. He is enthusiastically encouraged to join the activity, as they perform their concern for him. Michael, as a discursively produced subject, is afforded the unmarked children's tolerance. The threat of his disruption is managed by their tolerance of his transgressions, and the social order is restored, at least in the short term. How can we explain their actions in 'helping' and showing 'concern'?

Brown (2006) contends that the promotion of tolerance is prominent in particular forms of integration and assimilation. Tolerance is omnipresent in the 'inclusive' early childhood classroom. It is a political, moral and social discourse in this setting. "Almost all objects of tolerance are marked as deviant, marginal, or undesirable by virtue of being tolerated, and the action of tolerance inevitably affords some access to superiority" (Brown, 2006, p. 14). What is the work that a tolerance discourse does in this group time?

Brown (2006) maintains that tolerance is a "unique way of sustaining the *threatened* entity" (p. 27, original emphasis). In the classroom, the marked child threatens not only the social order but the boundaries of the 'normal', "tolerance is a practice concerned with managing a dangerous, foreign, toxic or threatening difference from an entity that also demands to be incorporated" (Brown, 2006, p. 27). Policies and practices in education promote the incorporation or inclusion of the potentially dangerous child with a diagnosis. In the 'inclusive' normative discursive context, the child is produced as disruptive and threateningly different and must be managed. The director's actions, in coming out of her office in such a vociferous way, contribute to the notion of something threatening. In a classroom saturated by special education practices, tolerance is relied upon to deal with and remediate threats. The director tolerates Michael's transgressions in an attempt to contain any potential disruption.

A tangible effect of tolerating is a noticeable separation. Separation of the marked and the unmarked is made visible here. A divide between the tolerated and the tolerating becomes visible. This delivers a significant challenge for 'inclusive' contexts, but also critically, a challenge for the becoming subjectivities of the children in the classroom.

In this discursive environment, only certain subject positions are made possible, while other understandings of conduct, or ways of being, are disqualified (Millei, 2005). Discursive positions that are disqualified, or mistrusted, become a concern due to their transgressions. As Petersen (2008) points out, "these people who get it wrong need some guidance; their problems need to be pointed out to them, they need to be enlightened, corrected" (p. 398). The unmarked children and teachers, in their actions and words, express a level of unease around the marked child. Michael, the object of concern, is in need of remediation, as he is considered unreasonable, volatile and unpredictable. The concern of the unmarked children, in trying to bring Michael in, suggests Michael's possible threat to the social order, and the 'normal', and legitimates the concerns of the concerned. In the 'inclusive' classroom, there is a "boundless sea of concern" (Petersen, 2008, p. 399) about getting the marked child to change, to become 'normal', and to keep the threat of their difference contained.

Tolerance is premised on and pertaining to difference, and viewed as a way of managing "the demands of marginal groups in ways that incorporates them without disturbing the hegemony of the norms that marginalize them" (Brown, 2006, p. 36). The tolerating unmarked children are afforded access to superiority in this power relation with the tolerated. These positionings have effects on subjectivities in the classroom, as they are continually repeated in discursive practices. Contrasting the way tolerance is practised on the marked child, the following observation shows how an unmarked child negotiates the rules with another unmarked child. The actions in this encounter provide a stark divergence to the ones that follow, when the interactions occur around the marked child.

Discipline Not Tolerance Is 'Dished Out' for the 'Normal'

> Alex (a child without a diagnosis) is sitting on the mat near the blocks playing alone with a Duplo train he has made. The teachers have declared pack away time, but Alex continues to play with the train. Joshua (a child without a diagnosis) moves toward Alex and tells him to put away the train. "Pack away time" he says loudly into Alex's face. Alex does not listen and continues with his train play. Joshua remains standing over Alex, so Alex pushes him away.
>
> Joshua responds with a loud "Ow", and moves away but only for a short time. On returning to the mat again he tells Alex to pack away. This time Joshua takes the train from Alex, when Joshua picks it up, it breaks in half, in mid-air, crashing over the mat. Joshua puts the piece in his hand into the Duplo bucket. Alex then unhappily puts the rest of the train away and puts the bucket on the shelf. As he gets up, he pushes over some children who are standing nearby. (Field Notes, 4/6/12, S1, p. 129)

Packing away, as already deliberated multiple times, is a heavily regulated part of the preschool day. It is a disciplined time for restoring order to the classroom. The children, along with the teachers, usually discipline those children who transgress, and those who cooperate, receive praise. Children enthusiastically and regularly step in to correct any deviance, so to restore the social order of the classroom (Davies, 1983). Unless, as we have seen before, those who transgress, are children marked with a diagnosis.

Joshua disciplines Alex's deviance and his indiscretions are not tolerated. His actions are not ignored but quickly regulated. Joshua takes control and removes the train from Alex's hands putting it in the bucket. Alex concedes and puts the rest of the train pieces away, but also shows his displeasure by giving some bystanders a push as he goes. Alex's actions could subject him as 'naughty' but the 'naughty' are not tolerated in the classroom, they are disciplined. This interaction between two unmarked children, where the transgressor is disciplined and conforms, with only a short burst of resistance, provides a contrast to the interaction that follows between Hugo (a child with a diagnosis) and Leah (a child without a diagnosis), where tolerance, not discipline, is taken up as a discursive practice.

Tolerating Transgressions

> At packing away time the children are divided into their class groups and sent to separate parts of the yard to put things away. Most of the children seem to do some packing away. However Hugo (a child with a diagnosis) is observed to resist this activity regularly. On this occasion he has spent the morning playing in a 'fire truck' and has been asked repeatedly to pack it away by a teacher. Instead of following these instructions he takes himself up onto the high fort and lies down in the fort. Leah (a child without a diagnosis) follows Hugo up into the fort trying to encourage him to come down and do his share of the packing up. She bends down next to him touching him gently and talking to him softly. "Come on Hugo, you have to pack up the fire engine that you were playing with." He wriggles away from her touch saying "no' several times, each time with increasing volume. She repeats similar words several times. One of the teachers calls to her, "Leah, are you going to get out of packing up?" Leah explains that she is trying to get Hugo to help. After a few minutes she gives up, comes down from the fort and starts to pack away the fire engine. She is told by the teacher to leave some for Hugo to do. Eventually Hugo comes down from the fort and with the teacher standing over him he puts one thing away. (Field Notes, 6/11/12, S3, p. 48) (Watson, 2016)

This observation from chapter three is repeated here. Jackson and Mazzei (2012) challenge the qualitative researcher to think *with* their data and challenge the idea of simplistic and single readings of data. Instead they argue for opening up to a "dense and multi-layered treatment of data" (p. vii). In reading and re-reading this observation I hope to "avoid being seduced by the desire to create a coherent and interesting narrative that is bound by themes and patterns" (Jackson & Mazzei, 2012, p. viii).

Pack away time begins in this classroom with the shaking sound of the tambourine. The director gathers the children together on the ground and assigns them areas of the yard that need to be cleaned up and packed away. In a conversation about packing away Joseph (a child without a diagnosis) told me that "If you're in the 'reef room' and they are carrying the board down, you can't help with the mountain (room)" (Field Notes 20/11/12, S3, p. 99). Each class group has separate responsibilities and the routine is structured and well understood by the unmarked children.

Hugo transgresses from the 'normal'; he does not help to pack away in the expected 'normal' way. One reading of this scenario might be that Hugo enjoyed the morning 'fire engine' play so much that he was not happy to put it away, and he did not take up the regulatory discourses regarding timetables, but rather skilfully resisted them by hiding. In this way Hugo did not conform to the discipline that works to 'civilise' young children (Leavitt & Power, 1997). Nevertheless, Hugo is subjected by these discourses. Instead of doing what he is supposed to do, he moves to the top of the fort. He appears to be hiding from those who might discipline him. He lies down to make himself less visible. In this discourse, at this time, Hugo is positioned as a transgressor, and as such, he is in need of regulation and management. Hugo's resistance could have other interpretations but in this discursive context, these other ways of 'seeing' him remain unappreciated and not in view.

Leah (a child without a diagnosis) is frequently observed to 'move in' on Hugo and to help him to follow the rules (Watson, 2016). Leah moves up onto the fort showing her concern. As the "concern expresser" (Petersen, 2008) she positions herself as someone who might be able to assist. What subject positions are made available in this discourse of concern? 'Concern', as Petersen (2008) argues, produces "exclusionary and de-legitimised" (p. 394) positioning. Leah is positioned as the autonomous, rational, 'normal' and legitimate subject, while Hugo is positioned, by way of his diagnosis, as the dependent, unreasonable and illegitimate subject. This concerned action works to shape and regulate Hugo's actions, Othering him in the process. When read in this way, these acts of concern problematise these 'natural' and taken-for-granted discursive practices of helping. As Leah gently tells Hugo that he needs to do his share of the pack away, she positions him as the immature subject, and tries to negotiate in a rational way with him.

Leah, after a few minutes, fails to do this but does not continue to coerce Hugo into packing away and moves off the fort. What informs Leah that she should not continue to coerce Hugo? She does not tell on him to the teachers, as she might tell on a 'naughty' child, but is patient and accepting, further marking him by tolerating his actions. Leah does not discipline Hugo in the same way that Joshua disciplined Alex. The teacher comments about Leah's actions, inferring that she is trying to avoid the work of packing away. Do the teachers want to avoid the possible disruption of Hugo, and evade 'setting him off', by telling Leah to pack away? What does it mean when the teachers separate them? When Leah moves down off the fort and does some of the packing up, how does this position her and Hugo? Hugo's transgressions are 'tolerated' by the teachers and Leah's are discouraged. Hugo at this time is left on the fort, separate from the other children.

Leah's enactment of tolerance produces and positions subjectivities (Brown, 2006). Leah in this context is positioned the 'normal' helper, the older, caring female, who is trying to help. Leah works to maintain the category of the 'normal' by taking up a discourse of tolerance, first performing a helping role asking Hugo to pack away, and then, when this does not happen, she tolerantly moves on. Informed by psychological, developmental, special education discourses, Leah positions herself as older and as the 'tolerator', as she acts to help Hugo follow the pack away rules. Brown (2006) contends that tolerance as a discourse moves around between state, civil society, and citizens, producing and organising subjects, as it is used by subjects to govern themselves and others. Tolerance in the classroom is institutionalised (Watson, 2016) and is exercised by the children and the teachers. Leah takes up tolerance as a practice to assist in the governance of the 'normal'.

Performing the packing away routine correctly and helping others in conducting their conduct, and managing their own and others' possibilities, creates the unmarked children as legitimate and superior, in this exercise of power. For Foucault (1982), "the exercise of power consists in guiding the possibility of conduct and putting in order the possible outcome" (p. 342). Tolerance practiced, is an exercise of power, and a political praxis enacted by the unmarked children. As the dominant group in the classroom, they confirm this position by offering protection or incorporation, or help to the sub-ordinated, and by doing this reveal their virtuousness in the process (Brown, 2006, p. 178).

Hugo is subjected by multiple discourses. The 'truths' and characteristics of his psychological diagnosis, and the therapeutic advice passed on by 'experts'. The take up of these discourses affect his inclusion and exclusion in this classroom. In an 'inclusive' classroom, a child's diagnostic characteristics come to represent who they are, as they explain how they might act, think and learn. The marked child is often described by their diagnosis, such as "he has ADHD and Atypical Autism, he is medicated and has been since the age of three" (Field Notes 4/5/12, S1, p. 11). The child is repeatedly not named, as their diagnosis is given as a description of them and only medical/psychological 'facts' are shared in conversations.

> Once a diagnostic label is attached there is the risk that all the child's characteristics are filtered through this diagnosis or explanatory mechanism resulting in a tendency to view the child's behaviour as symptoms, rather than as expressions of his or her unique personality. (Molloy & Vasil, 2002, p. 661)

The power of this knowledge over-rides all other knowledges of the child, creating the child with a diagnosis, as a unitary and fixed being. The discursive understanding that a diagnosis or a disability is a disease and a tragedy, is omnipresent in the 'inclusive' classroom. Teachers time after time commented on the 'sad life' of the marked child. On one occasion a teacher was observed reading a story to Sam (a child with a diagnosis). He was lying across her lap and she was pointing at and naming the pictures in the book. She looked toward me saying, "It's calming for him, can't imagine what it must be like for his poor parents", her face down-turned and head slowly moving from side to side, showing her melancholy (Field Notes, 4/6/12, S1, p. 134). The marked child is created as a subject of pity, and in need of sympathy and tolerance. Perceptions of disabled people in line with this discourse are nearly always negative (Swain & French, 2008). The tragedy model assumes that disability is about loss and that disabled people would rather be more like abled people. As Swain and French (2008) argue "disability, or rather impairment … is thought to strike individuals at random, causing suffering and blighting lives" (p. 7). This model evokes and seeks to arouse sympathy and concern in non-disabled people. "The ethical bearing of tolerance is high-minded, while the object of such high-mindedness is inevitably figured as something more lowly" (Brown, 2006, p. 178). Power then is exercised by the privileged 'normal' who can give sympathy and show concern. The 'normal' are constituted as the virtuous and the moral, and the Other as "undesirable by virtue of being tolerated" (Brown, 2006, p. 14).

Brown (2006) refers to tolerance as a civilisational discourse, as "to be uncivilised is to be intolerable is to be barbarian" (p. 182) and certain practices that are declared intolerable, are stigmatised as uncivilised. Routines discipline children and becoming civilised requires monitoring. Children are not passive recipients of classroom rules and are often observed to actively mediate and resist them (Leavitt & Power, 1997). Children who take up the 'civilising' practice, by performing within the norms, rules or codes of conduct, are positioned as the 'civilised', and from this position, draw on tolerance to 'civilise' those who remain 'uncivilised'. The asymmetry of power, between the tolerated and the tolerators, is observed in the 'inclusive' classroom.

Foucault (1977) tells us that the more subjects in a space are under surveillance the more they become regulated. Children's play in the classroom is regulated by teachers but children also act as regulators of themselves and others. "Within this heavily regulated space, play has been a key concept through which adults have tried to produce, understand, monitor, regulate and govern childhood" (Ailwood, 2003, p. 295). The play, and the packing away after the play, is recognised as part of this regulation and governance. The use of play equipment is monitored and specified. The child with a diagnosis however, is produced within these discourses as in need of remediation regarding their playing and packing away, and is helped rather than disciplined. Conversely, the teachers discipline the unmarked children, who in turn discipline each other, when they do not play or pack away correctly. Order is restored as everything is put back in the place where it belongs. In this classroom, the teacher makes comments about how the packing away activity has been conducted by the children, she calls out the names of the children who have been observed to have worked hard doing their share and she also names those who did not (Field Notes, 14/11/12, S3, p. 76, 28/11/12; S3, pp. 152–153). Praise again, as a reward, is used to discipline behaviours (Millei, 2011). Surveillance by the children, of each other, regulates packing away. The unmarked children position themselves as working hard at packing away, ensuring their recognisability (Butler, 1997) as a member of the 'normal'.

In a conversation stimulated by a photograph taken of Hugo on the fort, the question was asked about the rules of packing away and why Hugo didn't pack away, Joseph's response was, "Yeah … umm … cause they haven't told him the rules yet" (Field Notes, 20/11/12, S3, p. 99). This seems a notable response as the routine was the same every day. Joseph did not position Hugo as 'naughty' for not packing away, even though he knew that the rule applied to everyone else. "We see everyone packing away like that" (Field Notes, 20/11/12, S3, p. 99). Joseph positioned Hugo as not the same as him, as he had not been told the rules. In explaining Hugo's resistance to packing away in this way, Joseph expressed his acceptance and understanding of Hugo's difference, and possibly the need to 'tolerate' his lack of knowing. As Hugo hadn't been told yet, it was conceivably understandable that he didn't follow the rules. Hugo is created as a person who needs to be granted tolerance at least until someone tells him the rules.

> Tolerance is generally conferred by those who do not require it on those who do; it arises within and codifies a normative order in which those who deviate from rather than conform to the norms are eligible for tolerance. (Brown, 2006, p. 186)

The discourses that dominate this classroom inform the unmarked children that Hugo is eligible for tolerance. But what kind of subject does tolerance produce?

A Subject of Tolerance

In the following scenario we see how Hugo (a child with a diagnosis) seems to enjoy his 'tolerated' positioning during this play episode.

> Hugo (a child with a diagnosis), Leah, Audrey (children without a diagnosis) and Nancy (a teacher) are sitting and playing at the bottom of a rock water course that has filled with water, creating a pool. Hugo has a dolphin in his hand and he is moving it around in the pool of water.
> Nancy asks Hugo: "Is that a dolphin or a fish?"
> Hugo: "A dolphin."
> Leah: "Yes good!" (the pitch of her voice rising).
> Nancy: "Where do they live?"

Audrey: "In the ocean."

Hugo: "Yum yum yum" (making eating noises). Hugo moves his dolphin closer to some leaves that are floating in the water and pretends the dolphin is eating them.

The discussion continues about what dolphins might eat.

Leah stands and runs off returning with more dolphins and sea creatures. Hugo begins to squeeze his dolphin making a loud squeaky sound.

Hugo stands and moves to the top of the rocky water course and starts to balance his way down the rocks. The other children follow. Nancy attempts to discourage them. She takes Hugo's hand to help him so that he does not fall. The slope is very small. Audrey then holds Hugo's hand helping him walk down the wall again. After Hugo has balanced his way down the slope several more times he goes to the top again and stands waiting smiling and saying, "Are you going to help me Leah?" Leah is quick to help him, holding his hand as he moves down the slope. (Field Notes, 6/11/12, S3, pp. 46–47)

The whole group has come together to 'tutor' Hugo, in a similar way to how the group encouraged Michael to join them in clapping at story time. Leah and Audrey position themselves as teachers, helping Hugo to learn, as they draw upon normative caring and nurturing discourses. The teacher joins in the conversation about dolphins, drawing on pedagogical discourses when questioning Hugo. She directs her questions to him. The unmarked children's actions, in joining with the teacher in the lesson, shores up their legitimate membership in the category of the 'normal', and in this moment, expands the power of the 'normal' (Brown, 2006, p. 82) in the classroom. They perform in adult-like ways to teach and support Hugo.

When the children start to climb and balance on the rocks, the teacher repositions herself from pedagogue to safety expert, regulating the children's behaviour by reminding them to be safe. She enacts a helping performance by taking Hugo's hand enabling him to safely negotiate the small, insignificant slope. Safety, no risk, discourses powerfully manage and regulate children's actions in early childhood classrooms (Leavitt & Power, 1997). Audrey takes her turn at 'helping' Hugo. After several turns at safely traversing the slope, Hugo moves again to the top and this time waits for help. He now repositions himself at the centre of the game, more powerful, and parleying from his perspective. Hugo has now re-positioned the unmarked children as his helpers and he seems to be the one navigating the game and calling the shots, enjoying the girl's attention.

Hugo's positioning as the helpless, by the unmarked children and the teacher, is an acceptable and sanctioned way of positioning the marked child. The notion of helplessness pertains to a level of innocence and immaturity, and a degree of tolerance of the helpless, is necessary for remediation, development and civilising. Developmental discourses, where the rational adult-like being affords a degree of tolerance toward the irrational child-like being, are ubiquitous in the classroom. Hugo, at this time, accepts this subject positioning and repositions himself, renegotiating power relations in the interaction. Hugo now asks for help, he performs the position that he has been bestowed on him. He performs as if needing help, but there is also a hint of playfulness in Hugo's negotiation of the slope. Hugo is engaging in some politics of his own, he does not resist the positioning as he did before, but now appears to accept the position and the extra attention.

However at other times the marked child does not accept the positioning offered by the unmarked children.

Tolerating Indiscretions

> In the block corner early one morning, Michael (a child with a diagnosis) was putting the long blocks side by side, making them as wide as they were long. It looked like a square platform. He then started to put other blocks around this square shape.
>
> Michael (a child with a diagnosis): "I'm making a garage" (he says to himself, as he hammers with his fist on the outside of the blocks)
>
> Seb (a child without a diagnosis) from across the room approaches sitting opposite Michael watching him. He timidly starts to put blocks onto the construction, looking at Michael closely and following his lead. Seb puts the blocks down hesitantly.
>
> Seb: "There you go Michael."
>
> Michael then lies down on the mat, next to the construction saying "Good night, good night."
>
> Seb: "We haven't fixed it, we haven't built it."
>
> Michael then falls onto the construction noisily pushing it over and scattering the blocks. He lies across the pile of blocks. He then picks up one of the long blocks and holds it above his head, hitting a child who is playing nearby in the head. This other child picks up another block and tries to hit Michael, but then moves on (The noise attracts the attention of the teachers)
>
> Seb watching then attempts to fix the construction.
>
> Seb: "I'll make it up all nice."
>
> He tries for a minute or two, but Michael does not join in.
>
> Seb then stands and walks away from the area but returns minutes later.
>
> Seb: "Do you want me to build it again? Let's make a new garage."
>
> Michael: "It's all broken." (loudly)
>
> Odette (teacher) watching close by now approaches.
>
> Odette: "How did it get broken?" she asks as she starts to place the blocks back on the shelf. Seb watching Odette then starts to put the blocks away too.
>
> Michael continues to build. He tries to balance one long block on the ends of two long blocks that are vertical, creating an archway/bridge formation. The blocks are unstable and fall crashing loudly.
>
> Seb moves away saying: "I just don't want to get hit with those."
>
> Me: "Has it happened to you before?"

Seb:"Yeah just two times." (holds up 2 fingers).
He walks away to the other side of the room. (Field Notes, 1/6/12, S1, p. 97)

Michael is playing alone with the blocks when Seb moves into the area and starts to add blocks to the construction saying: "There you go Michael". He does not ask Michael if he can join him, which is often considered a regular entry to others' games, but at this time he just starts to add blocks. Seb positions himself as a 'helper' and more adult-like, and positions Michael as in need of help. As Michael is the object of concern, Seb draws on the multiple discourses that inform him of Michael's marked position. Michael's way of playing with the blocks needs remediation. Seb tries to convey to Michael how and what he should build. Seb's comment, "I'll make it up all nice", reinforces his position as the 'helper', while showing Michael how to do it the 'right way'.

Michael, unlike Hugo in the previous scenario, resists Seb's positioning of him and his uninvited help and management. He lies on the floor saying goodnight, as a way to communicate to Seb, and avoid his interference. As Davies and Harré (1999) suggest, people are capable of making choices in relation to the discursive practices that provide subject positions and there are many contradictory discursive practices that people can engage in (p. 35). Michael's actions show his refusal to be a part of this helping/helpless discursive practice that is being thrust upon him. Michael has finished with the game at this time. Seb, however, as the competent block player, tells Michael that he has not finished, as completing an activity independently is considered developmentally appropriate, and enforced in early childhood classrooms. To complete a task, shows one's autonomy, sensibility and intrinsic motivation (Carlton & Winsler, 1998), all considered favourably in educational contexts. Conversely, Michael's response in falling onto the construction, destroying it and scattering the blocks loudly across the mat, is viewed as senseless and unreasonable, as he lays his body across the pile of blocks.

After demolishing the building, Michael lifts a block into the air, hitting another nearby child in the head. This child tries to retaliate by hitting Michael back, but as the noise level starts to rise, this child moves on without complaint, when the teacher's attention is noted. There is an ever present risk to the social order when engaging with the 'not normal'. Michael is marked by his psychological diagnosis and the discursive practices of special education. He is closely watched by teaching staff at all times, as his diagnosis subjects him as impulsive and disruptive. Seb tries to 'normalise' Michael's play, or at least contain him, and return order to the block corner. Seb enacts the discursive practice of tolerance as a way to regulate Michael's difference. The irrational Michael is a potential and real threat and in need of supervision. Seb, drawing on these discourses, tries to calm the situation.

When Michael starts to lift the blocks above his head Seb leaves the scene, as he assesses Michael's dangerousness up close. Seb moves away furtively, he does not complain to the teacher about Michael's dangerous block behaviours. The child who is hit by Michael tries to retaliate but moves on quickly, without protesting when the teacher starts to take notice. How is it that neither of the boys complain? As Brown (2006) explains, "tolerance was coined to manage eruptions of the particular against the imagined universal, the marginal against the mainstream, the outsiders against the insiders" (p. 86). Michael's eruption is afforded tolerance by the imagined universal, the 'normal', to manage him. Where does this leave 'inclusive' education if the unmarked children tolerate and separate themselves from the marked children? Phillips (1999) argues that tolerance "reinforces inequality between the majority and minority groups as it confirms the 'normality' of those who are dominant, defining the others (even to themselves) as 'deviant'" (p. 129). How can tolerance enacted by the 'normal' be 'inclusive'?

As the teacher puts the blocks back into the shelf, Michael builds other structures, that also crash and make noise. The teacher in putting some of the blocks away attempts to contain the noise and disorder, displaying her close supervision of Michael. She says nothing to Michael about hitting the other child or to Seb about his helping. The teacher's performance of concern could be read as avoiding a confrontation with Michael. Petersen's (2008) metaphor of the "runaway train" (p. 401) might be useful here. The teacher, as the 'concern expresser', might see Michael as the potential 'runaway train', "an uncontrollable force" (p. 401). It is her role to rescue other passengers, the unmarked children, so that they maintain their position and don't jump on the same train as Michael. Michael's marking is reinforced and his 'not normal' way of playing is tolerated by a concern for order. The unmarked children, including Seb, tolerate his actions, and in doing so keep the peace, manage the 'threat', and control the risk of the 'runaway train'. Tolerance is "conceived as a tool for managing or lessening this hostility to achieve peaceful co-existence" (Brown, 2006, p. 157).

Tolerating Michael is taken up as the better alternative to other ways of interacting with him. As Brown (2006) suggests, there seems little or no choice about living or playing with other people to which we object and we have to accept that tolerating is perhaps a better alternative (Brown, 2006). Michael is not corrected for his actions. He is not asked to be more careful. He is tolerated. But tolerance does other work, as the individual who is the bearer of tolerance, carries "an authority and potential subjection through unavowed norms" (Brown, 2006, p. 14), while all objects of tolerance are marked as deviant, marginalised and undesirable by virtue of being tolerated.

Seb is a bearer of tolerance. Tolerance is granted by those who do not require it on those who do (Brown, 2006, p. 186). Michael's violent and unruly actions in swinging the block around above his head is not met with more violence, but with a 'civilised' response, as tolerance is thought to work to repress violence (Brown, 2006). Are Seb's actions, along with the teacher's response, virtuous and civilised or exclusionary? Is this exclusionary practice a form of violence?

Is it possible that Michael could have a different way of understanding how to play with blocks? Michael lifts the block above his head to show his strength or is it just his game at that time? Conceivably, his striking of the other child with a block was just a bit of clumsiness or carelessness and was not enacted with any violent intent. However, it is read as a threat and some level of 'fear' is sensed in Seb. Michael is best left alone, if order is to be restored. As Michael continues to build, erecting a bridge that subsequently crashes and falls, Seb decides that he will move away to avoid getting hit by the blocks. He fears for his own safety. Seb's fear of Michael's actions, as the discursively produced Other, is tangible and through this action the threat materialises.

The scenarios, in this section on helping, make visible the discursive practices of tolerance in the classroom under the guise of helping and concern. These practices however, are also modes of exclusion, with each scenario divulging different and more nuanced way of performing these practices. In the next section, how tolerance is made visible in a different way is examined, as the unmarked children enact a kind of resignation around the marked child. Tolerance is further considered in the way the children seem to just give in, and endure the marked child and their actions.

Giving In, Giving Up, Putting Up With: Performances of Resignation as Toleration

Giving Up

Spencer (a child without a diagnosis) is up in the climbing tree. The rule is that only one child is allowed in the tree at any one time. Michael (a child with a diagnosis) starts to climb up the tree. Spencer tells Michael to get down, reminding him several times of the rule. Michael does not listen and moves further up the tree. Spencer then climbs down out of the tree, walking away shaking his head, and looking back at the tree as he goes. Spencer: "He always do's that!" he says with a sigh and a degree of resignation. He walks away looking unhappy, his face wrinkled up and eyes narrowed and looking back at Michael as he moves off. (Field Notes, 18/5/12, S1, p. 52) (Watson, 2016)

The climbing tree is very popular and conflicts over the tree are observed on many occasions (Field Notes, 25/5/12, S1, p. 68). Spencer moves away from the climbing tree and 'gives it up' to Michael. This action by Spencer could be read as an act of category boundary recognition, but also of tolerance in his acquiescence. Spencer maintains himself as recognisably 'normal' as he knows the 'tree' rules. He unhappily tolerates Michael, who is subjected as not having to follow the rules, unreasonable, and possibly threatening. To maintain the 'normal' order and to avoid confrontation with Michael and the teachers, Spencer practices tolerance. Drawing on permissible tolerance discourses, Spencer understands that he cannot challenge Michael over being in the tree. He does not want to 'set him off'. As Michael starts to climb the tree, Spencer tells him about the one person rule. This rational rule protects climbers and avoids accidents.

Children use pervasive safety discourses as justification for others to keep the rules in the classroom and in the playground. These same rules of play moreover, produce authorised exclusionary practices (Field Notes), as we saw beforehand in chapter three with James. The rules enforce who can play, who cannot play, how many can play and how play can happen (Watson, 2016). The unmarked children talk about the rules and how it is not safe if more than one person climbs the tree (Field Notes, 25/5/12, S1, p. 68). They take up the rules and enforce them. Spencer tells Michael several times to get down, but Michael does not respond, staying in the tree and climbing even higher.

Spencer was aware of my presence as I observed this encounter, and his comment on leaving the tree was directed toward me. His actions may have transpired as he could see that I was watching. He wanted to remain recognisably a member of the 'normal' category, showing his awareness of what is right and what is wrong. He may have imagined that, as an adult in this classroom, I would have the same expectations as the teachers, and so he positioned himself as the 'tolerator'.

Spencer accepts Michael's position as Other, by keeping the peace and tolerating his invasion of the tree. Yet his practice of tolerance is enacted differently to the actions described earlier in the chapter. He does not act to help Michael, but shows a submission or a resignation, accepting that he must move on. He demonstrates a rational self-control, by keeping the peace, and maintaining the social order. Tolerance involves the "withholding of speech or action in response to contingent individual dislikes or violations of taste" (Brown, 2006, p. 13). This withholding of speech and action, performed by Spencer, is a less visible form of tolerance than the helping work accomplished by the children in the previous scenarios. However the work it does in de-legitimising and excluding is nonetheless powerful (Watson, 2016). The effect maintains Spencer's 'normal' membership category, strengthening Michael's association with the 'not normal'. Even though Spencer is not particularly happy about performing this tolerant act, his charitable actions work to keep the tolerated separate (Brown, 2006). Tolerance here again contributes to the separation of the 'normal' from the 'not normal'.

Tolerance is often judged to create neutrality and respect toward the tolerated, and is readily taken up into civic ethos and the social practices of our modern society (Brown, 2006). The ideals of toleration are commonly associated with equality (Phillips, 1999), and the obligation to tolerate is regarded as a consequence of citizen equality, "but toleration is oddly out of tune with equality and does not lend itself easily to egalitarianism" (Phillips, 1999, p. 128). Tolerance conceals power relations, the power of authority, and the power associated with discourses of normativity, as "tolerance checks an attitude or condition of disapproval, disdain, or revulsion with a particular kind of overcoming" (Brown, 2006, p. 26). This 'kind of overcoming' includes modes of incorporating and regulating the presence of this Other within.

The practice of tolerance contributes to the moral education discourses that dominate the early childhood classroom, creating individuals who understand the 'right' way to be with 'others'. To be 'tolerant' is to be ethically virtuous and socially conscientious (Brown, 2006), to be a moral being. Within the discourses, children are deemed to be developing social and emotional competency, and are expected to enact tolerating practices. To be tolerant of the marked child, who is 'threateningly different' (Brown, 2006), displays a 'maturity' of ethical and civic understanding. The children take up this discourse if they wish to be subjected in this way. The same discourse positions the marked child as the uncivilised, deviant and an object of tolerance.

Putting Up With

Sam (a child with a diagnosis) is standing at the classroom door banging on it with his hands and making a whining noise. A teacher (casual staff) moves toward him holding her guitar, sits near him and starts to play. Sam sits on the floor nearby but continues to make a noise. When the teacher plucks the strings Sam moves her strumming hand away and hits the guitar. Several other children (without a diagnosis) have now gathered around the teacher with the guitar watching and waiting. Sam continues to whine and tries to stop the teacher from playing, by roughly and abruptly, pulling her hand away from the strings. The unmarked children watch him trying to stop the guitar playing. Sam gets up

and moves back to the door pulling at the padlock that keeps the door shut. He continues to make loud sounds. I take a photo of the children gathered around the guitar. Sam
notices the camera and grabbing it off me starts to push buttons on the camera. The other
children watch him, wide eyed, as he takes the camera and starts to use it. The unmarked
children do not say anything. He spends several minutes focused on manipulating the
camera. Sam becomes calm and is no longer making the noises. The other children just
watch him exploring the camera. They do not ask to have a turn of the camera or the
guitar even though Sam has had a turn of both. (Field Notes, 11/5/12, S1, p. 36)

Sam's transgression in banging on the door to get out, is overlooked at this time
and the teacher instead presents him with the guitar. Distraction is a technique
used in special education as a management strategy for behaviours that might be
deemed difficult to control (Johnson, Lashley, Stonek, & Bonjour, 2012; Myles &
Southwick, 2005). It is also used as a pedagogical tool with younger children to
gain or maintain attention. Sam, as the discursive Other, cannot be regulated by
'normal' disciplinary techniques, so distraction is used to change his behaviour.
Distraction furthermore avoids confrontation and additional disruption to the
social order.

A group of about five unmarked children sit down around the teacher on the
floor showing their interest in the guitar. As she strums the guitar, Sam moves the
teacher's hand away to stop the teacher playing, hitting the guitar and whining
loudly, as the teacher tries to play. The unmarked children watch on, as Sam cries
out and forcibly moves the teacher's hand away from the strings. The unmarked
children do not touch the guitar, they remain quiet, watching. As I take a photograph, Sam becomes interested in my camera and he grabs the camera from me.
The unmarked children sit quietly staring at him, with some disbelief. They do
not ask for a turn of the camera. They do not comment on Sam using the camera.
How do they know that they should not ask for a turn, or make a comment, and
how do they know that Sam's actions should be endured, but not copied? They
did not tell him to stop what he was doing, they did not interfere. They did not
ask for a turn to play with the camera or the guitar. Sam's transgressions, in trying
to stop the guitar playing and in snatching the camera, are not regulated by the
children, by the teacher or by me.

Using Reflexivity…

*Watching the children, watching Sam with the guitar, I wondered at first why they
did not ask for their turn. When Sam's attention moved onto my camera, I allowed
him to take it as I had no objection to him, or anyone else using it. At this point I*

think I might have repositioned myself as a teacher attempting to show how I could include Sam just as the teacher with the guitar had done. The teachers had told me that Sam enjoyed technology, using computers, Ipads and cameras and I thought that my actions would 'include' him, perhaps creating him as a clever technology user. I then again repositioned myself as a researcher trying to observe the 'normal' and their reactions to the transgressions of the Other. I offered the camera to the other children when Sam had finished with it but nobody wanted it. I contributed to Sam's marking at that time as I allowed him to do something that the unmarked children thought they could/should not do. I did not realise at the time they would decline my offer, but my actions in thinking I could disrupt in a small way Sam's subjection, merely occasioned the maintenance of the 'normal' and reinforced Sam's marked position within the available circulating discourses. This was one of the few occasions where I had a direct encounter with Sam, as he was kept at a distance by the teachers and the wrist band.

The unmarked children look shocked by Sam's actions but nevertheless seem resigned to them. Tolerance is enacted by the unmarked children, as they accept Sam's 'objectionable' actions, rather than preventing him from doing it (Horton, 1996), or even commenting on it. They demonstrate that they understand their place within the discourses as they work to maintain their positions. They cannot hide however their disbelief and disapproval of Sam's actions. They tolerate, as tolerating bestows on them an "additional badge of superiority" (Phillips, 1999, p. 129).

Giving In

At indoor play time Liam (a child without a diagnosis) and Michael (a child with a diagnosis) are standing at a small table in the corner of the room. The table has a light under it to illuminate whatever you put on top. One of the teachers commented that the children had looked at medical x-rays using it.

Michael is lining up colour pegs on the table. Liam has some pegs and some small shapes and he appears to be categorising them according to their brightness.

Michael starts to put the pegs into a small bag that is also on the table. He starts to take the pegs and shapes that Liam is using and Liam tries to take them back. Michael loudly responds, "No."

Liam then joins Michael putting the pegs into the bag. Liam however keeps a few pegs for himself.

Michael: "Put more in."

Liam: "Not my special things." Liam continues to put pegs into the bag that Michael is now holding open. Then Liam leaning across the table puts his arms around the remaining shapes he has placed on the table. Michael attempts to take Liam's shapes.

Liam: "No more."

Michael: "Please."

Liam: "No these are my decorations."

Michael: "Can I have some more please?"

Liam: "No."

Michael points to a purple triangle shape: "Can I have that one?"

Liam: "No."

The argument continues backward and forward. Liam hands Michael another bag.

Michael does not give up so Liam says: "Ok you can have one."

Liam hands him a shape but not the purple triangle that he has asked for. Michael grabs the triangle anyway and moves away with Liam calling to him: "Give it back."

Fiona, a teacher, moves closer to the boys as they become louder. Michael moves away with the triangle and puts it into the bag he has collected all the other pegs in. Liam talks to the teacher about the purple triangle and says that Michael took it from him. But as it has now disappeared, the teacher does not pursue Michael about it. Liam leaves the area looking unhappy. (Field Notes, 18/5/12, S1, p. 46)

In this observation, Liam and Michael are initially playing near each other and it appears that they are sharing the lamp table and the shapes and pegs. As Michael starts to put the pegs away and begins to take Liam's share as well, some conflict arises. Liam reclaims what has been taken from him. Michael responds with a loud "no". This retort from Michael elicits an immediate response from Liam, as he starts to join in with Michael putting the pegs and shapes in the bag, kowtowing to Michael's demands. How could Liam's response to Michael's loud "no", be understood? Was Liam 'giving in' to Michael or was something else happening as well? Michael's loud "no" response could be heard all around the classroom. This possibly 'threatening' and unreasonable loud sound, appeared to trigger in Liam, a degree of resignation and tolerance toward Michael.

As discussed previously, inappropriate levels of noise, and different kinds of noise in the classroom environment, need management. Excessive noise levels are discouraged, as they are argued to affect a child's cognitive growth, they are a distraction to one's attention and detrimental to learning (Evans, 2006; Shield & Dockrell, 2003). Too much noise reflects not enough learning. Rational cognitive growth requires one's full attention. Other noises like the ones made by the marked child are deemed to be in need of management, control and suppression. How do the noises made by the marked child come to be considered this way? How do the unmarked children and teachers respond to these noises?

The noises of the marked child are regarded as different to the 'normal' and attract a different response. They are viewed as immature in child development discourses. Words are valued and signal a privileged positioning in communication and development. Noises are regarded as problematic, sometimes impossible to understand, leading to confusion and anxiety. The noises made by one marked child in particular, Oliver, seemed to always result in general 'panic' among the staff as they tried to stop or minimise his noises. They offered him food, sleep or a nappy change, as a way of keeping him quiet. As he had no words, only sounds, they appeared to find his noises unsettling (Field Notes, 18/5/12, S1, p. 42) and they worked very hard to halt or contain them.

Returning to the scene above, Liam contains Michael's irrational noises by complying with his actions and tolerating him when he takes away the pegs and shapes. As Liam tries to keep a few, Michael tells him that he wants more. Liam does not fight against Michael, even though he continues to take his shapes. Liam tries to keep Michael quiet, being aware of the sounds that Michael might produce at any time, which could potentially position them both as 'unreasonable'. Just as Spencer was not happy about leaving the tree, Liam too is not happy about losing his shapes. Liam uses his body to create a barrier, putting his arms around the shapes trying to protect the last of them. The argument continues with Michael wanting more and Liam standing his ground. But Michael's noises, his persistence, and the potential threat of being associated with him, are signs for Liam that he should 'give in', to preserve the social order and his position as 'normal'. What kind of subjects does this kind of tolerating produce here? Michael's transgressions must be tolerated. Michael subsequently takes the prized purple shape. They argue again more loudly, which attracts the teacher's attention. As Liam is engaged with the teacher explaining his actions, Michael slips away with the desirable purple shape. Liam's requests for recompense go unheard. Michael's noise is contained by Liam's tolerance and the teacher's actions reinforce this. Liam, like Spencer, leaves the scene unhappy but recognisably part of the 'normal' and the tolerant.

Giving up and giving in are acts of tolerance performed by the 'normal', as they display their category membership around the marked child. Keeping the social order, by not setting the marked child off, or by keeping noises to a minimum, are ways that the unmarked children can 'do' this boundary work in the classroom. Giving up and giving in, position one as reasonable. Being resigned to the presence and actions of the marked child, and using tolerance as a discursive practice, produces a divide between the 'normal' and the 'not normal', those who are 'reasonable', and those who are not able to be reasoned with. Tolerance creates a separation. It produces a level of resignation and a silence around something that is not talked about, but nevertheless is 'put up with' and not addressed.

Who and What Can We Tolerate?

Cohen (2004) reminds us, "tolerance is not indifference" (p. 71) and the need to tolerate only emerges when we recognise something that we disapprove of, or dislike. Toleration, requires the tolerator, to have a negative response about something they 'care' enough about, to warrant the need for tolerance. In the following scenario, the unmarked children draw again on discourses of concern and tolerance, as they talk about the legitimacy of the marked child's appearance, as she wears an eye-patch on her glasses.

> Me: "I've noticed Jasmine (a child with a diagnosis) wears a patch on her glasses."
> Cody (a child without a diagnosis): "Yeah."
> Hamish (a child without a diagnosis): "Yeah cause that's because that eye can't see."
> Tyler (a child without a diagnosis): "No because that eye doesn't um … it's not so strong enough and that eye's strong enough." (He points to his own eye to indicate which eye he is referring to.)
> Cody: "Nah. This one's not and this one's strong." (He points to his eyes.) "It's a forty six and it's an eight." (Again pointing to each eye to indicate the difference.)
> Me: "Why don't you have a patch on your glasses?" (Both Cody and Tyler wear glasses.)
> Cody: "Cause our eyes can see properly."
> Me: "How do you know about Jasmine's patch?"
> Hamish: "Umm."
> Cody: "Andrea told us." (Andrea is the centre director and teacher.)
> Me: "Why did she tell you?"
> Hamish: "Ahh … because we asked Andrea one day and then she told me."
> Me: "Why did you ask her?"
> Hamish: "I just thought and said to Andrea … maybe you're not allowed to have that on … we just thought maybe we should ask the teachers if its allowed at preschool." (Field Notes, 20/11/12, S3, p. 102)

When I ask the unmarked children about Jasmine's eye-patch, they positioned themselves immediately as medical authorities, a knowledge of superiority. They talk numbers to describe Jasmine's eyesight, as numbers are created as a powerful and authoritative knowledge in educational settings. Knowing about numbers in preschool displays one's maturity and readiness for school. Using numbers calls attention to their authority and knowledge. They talk about Jasmine as not seeing properly, even though two of the three unmarked children in the conversation, are wearing glasses. Possibly they consider their eyes to be different to Jasmine's, as they are not wearing a patch. They comment that Jasmine has "one eye that can't see" and maintain that "our eyes can see properly". They do not position themselves with the same 'deficit' as Jasmine. Their questions regarding the eye-patch reveal how they position Jasmine as different, while maintaining their category membership. The eye-patch, as a non-human actor, contributes to the production of Jasmine's marked position and provides the unmarked children with particular understandings of her.

The unmarked children have conferred about the acceptability of this non-human actor before as they describe how they asked the director about it. Hamish wanted to find out about the validity and correctness of wearing this eye-patch at preschool. But, what else is going on here? Do the children's questions about the eye-patch intend to challenge Jasmine's legitimacy? Do they want to know whether Jasmine's eye-patch should be tolerated, or are they questioning the legitimacy of Jasmine in this classroom? Their enquiry, about tolerating Jasmine's transgression in wearing the patch, is not just about managing a potential threat to order or curtailing conflict, but is also about shoring up the legitimacy of the 'normal' and expanding its power and dominance. As Cohen (2004) reminds us, tolerance is not pluralism or an enthusiastic endorsement of difference (p. 73). After deferring to the expertise of the director, again legitimising the 'normal', to check if Jasmine should be tolerated, they discover that they must endure Jasmine's strangeness. The discussion about her medical issues reinforces this. The unmarked children show tolerance by following the protocol of checking with the teacher, as "toleration suggests an act of generosity from those who have the power to interfere but refrain from doing so" (Phillips, 1999, p. 128).

Tolerance involves a degree of non-interference (Cohen, 2004). The unmarked children do not interfere with Jasmine, and her eye-patch wearing, and in this way they are tolerating her difference. By consulting the teacher, as the authority in the classroom, the unmarked children are positioned as rational rule followers, who understand how the hierarchy operates, and how power is exercised in the classroom. The effect of tolerance, and non-interference, however reinforces Jasmine's marking and their category membership. The unmarked children's concern for Jasmine's conduct is not just about the eye-patch. However, in order to understand Jasmine, they can only draw on available discourses, which produce Jasmine as different and deviant, potentially unruly and in need of governing and management.

The discursive practice of tolerance is enacted here to quiet any unrest that Jasmine's patch or Jasmine might arouse. Tolerance placates and tries to bury "the social powers constitutive of difference" (Brown, 2006, p. 89). The powers that produce difference, and the differences that are discursively produced around the 'normal', are quietened by tolerance. Differences that reveal inequality, exclusion and marginalisation are "ideologically vanquished" (Brown, 2006, p. 89) when tolerance as a practice, hides what it wants to bury.

Teaching and Learning Tolerance

Tolerance creates a certain kind of social order and certain kinds of subjects. It regulates the presence of the Other (Brown, 2006, p. 8) and at times needs to be 'taught' when intolerance is observed.

> Sam (a child with a diagnosis) is in the preschool yard trying to climb through the holes in a hanging sheet that is being used as a goal for bean bag throwing. As he persists with trying to get through the sheet the other children continue to throw the bean bags with some of them hitting him on the head. Nothing is said to Sam or the children about this. A teacher moves Sam away from this activity. He moves towards a climbing frame that has been left near the storage garage. He starts to climb it but is stopped by the same teacher who comments to me, "He loves to climb, he does not need to be encouraged. He can climb out of the school yard, he's like a monkey". Sam tries again to climb up the frame and again the teacher takes him down. He tries to climb several more times but is stopped. He then moves over to the preschool gate and tries to put his foot up on the vertical bars like he might try to climb the fence. Eddie (a child without a diagnosis) has been following this teacher like her shadow all morning and he closely watches this interaction with Sam and the teacher, and he comments to me as I am observing nearby;
> Eddie: "Sam is really naughty."
> Me: "What is he doing?"
> Eddie: "Climbing on the gate and Anne was getting him down."
> Me: "Do you climb on the gate?"
> Eddie: "No!"(very definitely)
> Me: "Why?"
> Eddie: "I'm not naughty."
> Me: "Why do you think Sam climbs on the gate?"
> Eddie: "Because he's a naughty little boy. You can't climb on the gate."
> Anne, the teacher, hears Eddie's comment and looks at me with eyes wide. She starts to talk to him about Sam, but she has to move quickly chasing Sam. She says to Eddie; "Sam just hasn't learnt all the rules yet."
> Eddie shakes his head, frowning with a surly look. (Field Notes, 7/5/12, S1, p. 29)

Sam is climbing on a sheet that the children are using as a target for their bean bag throwing. The children continue to throw the bags even though they are hitting Sam. Sam is not playing with the equipment in the prescribed way. Were the children enacting intolerance by hitting Sam with the bean bags? Did they not see him? Sam did not move away, he did not protest. Were his actions viewed to be without reason? Was it okay to throw the bean bags at him because he did not respond to the bean bag 'assault'? How was this potential intolerance, or perhaps outright attack on or abuse of him, viewed by the teacher? How did I view this myself and why did I not step in to halt the assault on Sam?

The actions of the unmarked children illustrate how they regularise and normalise appropriate ways to play, while excluding Sam's way to play and learn. Clearly, Sam did not exhibit the appropriate or acceptable way to play with the equipment. At this time, Sam's actions in 'not playing within the rules' did not inspire tolerance. The rules of the game though, legitimised the unmarked children's actions of throwing bean bags, even if Sam was within the target range. Via the rules of the game, the children could exercise a sovereign form of power. The 'rules' suspended Sam's right to 'be' and 'do' in this space. The rules provided the children with an exception to tolerance. Sam did not follow the rules and he was in the wrong place. The disciplinary power of playing the game properly, did not have an effect on Sam, and therefore a more direct sovereign power was applied. As Millei and Cliff (2014) explain in drawing on Agamben's (2005) notion of the 'exception', the regulation of a target identified as 'exceptional', legitimises 'exceptional' action. The unmarked children are "at the point where disciplinary power is exhausted, [and] the project of 'civilising' the body no longer requires only 'regular' surveillance and normalising instruction by educators and other experts" (p. 260), but requires sovereign power to be exercised. This power is legitimised by the circulating developmental discourses and the rules of the game, suspending Sam's rights as a legitimate subject.

Sam is moved away from the area so that the unmarked children can continue to play the game in the approved manner. His way of playing with the activity is not recognised, or talked about, or given any degree of legitimacy. Again, we see the marked child separated, and moved on, but in this case, tolerance was suspended. This time Sam is separated from the unmarked children for his own protection. Nothing is said and no action taken as the rules of the game seemed to dissolve the need for toleration. An 'unreasonable' and 'not human' Sam, did not produce toleration in the children, the teachers, or me, at this time.

Using Reflexivity…

What was I doing as this was happening? As I watched the children throw the bean bags at Sam, I made a mental note that the 'missiles' could not physically harm him. Sam did not protest or move away and I did not step in to challenge the children's actions. At the time I was alarmed by their actions, I thought that perhaps the children were showing their disapproval and abjection of Sam in a 'legitimised' way, as they could claim they were just trying to play the game properly. As I continued to reflect on this scene my discomfort increased as I contemplated the disciplining violence enacted on Sam by the power of the 'normal'. Sam's objectification within the classroom dis-

courses made him 'less than human' and the children no longer tolerated him in this moment. How do these discourses operate and maintain their legitimacy when they violently marginalise and de-humanise in this way? I was a part of this observation, I stood around, probably open mouthed and surprised. The way Sam was moved on by the teacher without words, like a 'wheelbarrow' being manoeuvred on a path, also reinforced for me his 'less than human' positioning. The scene however seemed all too familiar to me as a teacher and researcher. The way the discourses produce the marked child as the anomaly, objectified and 'not normal', with deficits that create them as less than human.

I think my reading of this scene is uncomfortable as it disrupts the 'harmonious' image of the 'inclusive' classroom, and highlights the violence of relations when discourses create subjects that are 'right' and 'wrong', where the 'wrong' must be 'remediated'. Nevertheless I continue in this representation to challenge, disrupt and trouble the hegemonic structures that I have worked within and present new ways of thinking "pushing toward an unfamiliar, towards an uncomfortable" (Pillow, 2003, p. 192).

Sam, shadowed by the wrist band wearing teacher, becomes interested in a climbing frame and starts to clamber up. The teacher tries to stop him as she draws on regulatory and safety discourses. The teachers often talk about Sam's interest in and ability to escape (Field Notes, 30/4/12, 7/5/12, S1). Each time he tries to climb on something the teacher picks him up and moves him on. She maintains a level of patience in her endeavour to stop him climbing, modelling a tolerance toward Sam. "He can climb out of the school yard, he's like a monkey" is the teacher's comment. Sam is now positioned as 'other than human', or less than human, and a threat to himself and potentially to others. His climbing actions are viewed as unreasonable. He is compared to a 'monkey' climbing irrationally, unpredictably, erratically and without purpose. Sam's actions position him as barbaric or animal-like, and again as one who needs to be developed, using tolerance as a discursive practice, to civilise him (Brown, 2006). Sam's actions, and the knowledge of his diagnosis, contribute to producing him as a particular kind of subject. Sam is positioned by the 'normal' via his diagnosis, and his irrational (animal-like) behaviours. Sam, like a monkey, needs to be contained, controlled and civilised.

During all this, Eddie (a child without a diagnosis) follows closely behind the teacher, Anne. He is alongside Anne, as she watchfully monitors Sam's climbing. Eddie hears her comment about Sam being a monkey and remarks to me that Sam is being "really naughty". Eddie, drawing on regulatory discourses, is cognisant that Sam's climbing is outside the borders of appropriate behaviour. He pays close attention to Sam's actions. He does not ignore Sam, as many of the unmarked children do. From the tone of his voice, he is annoyed by Sam's rule-breaking actions and wants Sam to stop doing what he is doing.

Eddie desires more of the teacher's time than other children, as he follows her around, requesting her attention throughout the morning. He seems resentful of the time she spends with Sam, expressing intolerance towards him. Eddie positions himself as superior in knowing appropriate ways of being, while calling Sam 'naughty', using an irritated tone of voice. He positions Sam as one who needs to be punished, rather than tolerated and rewarded, with so much attention. The teacher Anne, however, hastily draws on tolerance discourses, and steps in to the conversation to regulate Eddie, teaching him to be more tolerant of Sam. She tells Eddie that Sam hasn't learnt all the rules yet. Eddie appears unhappy with this response from the teacher and doesn't seem to readily accept this idea.

Using Reflexivity…

This was one of only a few times when the practice of tolerance was interrupted, as the unmarked child resisted this discourse, positioning the marked child as 'naughty', just a regular 'naughty', not pathologised. When observing this I immediately and spontaneously positioned myself in the teacher's shoes and thought yes it is necessary to teach tolerance here and Eddie needs to know that Sam is not 'naughty' just not the same … What was I thinking? How can tolerating bring about a rethinking and re-positioning of subjects? Again I said nothing. The tolerance discourses that circulate in the 'inclusive' classroom informed my 'naturalised' and instantaneous response to this situation. I had to challenge myself to think otherwise about this, as I still struggled in the context to question the familiar.

Earlier, as Eddie watches on, while Sam is hit by the bags, he does not appear to take any notice. Conversely he watches very closely as Sam moves haphazardly from activity to activity without apparent reason. He observes him as he climbs on the equipment and the boundary fences, positioning him as an escape risk. Eddie can see that Sam does not obey the rules. He does not accept Sam's behaviour, he does not tolerate it, or become resigned to it. Eddie positions Sam as intolerable. The teacher urges tolerance by drawing on developmental and learning discourses, but this does not seem to impress Eddie.

Tolerance discourses can be drawn upon when individuals behave in ways that are offensive or disturbing. Here again tolerance is enacted by a negative response (Cohen, 2004). Eddie voices his negative opinion about Sam, saying that he is 'naughty', but a child with a diagnosis is not produced as 'naughty' in this classroom. They are produced as 'deficient' and often unreasonable, and as such, in need of sympathy and tolerance. This tolerance teaching, performed by the teacher, encourages Eddie to position Sam as something other than 'naughty'. Sam is not constituted as 'naughty', even though his actions could be read that way. To be positioned as 'naughty' is not always pathological. 'Naughty' attracts discipline, not tolerance or sympathy. Sam is constituted and read as pathological and 'deviant'. In trying to irrationally escape, by climbing like a monkey out of the preschool yard, he becomes other than human and other than rational. He is not positioned as the naughty or the 'bad', as they are considered somewhat rational. Following Laws (2011), it could be argued, that he is positioned as the 'mad'.

To speak of a young child as 'mad' may well be considered outside the domains of acceptable discourses. In sanctioned discourses, children are often regarded as 'untamed' or 'innocent', but never 'mad' (Laws, 2011). Utilising Foucault's (1967) work on the history of adult madness, as a tool for understanding the discursive constitution of the 'inclusive' classroom, it becomes appreciable that the marked child, via the dominant and marginalising discourses, is positioned as 'mad'. Positioned as different, delayed, deviate and in need of surveillance. The marked child is watched over, and their actions are scrutinised, as they present a threat to the 'normal' with their unpredictability. They are separated from the 'normal' group by the take up of multiple discourses, by teachers, by children and by non-human actors. A sense of anxiety is created around this child, as they might escape, they might make 'strange' noises, upsetting the peace and order, or they might hurt someone or themselves. Foucault (2006) argues that it is this sense of anxiety that reinforces and maintains the separateness, and the ongoing need to separate.

Is it possible that traces of the practices that have been used to 'deal with' 'madness' over centuries (Foucault, 1967) are still to be found in the way we talk about, the way we manage and the way we help the marked child? (Laws, 2011). The 'mad' attract a level of toleration, the 'bad' do not. Sam's diagnosis, its characteristics and his actions, require tolerance from the unmarked children, as his diagnostic deficits create him as the 'abject', object of 'concern' or the exceptional. The discourse of concern, constructed over centuries, is for the maintenance of the 'normal'. Sam's positioning as 'mad' requires containment and management to sustain a level of order (Foucault, 1967). The 'normal' must confine the 'not normal' to protect itself.

In maintaining and legitimising the 'normal', tolerance is encouraged as a preferred alternative to other reactions such as outright rejection, repression or exile (Brown, 2006). Tolerance is enacted on those things and subjects, that tolerators think they can change in some way, as "we do not tolerate what is outside of our reach, what is irrelevant to us, or what we cannot do anything about" (Brown, 2006, p. 29). Eddie at this time positioned Sam as 'bad'. The children who threw the bean bags at Sam positioned him as unable to be reasoned with. They did not tolerate what they saw as out of their reach. Eddie did not tolerate Sam because he did not think he could be changed. However, he was encouraged to tolerate and re-position Sam as 'mad', as having deficits and in need of help.

"Don't Stir Him Up"

> Michael's (a child with a diagnosis) play in the home corner was getting rowdier. He loudly called out across the room to Michaela and Rachel (children without a diagnosis). They had left the home corner to go on a 'holiday' but Michael wanted them to return to the home corner where he was waiting, lying in a small cot. A teacher, Edith, approached the home corner and engaged Michael in a game as it seemed the girls were not going to return. She played with Michael for a short time and then Patrick (a child without a diagnosis) joined the game. Both children were moving milk containers quickly in and out of the small refrigerator. Patrick commented: "Michael the milk might be getting hard … better get it out of the freezer" To which Michael replied: "Hurry, hurry, hurry" as he took all the containers out of the fridge frantically and noisily dropping them all over the floor. Michael and Patrick became very excited in the play. Containers were flying around, they were picked up, thrown into fridge and out again; a flurry of activity, with an ever increasing level of noise.
> A teacher, Anne, moved quickly to the area and said to Patrick, "Don't stir him up. You can still play with him because he likes it, but don't stir him up". With this comment, the game ended. Patrick with his eyes downcast wandered around in the home corner talking to himself and randomly touching objects on the table. Michael continued to play with the milk cartons alone. Anne, the teacher then turned to me, as she saw me watching, and said that Patrick had 'stirred up' Michael before by encouraging him to go and play on the computer keyboard and then telling another child to try and take it off him. Again the teacher Anne reinforced this saying: "Patrick tries to wind him up". (Field Notes, 4/5/12, S1, p. 15)

Patrick moved into the area quite quickly after the teacher, Edith, left. It appeared that he was keen to play with Michael. He seemed to be enjoying the game. He was smiling and trying to encourage Michael to play the game at a faster pace. However, the game got 'too noisy' for classroom expectations and the teacher Anne, stepped in. The teacher seemed to assume that Patrick's intentions for playing with Michael were questionable, harbouring negative objectives, as she commented that Patrick tries to wind Michael up. Did her actions aim to protect Michael, Patrick or the social order of the classroom? The teacher, drawing on discourses of regulation and special education, perhaps wished to 'protect' the 'vulnerable' child with a diagnosis while maintaining order. What were the effects?

Michael is constituted as easily unsettled, easily wound up and potentially a threat to the order of the classroom. 'Stirring him up' is thought and said to be ill-advised. Suppressing and containing Michael's potential 'threat' maintains the 'normal' and the social order of things. Discouraging Patrick from playing with Michael does other things as well. It both isolates and separates Michael from Patrick and arguably exposes traces of historic practices of confinement and expulsion (Foucault, 1967). Michael is isolated from playing with the 'normal' Patrick. Patrick removes himself, and Michael plays alone. Patrick is disciplined and somewhat embarrassed. He is reminded how to act around Michael. He must not play with Michael in this way and he must be more careful with Michael. He is told not to stir Michael up and be more cognisant of the potential risk that Michael poses. Michael's marked position is reinforced and his marginalisation maintained. Patrick can only play in a particular way with Michael, as only certain interactions result in behaviours that are tolerable for the classroom order.

'Regimes of truth' operate to individualise particular subjects, and those who disrupt or threaten to disrupt the social order, are more "strongly individualised" (Brown, 2006, p. 43). In modern disciplinary societies, the 'normal' subject can usually avoid this individuating discipline by disciplining themselves, via the 'normal', but those who deviate cannot. They are more often 'dissected', regulated and Othered (Foucault, 1977). As Brown (2006) recognises, the tolerated "will always be those who deviate from the norm" (p. 44). Michael deviates from the 'normal' and must be tolerated, and often the best way to do this is to leave him alone. The practice of separating Patrick from Michael contains the 'mad' and maintains the order.

The disorderliness of the noise created in the game and the spontaneous flurry of activity is stemmed by the teacher's response. The teachers keep a vigilant check on the possible threat that is Michael. What informs the teacher's actions? Was she concerned about Michael's response? Or was her concern about Patrick's involvement? What might happen if Michael was set off? How did this act of separation constitute subjectivities? Perhaps Patrick did like to stir up Michael. He might have enjoyed the noises Michael made, and the 'wild/mad' behaviour that Michael often exhibited. Possibly Patrick wanted to be able to play in this way too. Was there the potential that this 'madness/wildness' could propagate in the classroom? Foucault (1967) "argues that the confinement of 'madness' has nothing to do with any medical concept" (Laws, 2011, p. 52). Historically, practices of confinement arose to protect the population from the contagion of disease (Foucault, 1967). This practice over time moved to contain those who were considered a threat to social order, not just because of health alone, but also because of their unreasonable and irrational behaviours (Foucault, 1967).

'Wild', noisy play is not encouraged in educational settings and is viewed as 'unproductive', as already noted. Discourses of 'play as learning' (Grieshaber & McArdle, 2010) and 'play as work' (Cannella, 1997) dominate the setting. Children are thought to learn best through play by interacting with materials, other children and adults (Bredekamp & Copple, 1997). "Play is viewed as children's serious real-life work of constructing, organizing and shaping social orders" (Blaise, 2005, p. 37). Play is imagined as productive, not wild and noisy. This observation was one of the few times in the research where an unmarked child made a move to *play* with a marked child. Michael's 'wild' play, when he plays alone, is tolerated but when an unmarked child starts to play in the same way, this is not tolerated and dissuaded. Patrick possibly attempts to disrupt the 'norm' by playing with Michael. But the 'normal' is preserved by the teacher, as category boundary crossing is restrained and forbidden. Joining the 'mad', in 'mad' play, is not permitted, as the 'mad' should remain controlled and separate. The 'mad' must be tolerated but the 'mad' cannot endanger the 'normal' and its orderliness. The 'normal' in joining the 'mad' might blur or break down the boundary between the two and this could be dangerous for the 'normal'. If all the unmarked children enacted the 'wild/mad' play, what could happen to the classroom, what could happen to the children?

Tolerance is imposed in order to help regulate the Other and their interactions with the 'normal'. Eddie in the previous scenario, is encouraged to tolerate Sam, as he climbs around the playground like a 'monkey'. He is told that Sam is not 'naughty' or bad. Eddie is supported to understand Sam differently. If Sam is not 'bad' is it possible that he is produced in the classroom as 'mad'? In the second scenario Patrick is corrected for his play interactions with the 'unruly' Michael. Separation of the children is a priority for the teacher. A separate space between the marked and unmarked categories is a contributing constituent of the 'normal'. Eddie is taught to tolerate the 'mad', as they are not 'bad', and Patrick is taught that only minimal and controlled interactions with the 'mad' are tolerable. Tolerance keeps a distance.

Tolerance Hides Difference

Tolerance is often framed as a sign of steady progress toward a more civilised society, cultivated as a way to liberate and empower excluded populations. It is now dominant in both popular and state discourses (Brown, 2006) with toleration considered as the substantive heart of liberalism (Cohen, 2004). Tolerance, as a discursive practice in the early childhood classroom, offers little for 'inclusive' practices (Watson, 2016). The discursive power of tolerance positions subjects in particular ways that can include and/or exclude. The idea that tolerance creates a more 'liberal' classroom is not established, as the enactment of tolerance operates to regulate and civilise, by imposing the 'normal', on those considered different to the 'normal'.

In the classroom, inequalities and difference are suppressed by tolerance discourses (Brown, 2006). Phillips (1999) argues, that tolerance provides "no recipe for better understanding and does little to challenge the prejudice on which tolerance feeds" (p. 129). Those who agree to tolerate, see themselves absolved from any further moves towards better understanding, and difference is constructed together with deficit and danger. The hegemonic normative discourses remain powerful at the centre, marginalising those who are not members of this category. Toleration makes no obligation about rethinking the basis of the disapproval that warrants the toleration (Phillips, 1999). The marked children, as subjects in need of toleration, are consistently viewed and positioned in the category boundary work, as "undesirable and marginal, as luminal subjects or even luminal humans; and those called upon to exercise tolerance are asked to repress or override their hostility or repugnance in the name of civility, peace and progress" (Brown, 2006, p. 28). The discourse of tolerance makes no move to rethink the 'normal', or the disapproval of the Other (Watson, 2016). Examined in this way tolerance makes no move toward a more 'inclusive' classroom.

In the following chapter the practice of silence becomes the focal point of attention inside the classroom. The effects of the 'normal' become visible in the nuanced ways that silence is performed, when the unmarked children encountered the marked child in the classroom. Silences were enacted as Eddie was silenced by his teacher when he said Sam was naughty and Patrick was silenced as he played with Michael. Liam and Spencer became silent in their tolerant resignation of Michael and his actions. Tolerance makes a contribution to the multiple silences played out in the classroom, producing an environment where certain things cannot be talked about, or can only be talked about or addressed, in available and sanctioned ways.

References

Agamben, G. (2005). *State of exception* (Kevin Attell, Trans.). Chicago, IL: University of Chicago Press.

Ailwood, J. (2003). Governing early childhood education through play. *Contemporary Issues in Early Childhood, 4*(3), 286–299.

Blaise, M. (2005). *Playing it straight; Uncovering gender discourses in the early childhood classroom.* New York, NY: Routledge.

Bredekamp, S., & Copple, C. (1997). *Developmentally appropriate practice in early childhood programs serving children from birth through to age 8.* Washington, DC: National Association for the Education of Young Children.

Brown, W. (2006). *Regulating aversion: Tolerance in the age of identity and empire.* Princeton, NJ: Princeton University Press.

Butler, J. (1997). *Excitable speech. A politics of the performative.* New York, NY: Routledge.

Cannella, G. S. (1997). *Deconstructing early childhood education: Social justice & revolution.* New York, NY: Peter Lang.

Carlton, M. P., & Winsler, A. (1998). Fostering intrinsic motivation in early childhood classrooms. *Early Childhood Education Journal, 25*(3), 159–166.

Cohen, A. J. (2004). What toleration is. *Ethics, 115*(1), 68–95.

Davies, B. (1983). The role pupils play in the social construction of classroom order. *British Journal of Sociology of Education, 4*(1), 55–69.

Davies, B., & Harré, R. (1999). Positioning and personhood. In R. Harré & L. van Langenhove (Eds.), *Positioning theory: Moral contexts of intentional action* (pp. 32–52). Oxford: Blackwell Publishers.

Diamond, K. E., Hestenes, L. L., Carpenter, E. S., & Innes, F. K. (1997). Relationships between enrolment in an inclusive class and preschool children's ideas about people with disabilities. *Topics in Early Childhood Special Education, 17*, 520–536.

Evans, G. W. (2006). Child development and the physical environment. *Annual Review of Psychology, 57*, 423–451.

Foucault, M. (1967). *Madness and civilisation: A history of insanity in the age of reason.* London: Routledge.

Foucault, M. (1977). *Discipline and punish: The birth of the prison.* London: Penguin.

Foucault, M. (1982). The subject and power. *Critical Inquiry, 8*(4), 777–795.

Foucault, M. (2006). *History of madness.* Oxon: Routledge.

Grieshaber, S., & McArdle, F. (2010). *The trouble with play.* New York, NY: Open University Press.

Horton, J. (1996). Toleration as a virtue. In D. Heyd (Ed.), *Toleration: An elusive virtue* (pp. 28–43). Princeton, NJ: Princeton University Press.

Jackson, A. Y., & Mazzei, L. A. (2012). *Thinking with theory in qualitative research: Viewing data across multiple perspectives.* London: Routledge.

Johnson, N. L., Lashley, J., Stonek, A. V., & Bonjour, A. (2012). Children with developmental disabilities at a paediatric hospital: Staff education to prevent and manage challenging behaviours. *Journal of Paediatric Nursing, 27*, 742–749.

Laws, C. (2011). *Poststructuralism at work with marginalised children.* Sharjah: Bentham Science Publishers.

Leavitt, R. L., & Power, M. B. (1997). Civilising bodies: Children in day care. In J. Tobin (Ed.), *Making a place for pleasure in early childhood education.* Michigan: Edward Brothers.

Millei, Z. (2005). The discourse of control: Disruption and Foucault in an early childhood classroom. *Contemporary Issues in Early Childhood, 6*(2), 128–139.

Millei, Z. (2011). Thinking differently about guidance: Power, children's autonomy and democratic environments. *Journal of Early Childhood Research, 10*(1), 88–99.

Millei, Z., & Cliff, K. (2014). The preschool bathroom: Making 'problem bodies' and the limit of the disciplinary regime over children. *British Journal of Sociology of Education, 35*(2), 244–262. doi: 10.1080/01425692.2012.761394

Molloy, H., & Vasil, L. (2002). The social construction of asperger syndrome: The pathologising of difference? *Disability & Society, 17*(6), 659–669.

Myles, B. S., & Southwick, J. (2005). *Asperger syndrome and difficult moments: Practical solutions for tantrums, rage and meltdowns.* Shawnee Mission, KS: AAPC Publishing.

Odom, S. L. (2000). Preschool inclusion: What we know and where we go from here. *Topics in Early Childhood Special Education, 20*(1), 20–28.

Petersen, E. B. (2008). The conduct of concern: Exclusionary discursive practices and subject positions in academia. *Educational Philosophy and Theory, 40*(3), 394–406.

Phillips, A. (1999). The politicisation of difference: Does this make for a more intolerant society? In J. Horton & S. Mendus (Eds.), *Toleration, identity and difference* (pp. 126–145). New York, NY: Palgrave Macmillan.

Pillow, W. S. (2003). Confession, catharsis, or cure? Rethinking the uses of reflexivity as a methodological power in qualitative research. *Qualitative Studies in Education, 16*(2), 175–196.

Shield, B. M., & Dockrell, J. E. (2003). The effects of noise on children at school: A review. *Building Acoustics, 10*(2), 97–116.

Slee, R. (2011). *The irregular school: Exclusion, schooling and inclusive education.* Oxon: Routledge.

Washbrook, E., Propper, C., & Sayal, K. (2013). Pre-school hyperactivity/attention problems and educational outcomes in adolescence: Prospective longitudinal study. *The British Journal of Psychiatry, 203*, 265–271.

Watson, K. (2016). Talking tolerance inside the 'inclusive' early childhood classroom. Bank Street. *Occasional Papers Series 36, Part II.* Retrieved from https://www.bankstreet.edu/occasional-paper-series/36/part-ii/talking-tolerance-insixe/

6

Nuanced Silences and Their Effects

Careful consideration has been given to what was 'seen', 'said', 'heard' and assembled in the classroom. In this chapter, attention is turned to the things that were not seen, not said and not heard. An exploration of silences is a critical part of looking at the whole, as it is "the relevant speech act 'spoken' beneath the surface" (Mazzei, 2007b, p. xii).

> Silence itself—the things one declines to say, or is forbidden to name, the discretion that is required between different speakers—is less the absolute limit of discourse, the other side from which it is separated by a strict boundary, than an element that functions alongside the things said, with them and in relation to them within over-all strategies. (Foucault, 2008, p. 27)

Keeping 'silent', being 'silent' or not speaking, or speaking about something in different terms in order to avoid speaking, are examples of what could be cogitated as discursive moves (Mazzei, 2007b). Silences are essential components in the analysis of classroom encounters as they contribute to the 'meaning between words' (Mazzei, 2007b). Silences not only shape the category of the 'normal' but are produced as an effect of it, and its category maintenance work. How does silence position subjects? What does silence do? Silences have much to teach the researcher (Mazzei, 2007b).

In examining silences, there is no desire to create a binary between speech and silence, that is between what one says and what one does not say, but instead theorising with Foucault it seems that;

> we must try to determine the different ways of not saying such things, how those who can and those who cannot speak of them are distributed, which type of discourse is authorised, or which form of discretion is required in either case. (Foucault, 2008, p. 27)

Silences pervade discourses and are visible in discursive practices. As discourses are taken up, silences can powerfully exclude and oppress those who do not speak from the authorised discourse. The silences taken up and performed by the authorised 'normal' contribute to the noticeable and continual separation of the marked and the unmarked. A separate space for the marked child is produced in the many silent practices employed by human and non-human assemblages in the classroom. Traces of historical discourses from centuries past, where 'madness' was silenced and confined to places of asylum (Foucault, 1967, 2006), are discernible. The silences reveal a shared understanding among the children that some things cannot be spoken of.

To begin, a contrast to the silences created around the marked child is presented. In what follows, the misdemeanours of the unmarked children in their everyday encounters with each other are loudly resisted and protested. Silence is not the practice taken up here. Drawing attention to this interaction juxtaposes the subsequent scenarios, as encounters with a marked child produce very different effects.

Not So Silent

> Elliot (a child without a diagnosis) is in the sandpit digging a deep hole and I am sitting nearby.
> Elliot: "Come and see how big my hole is."
> Me: "It's huge!"
> Kane (a child without a diagnosis) moves closer to take a look and stands in Elliot's freshly dug hole.
> Elliot: "Get out of it!" (loud and angry)
> Kane: "No, I'm not."
> Elliot: (to me) "He's in my hole … he's in my hole."
> I do not respond verbally but give Elliot a sad look.
> Kane: "I'm not getting out … it's everyone's hole." (Kane is now stomping in the hole making the sides collapse inward; the big hole is getting smaller)
> Elliot: "No, stop doing it … I'm strong!" (standing his ground and looking into Kane's eyes)

Kane: "I'm strong." (staring straight back at Elliot)
They start to push each other. Kane uses a spade and pushes it into Elliot's chest.
Elliot's twin sister Penny (a child without a diagnosis) moves in on the scene. She gives
Kane a big shove in his chest and says: "Don't do that."
Kane falls backward onto the sand and out of the hole.
Kane: "I'm going to play somewhere else!" (angry and defeated)
Elliot: "Good!"
Kane runs off and Elliot re-digs his hole.
A teacher who had been sitting at the other end of the sandpit approaches me and asked
me why I did not intervened. I said that I thought the children could best resolve it them-
selves. She looked at me with surprise. (Field Notes, 18/6/12, S1, pp. 166–167)

The scene of children digging a hole in a sandpit is a 'normal' activity in any preschool day. Sandpits adorn most, if not all, preschool playgrounds in Australia. Pedagogical, developmental and historical discourses inform early childhood practitioners of the value of 'sensory experiences' (Winderlich, 2012) and the potential of sensory learning for development (Froebel, 1974) made available in sandpit play. In addition, the sandpit provides a place for social interactions and social development, as well as a space where fine and gross motor skills can potentially progress (Jarrett, French-Lee, Bulunuz, & Bulunuz, 2010). Sandpit play also encompasses rules about particular ways of playing and being in the sandpit. As a discursively constructed activity, sandpit play produces a code of conduct that individuals take up to manage the space and each other. This arguably could turn out to be problematic for children who do not play, or 'be', in the sandpit in the correct way.

Elliot draws attention to the hole he has dug and enthusiastically asks me to look at it. He positions himself as playing in the correct way. To dig a big hole is considered one of the sanctioned ways to act in the sandpit. His hole digging performance demonstrates his category membership and by drawing adult attention to his achievement reinforces this. With the arrival of Kane, however, Elliot now needs to re-position himself to defend his play. Kane disrupts the acceptable way to play by standing in the hole and making movements to cave it in. Elliot responds by asking for my assistance to reconcile the situation.

Subsequently, Elliot uses the vigorously endorsed resolution strategy of "use your words" to tell Kane to get out of his hole. "Use your words" is a ubiquitous phrase, encouraged by adults and children, in Western early childhood settings to assist in resolving conflict (Blank & Schneider, 2011), as discussed in chapter three. Kane uses, in his response, an equally acceptable strategy saying: "it's everyone's hole". Children are often reminded that preschool equipment and toys 'belong' to everyone in the classroom. This expectation is thought to inspire children to learn to share, as sharing is encouraged. Sharing with others is argued to show a developing theory of mind and growing moral awareness (Arthur, Powell, & Lin, 2014). Sharing with others is an indicator or a milestone in social competency, as it encourages young children to develop friendships (McDevitt & Ormrod, 2007). Everyone is to share everything at preschool.

Both children draw on these acceptable and sanctioned discourses in this 'standoff'. Elliot then comments on his physical strength to which Kane replies the same. The children's voices increase in volume and emotion, exercising more power with each utterance. They take up masculine hegemonic discourses (Blaise, 2005; Davies, 1989) also acceptable in this context, and the 'standoff' continues. They become more physical and start to push each other. Elliot's twin sister Penny moves in to provide a resolution. Penny, drawing on sisterly protective discourses, is looking out for her brother, exercising her power in delivering a determination. She is drawing on parallel discourses that produce a particular code of conduct in the sandpit, where it is not acceptable to jump into another person's hole, or push someone using a spade.

Elliot at first tries to maintain his category membership, by using various strategies to remain recognisable, but as Kane becomes more aggressive, while drawing on equally acceptable discourses, Elliot appears to run out of options. Penny reclaims the hole for Elliot. Kane exits the sandpit with the comment "I'm going to play somewhere else". His way of playing in the sand is not tolerated and Penny and Elliot let him know this. What is interesting here is that Kane's behaviour is not ignored, it is confronted, spoken about loudly, and dealt with. He is disciplined, put back in his place, to uphold the social order and a distinct code of conduct. Kane challenges the social order but the children themselves eventually maintained it. Adult discipline is not necessary as the 'normal', with the support of Elliot and Penny, did its disciplinary work on Kane.

Using Reflexivity...

I recall at the time thinking about the many conflicts between children I had witnessed in classrooms over the years, and the way the children positioned teachers as mediators. Elliot wanted me to be a mediator but I declined this invitation. I think at the time I was struggling to position myself as a non-teacher. At an earlier group time session I had observed as Anne (the teacher) instructed the children in how to resolve conflicts between peers. "You need to say, I don't like it, not one, not two, but three times, you need to ask them to stop doing it and if they're not listening to you, then you go and tell the teacher and ask them to help you" (Field Notes, 15/6/12, S1, p. 161). Using your words first and then enlisting the help of an adult is accepted protocol. My lack of response to Elliot's request for help was partly due to my resistance to this protocol and also due to the way I was positioning myself with the children.

As the scene unfolded, the children came to a resolution on their own. I avoided involving myself as I chose to position myself as unable to exercise the power of a teacher to tell others what to do. As a researcher I had decided not to step in and solve the children's problems but instead observe their negotiations. I was positioned afterward by another teacher as somewhat neglectful in my adult/teaching duties. According to Wohlwend (2007), "in conflicts among young children … teachers are expected to act as neutral guides who provide emotional support to all children on both sides of a conflict and encourage compromise between cooperative peers" (p. 79). I felt as though I had been positioned as an inadequate teacher in this process as I provided no guidance or support for the children in the conflict, as I saw them as quite capable of compromise without it. The teacher had tried to regulate my actions. Nevertheless I did feel somewhat triumphant that I had resisted the protocol and troubled, if only for a moment, the acceptable discourses.

The sandpit scenario with Elliot, Kane and Penny, fashions a lucid contrast to the unmarked child's interactions with the marked child in the sandpit.

Silence 'Does' Things

Silence—Avoids

> On this morning there is a lot of activity in the sandpit. There are about ten children digging and building. As I start to observe I notice that Michael (a child with a diagnosis) is on the edge of the sandpit with a teacher nearby.
> Anna, Michaela and Lucy (children without a diagnosis) are sitting in the middle of the sandpit in a circle formation digging a deep hole. Michael, who has been digging on his own about a metre away, stands and moves over towards them and starts to stomp on the hole they have been digging. Nothing is said. The girls look at him with their eyes wide and open mouthed. They wait. After about a minute Anna stands and moves, "Hey let's make a castle over here … (pause) over here." Anna beckons the others to follow, as Michael has now destroyed the hole they have dug. (Field Notes 18/5/12, S1, p. 50)

In the early childhood classroom, normative discourses of social competency and social development contribute to the developmental/psychological focus. Authoritative regulatory discourses regarding the right way to play are understood here by Anna, Lucy and Michaela. Sandpit 'etiquette' is shared by them, as it was with Elliot. In performing this positioning one must know how to act in the sandpit and cooperate with the other children, among other things. A 'normal' sandpit player knows that destroying other children's constructions is not the 'right' way to act.

Nevertheless, when Michael destroys the hole the children have been digging, they do not outwardly protest, they say nothing. It is the unsaid that makes the discourse visible and their silence speaks. It articulates and makes public their position within the discourse and their positioning of Michael. Ferfolja (2008) acknowledges that normative discourses on some levels impose silences which consequently marginalise those who are positioned outside the 'norm'. The children, without a word, look at Michael, 'silent', eyes wide, mouths open, and referring to each other, they wait momentarily and then move away together. They look in his direction only fleetingly, but do not engage with him. There is a sense of anxiety about Michael's actions, as they are viewed as irrational, and outside the boundary of the 'normal'. To maintain themselves as members of the 'normal' they separate from him. Their category boundary work has maintained their recognisability, while also reinforcing Michael's positioning as marked.

This sandpit scene completely contrasts Elliot and Kane's overt, loud and physical encounter. Elliot challenged Kane, and with Penny's assistance, regained his hole in the sand. When Michael takes over the hole the unmarked children respond very differently, 'silently' leaving him to it. How did they come to this decision? How did they all know how to act in unison?

Nothing is said to Michael, they all quietly move on, he is the 'abject' (Butler, 1993). Foucault argues, that "people know what they do; they frequently know why they do what they do; but what they don't know is what what they do does" (Dreyfus & Rabinow, 1982, p. 187). The children in their silence and in their actions 'do' something; their actions exclude Michael subjecting him as 'not normal', irrational, unreasonable, and not the same as them. From their vantage point, they do not acknowledge his way of being and acting. The children's embodied response and resistance to Michael is made visible as they move away, with scandalous looks on their faces. Again the children's actions reveal traces of historical discourses, where fear and anxiety were created around the 'mad' (Foucault, 1967, 2006), and silencing the 'mad', was thought of as a protection for the 'normal'. The marked child, as a discursively produced subject, is not spoken of, not spoken to, or about, but nevertheless present.

The produced subject of the marked child is the ever-present, but unaddressed 'elephant in the room'. The silence around the marked child reveals a shared taboo (Douglas, 1966). Everyone in the sandpit space is very aware of the presence of Michael, but they are compelled by the discursive context, to remain silent about it. There is a sense that the marked child is 'obvious' to all but nonetheless 'silently' avoided. The 'obviousness' (Althusser, 1984) of the subject of the marked child is shared and understood by the members of the 'normal' category in order to maintain their membership and the overall social stability. Correct membership, involves being able to position oneself as a member of the group, who knows and takes for granted what others might know (Davies, 1993, p. 18). The unmarked children, in their relations with the marked child, declare the 'obviousness' of their membership as they move away together. While at the same time, the 'obviousness' of Michael's position, as a potential disruption to the social order (Davies, 1993) is tangible. How can this taboo be understood? How is the 'obviousness' created around the discursive subject of the marked child?

Douglas (1966) asserts that in any social system there is a fear of the marginal. The precautions against the dangerousness of the marginal, must come from the 'normal', as the marginal "cannot help his abnormal situation" (p. 97). Douglas claims that if a person has no place in the social system, they become regarded as a marginal being. All 'cultures' have ways of dealing with anomalies. One way of dealing with difference is to 'avoid' the anomalous, which "affirms and strengthens the definitions to which they do not conform" (Douglas, 1966, p. 39). Avoiding the discursively produced marked child affirms the 'normal' membership of the unmarked children. Another way of dealing with anomalies, and the events that occur around them, Douglas (1966) continues, is to label them dangerous. Individuals can feel anxious when they are confronted with anomaly, and so attributing danger to the anomaly, is one way of putting it above dispute and again enforcing conformity (p. 40). These cultural provisions for dealing with difference, have the effect of producing exclusionary practices in the classroom, made visible in the shared and obvious taboo.

Thinking about and reading this scene differently, Michael may have an alternative perspective on sandpit play. In the circulating and authorised discourses however, his way does not fit the prescribed normative way. Michael's way is 'not normal'. These discourses provide only limited ways of 'being' and 'doing', producing constraints on all children, and how they position themselves and each other. The discursive constructions of the knowable and rational sandpit playing subject, disciplines the unmarked children, and marginalises the marked.

Via the normative discourse, the children have the power and knowledge to discipline each other. The actors in the classroom are entangled in social relations producing power that can be applied in regulating how subjects conduct themselves and monitor others, as "the exercise of power is not simply a relationship between partners, individual or collective; it is a way in which certain actions modify others" (Foucault, 1982, p. 788). In the sandpit, the unmarked children's actions, in their silence, exercise power in producing the 'normal' among themselves, one beckoning the others to move away, creating a way of behaving that is possible in this place. This "exercise of power consists in guiding the possibility of 'conduct'" (Foucault, 1982, p. 789) of both the unmarked children and the marked children. The norm, in providing a code of conduct, produces identities and regulates individuals, as it shapes how problems and behaviours are to be understood. It ascribes appropriate ways of dealing with and governing conduct (Millei, 2011).

Silence — Ignores

> Ben (a child without a diagnosis) and Charlie (a child without a diagnosis) are busily building and discussing the constructions they are making at a table in the playground. I had been sitting down at the table with them asking some questions about the photos I had on my computer and taping the conversation. The taping had finished when Ethan (a child with a diagnosis) approached the table and sat on a chair that was not at the table but a small distance away but he could still reach the construction toys.
>
> As Ethan sat down, the other two boys did not appear to notice him. He did not attempt to touch the construction sticks but sat on the chair and stared into space. Ben and Charlie continued to take more pieces of construction out of the basket and talked about what they would build next.
>
> Ethan began to make noises, not words just sounds in a variety of pitches. Charlie looked up from his construction staring with wide eyes at Ethan for several seconds and then looked down again at his construction. Ben did the same but for a shorter period of time. Ethan continued making the noises which got louder and louder. Charlie again looked up but this time with wide eyes and his face wrinkled showing some animosity. Ethan asked, "What's that … a person on the table?" (There was a wooden doll from the doll's house on the table). Charlie and Ben did not speak to Ethan. They ignored him and continued their game for a few more minutes. They then got up and moved away. I sat with Ethan and talked about the other wooden figurines. (Field Notes, 21/8/12, S2, p. 149).

As mentioned many times already, particular noises are sanctioned in the classroom. Moreover, sounds are differentiated in the classroom according to their educational value (Millei, 2005). Noises that are not 'recognisable' as speech are generally not encouraged. Decipherable speech has legitimised authority with indecipherable speech labelled as deficient. The development of speech and language, regarded as developmental progress, is discursively produced as a universal truth for all human beings (Cannella, 1997). Conversely the 'noises' made by the marked children are sometimes unrecognisable and consequently not regarded as appropriate preschool speech. They produce an uncomfortable silence in the unmarked children and the teachers. As Charlie, and then Ben, stared wide eyed at Ethan, they try to ignore his presence and his sounds, showing a level of discomfort or disapproval of him at the table, by moving away and separating themselves. This uncomfortable coming together quickly comes to an end.

Ben and Charlie do not speak to Ethan as he joins them at the table. Even when Ethan asks them a more audible, decipherable and 'rational' question, they do not respond. Non-speech noises position children within the normative developmental discourses, as much younger: "he can't talk", "he's a baby" (Field Notes, 21/5/12, S1, p. 55). The unmarked children know that Ethan is not a baby. They also know that he often talks to himself and does not always use words in a way they can understand or communicate with. Ethan's unpredictable behaviours perhaps make it awkward to engage with him in this normative environment. They do not and possibly cannot respond to him, or even ask him to 'be quiet', they must ignore or at least show they are tolerant, by paying no attention to his sounds. They disregard him together to show they are different to him, demonstrating their category membership.

Ethan's noises could have been his way of saying "Hi I'm here!" But his way is not recognised as the 'right' way of being, or the 'right' way to join others at a table. Having a speech and/or language delay or difference in the early childhood classroom, is regarded as a concern, and special remediation is needed, as 'experts' contend that if it is left untreated, difficulties in learning and socialisation will result (Wankoff, 2011). Additionally, a connection between communication impairments and psychiatric disorders is reported in medical research, with speech and language deficits contributing to the criteria for the diagnosis of many developmental disabilities (Wankoff, 2011). Psychological and psychiatric discourses often attribute non-speech noises to a 'lack of reasoning', irrationality, and the potentiality of a threat (Foucault, 2006). Ethan's noises are attributed to his diagnosis and his difference. How does this type of 'truth', constructed as expert knowledge, position children? The category boundary work around the 'normal' positions those who make 'noises', that are not speech or part of a recognisable game or behaviour, as outside the category, possibly delayed and possibly a developmental error. In order to maintain the category, recognising and responding to the noises of the marked child is avoided, a shared silence is the solution, and moving away is a preferred tactic.

Butler (1997) posits that, in the process of becoming a subject, the starting point is the 'bad' or unformed subject. Each person has to continually work on realising themselves as the 'not bad', in order to become recognisable as an "acceptably formed subject" (Laws & Davies, 2000, p. 209), the 'normal'. The unmarked children engage in this continuous work to stay recognisable as the 'not bad', and ignore and avoid the Other as part of this work. Ben and Charlie are working at making themselves the "acceptably formed subject" (p. 209). Ethan, on the other hand, is positioned as the unformed subject.

Ethan is the discursively created 'unreasonable' being who makes unrecognisable noises, a potentially threatening subject, better ignored or avoided by the 'normal'. Foucault (2008) recognises that discourses, are made up of things unsaid that may be in some way, forbidden (Ward & Winstanley, 2003). The forbidden, the sharing of a taboo, is preserved in the classroom around those who make unrecognisable sounds. The things unsaid, and the silence produced within the discourses are however dangerous, since as St. Pierre (2000, p. 485) explains, "once a discourse becomes 'normal' and 'natural' it becomes difficult to think and act outside it".

Silence—Moving Away

> As the children in the group finish their morning tea on the verandah they move out into the playground. Sam (a child with a diagnosis) is already in the yard accompanied by a teacher. (He has been making a lot of noise trying to get out of the classroom and into the yard beforehand). Sam is looking at and touching some hanging orange balls that are attached to a wooden frame and have been set up as an activity in the yard. He is moving them around hitting them with his hand and attempting to catch them. Two children (without a diagnosis) from the group on the verandah move enthusiastically toward the hanging balls activity to play however one of the children pulls the other child away from the area shaking her head and pointing at Sam. They quickly move to another part of the yard. (Field Notes, 30/4/12, S1, p. 8) (Watson, 2016)

As the unmarked children move into the playground at 'outdoor time', Sam is already in the yard. The unmarked children do not talk about Sam being in the yard before the 'correct' time. The teacher has released him as he was making loud 'noises' banging on the locked door, trying to get outside. Sam's noise creates a level of anxiety in the classroom. By allowing him to move out before the rest of the group, the teachers avoid the potential risk of a 'scandal' (Gordon, 2013) to the 'normal', posed by Sam's 'out of control' and unreasonable actions (Foucault, 2006). Again the 'noises' of the marked child create an uneasiness in the classroom. Anxiety and awkwardness contribute to the need to liberate him from the room, and in so doing, silence the noise. Sam's 'noises' disrupt the established orderliness, as they pollute the stable classroom and generate a level of disorder

(Douglas, 1966). Stopping the 'noise' is necessary to return order (Watson, 2016). The unmarked children understand and share the need for the silencing. Separation from the unmarked children is again sanctioned in these actions.

Medical, psychological and psychiatric discourses subject Sam as 'unable' to follow the 'normal' rational routines of the classroom and so he is permitted to separate from the other children (Watson, 2016). Schegloff (2007) contends that a "failure to measure up to an identity category does not generally lead to an expansion of the scope of the category; rather it leads to pathologising" (p. 469). Sam's diagnosis declares that he has impaired communication skills and behavioural problems (Watson, 2016). He is provided his own space to move in, his own rules and his own time. He is made separate to facilitate his remediation, reflecting the teachers' understanding of his discursively produced diagnosis. The children's collective avoidance of Sam, again reveals the taboo that is produced around the marked child. This pathologising produces the deviant and the dangerous subject, labelling the difference and enforcing the conforming and 'normal' category (Douglas, 1966).

In the above scenario two unmarked children approach the new activity and appear eager to have a turn. They stop in their tracks when they notice that Sam is already playing with the hanging balls. They don't speak to each other, but through bodily movements and gesturing, move on and do not have a turn. A shared 'obviousness' about Sam, his difference and his anomalous status is noticeable. Interacting with Sam, and talking to or about Sam with words, is taboo. As one child pulls the other away in silence, they embody this shared understanding.

In another reading of this scene, the unmarked children could be seen to be taking up special education discourses, that inform them that as Sam needs teacher remediation at all times, staying out of his way, is the 'right' and 'normal' way to act around him. Alternatively, moving away could be read as the children drawing on moral or tolerance discourses, as discussed in chapter five, as they give Sam his own space to be with the teacher, politely not interfering. In taking up these either of these discourses, the unmarked children powerfully legitimise themselves as a member of the same group, and custodians of the moral order. Members seek to defend their status through maintaining the moral order but "membership categorisation is a 'moral order' fraught with consequences for the participants" (MacLure, Jones, Holmes, & MacRae, 2012, p. 452) and making decisions about the right and wrong way to 'be', and also how to 'be' with others, has consequences for the subjectivities of the children in the classroom.

The children's actions could be read as a taking up of the governing discourses that circulate and encourage a 'civilised' (Leavitt & Power, 1997) way to 'be'. The unmarked children stay away from Sam because they don't want to be recognised as being like him, as his actions, inside and outside of the classroom could be considered 'uncivilised' (Watson, 2016). As Davies (2006) suggests, "category maintenance work is actively going on as part of the hard work that individual subjects engage in to separate themselves out into the binary category to which they have been assigned" (p. 73). The category maintenance work upholds their recognisability, keeps them 'separate' from the discursive 'deviant'. Reason and unreason are kept apart by discursive practices.

In Foucault's original thesis, *The History of Madness* (2006), he traces the silencing of unreason, along with the limitations placed on unreason, by reason. Unreasonable beings were thrown into 'oblivion' at the end of the 18th century, in a battle with the dominance of reason (Carrette, 2000). The exclusion of those who do not 'fit in' is a distinctive focus of Foucault's work. Those without reason were produced as disruptive subjects, incapable of work, unmanageable and undisciplined. They became the "objects equally of fear, revulsion and human sympathy" (Gordon, 2013, p. 93). The power and knowledge exercised by medical science and other psy-sciences (Rose, 1999) initiated the call to separate, segregate and intern unreason. Foucault's (2006) work examines how past societies, experienced and defined the limits of unreason, and how these limits were produced, based on a fear. It seems that the discourses in the classroom produce the marked child as unreasonable and irrational. The practice of silence employed to manage unreason, is historically traced in Foucault's work, where silence works to both protect the 'normal' but equally, to allay any created fear or anxiety.

Silence—Moving Past

As I walked toward the preschool car park one morning I could see a woman getting out of her car with an infant on one hip and holding the hand of a crying preschool aged child. I recognised this child as I got closer as Hugo (a child with a diagnosis). He was crying loudly and resisting his mother's attempt to take him through the preschool gate. His mother persisted and dragged him into the preschool building with difficulty. As I followed them and moved into the foyer of the building I saw Hugo just inside the door lying sprawled out with a sheet covering him. He was now alone.

Another parent and child pair had followed me into the foyer and they stared down at Hugo as they moved around his body in the restricted space. As I stood in the foyer a teacher approached Hugo and tried to coax him further into the building but this was unsuccessful. As I moved down the hallway I could hear the mother discussing with the teacher her resolve to leave him at the preschool, as she was sure that he should not "get what he wants if he chucks a tantrum". I did not hear what the teacher's response was.

The mother then returned to the foyer and picked up Hugo by the arms saying, "You can't stay here someone might trip on you and sue me." The mother took Hugo to the classroom and left him on the floor, but he immediately stood up and returned to the foyer crying loudly. Many parents, carers and children were arriving through the front door during this encounter. The adults stopped briefly, looked and frowned, all the time holding the hand of their child. The children moved through the area, they glanced briefly at Hugo and then moved on. (Field Notes, 23/10/12, S3, p. 15)

Hugo is upset at the beginning of the preschool day, as children often are, and his actions make this position quite clear. As the unmarked children enter the centre they move quickly and silently passed him to reinforce their unmarked 'normal' category membership. They positioned themselves as being independent by not crying, or showing their emotions, at the beginning of the preschool day. They try to disregard Hugo's loud, wild crying. Positioned as a special child with a diagnosis, his actions reinforced the characteristics of this diagnosis. This diagnosis, *his* diagnosis produces him within a deficit discourse (Nutbrown & Clough, 2009; Purdue, Gordon-Burns, Gunn, Madden, & Surtees, 2009) and a member of a homogenous group of other subjects similarly diagnosed. *His* diagnosis describes 'who he is', a unitary (Davies, 1989) and an irrational (Rose, 1999) being.

Special education knowledge is valued in the classroom as it makes available specific strategies to remediate deficits. Leaving Hugo in the foyer and waiting for him to calm down could be one strategy. Hugo, as a pathologised subject, is an individual of concern, and as such in need of careful scrutiny. Reading this scene via special education discourses, one might judge that Hugo needs extra support, patience and tolerance for his morning transition to preschool. From this perspective, Hugo might be remediated given time, and become more like the 'normal'.

Alternatively, by turning the scrutinising gaze away from Hugo, the individual child, and towards the non-pathologised group, another reading of this scenario could examine in more detail the actions of the unmarked children and teachers; the 'silent' way they move around Hugo's noisy and unavoidable body, sprawled across the foyer floor. If one's body does not seem to fit the 'normal', one is still produced in relation to the 'normal' (Cadwallader, 2007). Hugo's body collapsed in the foyer does not 'fit' the 'normal'. In their shared silence, the unmarked children position Hugo as Other, the abject. They see and hear him because his presence is 'obvious', but they do not *see or hear* him, as any recognition of him is taboo since his behaviour at this time is 'scandalous'. Hugo as a discursive subject is '*the elephant in the room*'. Very present but avoided by everyone. Evading Hugo's discursively produced being, affirms and strengthens the definition to which he does not conform (Douglas, 1966).

Hugo, in locating himself in the foyer and loudly expressing his 'unbridled' emotions, makes his position very visible to everyone as they arrive. This public space performance may have worked for him before. His actions remarkably are not attributed to his dislike of preschool but are read as a characteristic of his diagnosis. His mother also positions him in this way. She enters the space seeking the assistance of the teacher 'experts' to transition him into the classroom. She positions herself as the mother of the Other, somewhat 'helpless/powerless', while positioning the teachers as the ones with the power to advise and help, and relieve her of the embarrassment of her son's actions. She conceivably wants to drop her son off in the same way that other mothers do, the 'normal' way. Hugo's mother, drawing upon the dominant circulating discourses, joins in with the teachers, in attempting to 'correct and coerce' (Foucault, 1977) Hugo.

Moreover, her positioning as the marked child's mother might attract sympathy, as being the mother of a diagnosed child is often constituted as tragic. Discourses position the parents of a diagnosed child as different to other parents whose children are not diagnosed. The parents of the diagnosed are deemed to have needs that require them to learn special skills to help with their child and the difficulties they present (Grace, Llewellyn, Wedgwood, Fenech, & McConnell, 2008). Burman (2008) notes that as developmental discourses pathologise difference, they render parents subject to blame and scrutiny (p. 50). Hugo's mother could just as easily be regarded as a 'bad' mother who cannot control her child, but because of Hugo's marked status, his pathology affords her sympathy. Stereotypes frequently depict 'disorderly' children and their families as problematic and include value judgements about their caregiving abilities (Harwood, 2006).

Overall, there is a feeling of angst, awkwardness and anxiety, in the foyer on this morning. No one seems to know what to do. When Hugo's mother picks him up and moves him into the classroom, he goes back to the foyer, so that his 'protest' powerfully remains on show. Hugo seems to understand the powerful effects of using this public space, at this public time. As Laws and Davies (2000) contend, power acts on the subject, making the subject possible, the condition of its possibility and its formation. Additionally, power also acts as what is taken up by the subject and retold in the subject's own acting (Laws & Davies, 2000, p. 207). The angst of the teacher and Hugo's mother could be explained by Hugo's power in lying in the foyer. They become positioned as unable to act, powerless, as Hugo's actions cannot be managed in a rational way, as he is subjected as irrational. Hugo's subjection is made possible by the power of psychological discourses, but also by his own acting.

Hugo's irrational behaviour is 'loud and large' in the foyer. Hugo's mother's comment about him having a tantrum, is possibly an attempt by her, to draw from 'normal' discourses about young children's behaviour, to describe her son. How would an unmarked child acting in a similar manner in the foyer be positioned? Would they be regarded as naughty and 'bad' and be disciplined? Would the adults have a rational discussion with the child? Hugo's diagnosis subjects him as 'not normal' and his tantrum is seen to be pathological rather than normative. As pathological behaviour, the tantrum is no longer normative but an act of the unreasonable. Silence becomes the best way to contain this subject, as unreason must be curtailed and silenced (Foucault, 2006) as it cannot be reasoned with.

Using Reflexivity…

I wondered whether this was a common scene. I felt uncomfortable and awkward for Hugo, for his mother, and for myself, as I stood around watching, taking down a mental note (as a good researcher should) and then jottings in my notepad. This was potential data wasn't it? As the children moved past Hugo I moved past him too, but I went back to have another look, like a member of the 'paparazzi' trying to gain the best vantage point. As a researcher of 'inclusive' practices this was the kind of data I wanted and needed to collect. How would the classroom manage this disruption to the order? I wanted to see how the children would react but I was also surprised by my own reaction. I stood around nearby and waited to see what would happen, but I felt uneasy as though I didn't want to be caught watching. Thinking about this more and turning back on myself (Pillow, 2003) I wanted to be positioned as the 'normal' too. I wanted to be seen as ignoring Hugo too. I did not want to be the one who disrupted the scene by getting in the way or looking for too long or giving Hugo too much attention. I now think that the position I took at the time and my actions shows the 'gravitational pull' of the 'normal'. At that moment it contained and constrained us all.

The performance of silence speaks and requires our attentiveness (Mazzei, 2007a), as it is shaped by, and shapes subject formation and discursive practice. Derrida (1992) affirms that silence is a strategic response and, "polite silence can become the most insolent weapon" (p. 18). The children do not say anything to Hugo, as they make their strategic move (Mazzei, 2007b, p. 28) around him, nor do they say anything about his actions, as that is taboo. It is the 'unsaid' that contributes here to the production of subjectivities.

Historical discourses have constructed unreason or 'madness' in a way that obliges the 'normal' to silence it, to separate it and contain it (Foucault, 2006). The 'asylum' was created to perform these functions. However, in the classroom the silence, separation and containment observed in the children's everyday encounters is not a physical containment composed of walls, doors and locks but nevertheless, a performance powerfully enacted to protect the 'normal', to maintain the social order and to remediate the 'mad'. The discursive practice of silence, as an exercise of power, maintains and protects the 'normal' from 'madness'.

Silence—Keeping the Quiet Order

> Teacher Odette has been struggling with Sam (a child with a diagnosis) for about 15 minutes trying to keep him away from the door. She looks to Anne, another teacher, and says, "Just debating whether I should let him go?" As she speaks the director Sue arrives on the scene, leaving her office possibly because of the noise Sam is making, crying and banging on the door. Sue picks Sam up off the floor near the door and takes him back inside the room. He kicks and screams even more loudly. A group of children are sitting on the verandah nearby eating their morning tea but only two of the group turn to look briefly at Sam and the director Sue. The rest of the children just continue not seeming to notice the disruption. (Field Notes, 28/5/12, S1, p. 79)

How did the children not respond to Sam's loud crying and screaming or did they? Their response was to silently ignore and maintain correct conduct. By not noticing or talking about the unreasonable marked child *'the elephant in the room'* emerges. Silence creates and preserves the taboo of not addressing unreason, keeping reason safe and separated.

Psychological and psychiatric discourses, that disseminate the concept of the developing rational being (Rose, 1999), are persistent in the classroom. The rational being, produced in the 'age of reason' (Foucault, 1967), contrasts the irrational, the 'mad', as not fully human (Hekman, 1990). Reason privileges particular knowledges and ways of being, marginalising and violating others. The concept of reason is established as an objective 'truth' or a foundation of 'true' knowledge (St. Pierre, 2000, p. 488). Foucault (1984) argues the need to interrogate the substance of rationality in his examination of history and reminds us that the history of reason:

> was born in an altogether 'reasonable' fashion—from chance; devotion to truth and the precision of scientific methods arose from the passion of scholars, their reciprocal hatred, their fanatical and unending discussions, and their spirit of competition—the personal conflicts that slowly forged the weapons of reason. (Foucault, 1984, p. 78)

Rationality, it seems, was produced through passion, not objectivity, but is nevertheless presented as an 'objective reality'. Rationality and its expected development in each individual, contributes powerfully to the 'normal' in the early childhood classroom. It delimits possibilities and marginalises those who do not perform within its restricted boundaries. Through, and within historical discourses, it creates the Other as a subject to be feared, a contagious and 'tainted' subject. Medical knowledge, the "*homo medicus*" and its associated knowledges came about "as a guardian to protect others from the vague danger that exuded through the walls of confinement" (Foucault, 1967, p. 195). The discourses that continue to prevail in the classroom, are taken up in order to contain what might be contagious, and to mitigate and minimise any anxiety about this contagion.

Silence—Shows Disapproval

> Michael (a child with a diagnosis) is inside a large, hard plastic, blue ball. It has large holes in the sides of it and has been set up with a balance beam going through it as a climbing activity out in the yard. The children walk along the beam and then climb over the large, blue ball shape to continue on the other side. Michael is sitting inside the ball and he is kicking the sides with his feet and hitting the hard plastic with a wooden spoon from the sandpit. The children are staring at him looking unhappy and alarmed about this. Anna: (a child without a diagnosis) "Stop it Michael!" she says loudly as she crosses over the beam. Michael starts to squeal, making wooing noises. He looks to be having a good time but is not listening to Anna. Rachel (a child without a diagnosis) is standing on the balance beam waiting her turn to cross over on the beam following Anna, but she hesitates. She looks worried about moving any further, closer to Michael. She stares at Michael eyes wide with her mouth open. She wants to climb over the blue ball but stops to watch Michael. More of the children start to tell Michael to stop. A staff member moves towards the scene reminding the group of the rules about the equipment. The rule is that only one child at a time can be on the beam. Rachel's hesitation has meant that several children are waiting their turn on the beam, breaking this rule. Nothing is said to Michael by the group of children or teacher. With the arrival of the staff member all the children move away leaving Michael alone. (Field Notes, 4/5/12, S1, pp. 20–21) (Watson, 2016)

Michael's presence in the blue plastic ball in the middle of the climbing game is not welcome. The game and using this equipment has particular rules or expectations about how it 'should' be played. Play is organised, classified and divided into tasks (Foucault, 1977) in early childhood classrooms. This leads to its normalisation as activities are regulated and monitored (Foucault, 1977). Activities prepared by teachers are programmed to produce certain actions and ways of playing that will potentially stimulate development or learning outcomes (Watson, 2016). The unmarked children unreservedly take up the normative discourses of play and associated regulation. Michael however at this time does not follow this same understanding of the game. He plays in the blue ball, squealing and calling out, enjoying himself as he laughs and repeats his actions over and over. Michael actions are 'out of the ordinary' and the children recognise this. However, they continue to follow the expectations of the activity, all the while positioning Michael as outside the 'normal' and in need of correction.

When Anna repositions herself and attempts to discipline Michael saying loudly "Stop it Michael", she draws attention to Michael's actions, possibly trying to engage others to help discipline him. Anna's attempt at disciplining Michael made his actions all the more 'obvious'. This interaction was more unusual, as the unmarked children do not often discipline the marked child, as commented beforehand. Anna's attempt to normalise or remediate Michael's actions did not seem to work. Michael's response to the disciplining was to add some extra volume and 'wooing' to the noise mix. When Rachel moves onto the beam but stops short of crossing over the top of Michael, she stands still and silent. She looks down at him with trepidation. She does not speak, but waits, possibly wanting some intervention from someone. The silence does its work here to position the children (Watson, 2016). Michael, inside the blue plastic ball is positioned as the noisy, irrational, and the 'normal' are positioned as the rule following, rational. Rachel takes up silence as a discursive practice, to show her disapproval of Michael's actions, and to attract attention and support. In her silence she expresses a level of fear and anxiety. She does not act as Anna had done in her attempt to discipline Michael. She instead imposes a silence, the effect of which creates Michael as the unreasonable being, obvious but unaddressed. Her silence moreover maintains her membership in the category of the 'normal'.

As more children line up, they are unable to cross the beam and some of them try to rein Michael in with their words, but with no success. Again the 'use your words' (Blank & Schneider, 2011) strategy, for resolving the situation, does not seem to work. The 'noise' they create in trying to stop and remediate Michael, along with the 'noise' being made by Michael, catches the teacher's attention. The teacher defers to the rules and regulations of the game and the number of children on the beam at one time. The teacher curiously avoids an encounter with Michael, keeping silent about his actions. The unmarked children having 'broken' the rules of the game, move away in silence (Watson, 2016).

Unreasonableness is managed by silence. It is not managed by addressing it or by disciplining it, as there is a fear of 'setting him/it off'. Setting Michael off cannot be tolerated as discussed in chapter five. The teacher's actions, or lack of actions, clearly reinforces the taboo, as this has been constructed as the best way to operate around the marked child. Sharing the taboo, the unmarked children move away as they are re-positioned as rule breakers, a position they do not wish to occupy (Watson, 2016). Michael is left inside the blue plastic ball alone, playing the game differently and unacceptably. Reason and unreason are separated again, as Michael's way of being is excluded, as it does not 'fit', and he is left isolated in his own space.

Silence is nuanced. Silence has many moves and manifestations and as a discursive practice, silence has many functions. It works to avoid the marked child, separating them from the unmarked children, who learn to take up and share this discursive practice. Silence quietens disruption and shows disapproval (Watson, 2016). The enactments of silence produce and re-produce the 'normal' and maintain it. Taboo, as a shared understanding, requires no discussion, it is a silent engagement. It works to contain any danger. Whatever we imagine the taboo to be and whatever form it could take, it seems that there is *something* in the 'inclusive' classroom that cannot be spoken of, and cannot be addressed. Is it the diagnosed child? Is it disability itself? What is '*the elephant in the room*' that cannot be attended to?

Sometimes in the classroom silence takes a different form. The silence is not an absence of words, but a limitation on words, as only certain things can be said and only certain discourses can be drawn on. The normative discourses act to silence certain ways of speaking, and ways of 'being' and 'doing', while producing sanctioned ways of describing the actions of the Other.

Silence Produces Other Ways to Speak

Talk about Something Else: Speaking Only in Certain Terms

This conversation occurred after a group of children (without a diagnosis) witnessed Jasmine (a child with a diagnosis) resisting a teacher's request to complete an activity.

> Me: "What has happened to Jasmine?"
> Chelsea: "Who?"
> Me: "Jasmine over there?"
> Jackson: "She's having a heart attack."
> Me: "Does that happen often?"
> All: "Yeah, yeah, yeah."
> Me: "Does that happen to you?"
> Both children: "Nope."
> Jackson: "We don't have a heart attack."
> Tyler: "Someone on the TV I saw had a heart attack."
> Me: "Tell me more."

Tyler: "...Well ummm a doctor was trying to fix someone and then he's gone out ... so ... he goes outside and then he just had a heart attack."
Me: "How did you know he was having a heart attack?"
Tyler: "Cause he just fell over."
Me: "Why does Jasmine do that?"
Tyler: "Cause she always sits down when she tells ummm ... when the teachers tell her to do something, like painting and ... er ... drawing."
Me: "Why does she have to do that?"
Chelsea: "Cause she has to do what the teacher tells her to do."
Me: "Do they tell you to do it?"
Chelsea: "No but we do it."
Me: "Why do you do it?"
Chelsea: "Cause we know we will get in trouble."
Me: "And she doesn't know that?"
Tyler: "No cause she's little."
Chelsea: "And she's just learning."
Tyler: "She's just learning ... she's five ... she is a big girl."
Chelsea: "She doesn't know a lot of things cause she's talking really young and she's talking funny."
Tyler: "Yeah ... she's talkin funny yeah ... but she can say hello good like bye, bye." (Field Notes, 20/11/12, S3, pp. 93–94) (Watson, 2016)

Jackson is quick to explain Jasmine's actions of lying on the floor, screaming and struggling with the teacher, as a 'heart attack'. He has seen it before and does not appear concerned about it, as he returns quickly to the conversation with his friends. Jasmine has obviously recovered from her 'heart attacks' in the past. He draws upon available discourses, and sanctioned ways of being, to understand Jasmine's actions. He does not have heart attacks, he is 'normal'. Tyler draws on medical discourses and plausible knowledge gained from television viewing. Drawing on these authoritative discourses from outside the classroom, both children positions themselves as somewhat imperious. They are confident in the way they deliver this information, as the normative discourses privilege the mature and conversant as 'being' more adult-like. The discursive 'normal' in the classroom produces and maintains limits around speakability; what can be said, who can/cannot say it, and what cannot be said.

The unmarked children talk about Jasmine as if she is quite different to them, and taking up regulatory discourses, explain how she does not want to do what the teacher wants. They do what the teacher wants to avoid getting into trouble. Doing what the teacher wants is viewed as important. They position themselves as knowing the rules and conforming to them, avoiding punishment and securing their membership in the category of the 'normal'. In a setting where the adult/

child binary dominates, being positioned as a knowing, more adult-like being, is privileged with power (Watson, 2016). They position Jasmine as not knowing how to act, explaining that she is only "little" and "just learning". Tyler comments that Jasmine is little, but then corrects himself, saying she is just learning, "she's five … she is a big girl." Tyler knows that being five is supposed to position a person as big. He seems to be struggling with himself on how to position her, as her age and actions do not fit together within the normative discourses that inform him.

The silence is expressed and performed differently in this observation. The children are not silent but instead draw on the available and tolerable discourses to talk about Jasmine. They do not talk about her as being 'naughty', 'bad', or misbehaving as they might about another child who avoids doing what the teacher wants. Instead they explain her actions as a "heart attack", a medical concern, something that perhaps Jasmine cannot control or regulate. She is described as young, and "just learning". The silence is not an absence of words but a discursive practice (Foucault, 2008), where only certain things can be said. The unsaid is replaced by what is permissible and available. The power of the silence, or the unsaid, or that what is said in its place, is made visible as the unmarked children draw on sanctioned knowledges that are privileged in this context. The children could have discussed the "heart attack" as a 'normal' tantrum, like Hugo earlier, but the medical terminology used produces a difference, and places an emphasis on the medicalised and pathologised discourses, and ways of being. The medical is approved of and can be spoken of, but interestingly only in terms of a medical condition, a biological condition, and not in terms of the psychiatric, the unreasonable or irrational. Jasmine is not described as having a tantrum, as she is 'not normal' and only the 'normal' have tantrums. She has something else going on and to use the sanctioned medical terms produces her and her actions as something quite different.

The unmarked children give the impression that they are comfortable in their knowing, positioning themselves as different and more grown up than Jasmine. Walkerdine (1999) contends, that discourse informed by developmental psychology, privileges a certain representation of normality, to the degree that particular children are Othered, and they become the object within and of pathologising discourses (p. 2). Jackson's description of Jasmine's actions announces his adoption of these pathologising discourses (Watson, 2016). However, as Butler (1997) argues, this is problematic as "these pathologising discourses are, central to the formation of the subject" (MacLure *et al.*, 2012, p. 449), and position Jasmine outside the limits of the discursive 'normal'. These discourses create her as a subject, or object of pathology, the 'abject', possibly a patient and someone who needs medical attention. Jasmine is firmly consigned, at this time, as the unreasonable, and in need of the teacher's containment. The unmarked children expect that the teachers will control and monitor Jasmine, protecting her and them in the process.

How do the medical and psychological discourses inside the early childhood classroom produce separation and fear of the 'not normal'? In the following scenario I grapple with this question and note in the analysis how the presence of the Other creates a sense of discomfort and a level of anxiety.

Silence—No Way to Speak

Not Seen, Not Heard

A group of children Michaela, Spencer, Patrick, Ethan, Anna and Rachel (children without a diagnosis) have gathered to look some photos taken in the classroom. The first photo shown to them is of Oliver (a child with a diagnosis) in his wheelchair. He is accompanied by two teachers who are standing either side of him. Oliver is in the centre of the photo frame.

Me: "Let's look at this picture here."

A child is coughing in the background so I ask again.

Michaela: "Chris." (teacher's name)

Me: "Can you tell me what's happening in this picture?"

Long pause (in the picture the two teachers are standing either side of Oliver trying to get his headphones to operate)

Patrick: "That's ... Edith ... ummmmm" (another teacher)

Me: "What is happening in the picture Spencer?"

(silence)

Patrick: "I can see ... ummmm ..."

(silence)

Spencer: "Ummm ... there's ... umm I can see umm, I can see something citing." (exciting)(moving in his seat, not wanting to answer)

Me: "Who's in the picture?"

(silence)

Spencer: "Thomas."

Me: "Thomas? Where's Thomas?" (Thomas is not in the photo). "Who is in the picture Ethan?"

Ethan: "Chris."

Michaela: "And Edith" (a teacher)

Anna: "And not me I can't see."

Me: "No you're not there Anna. Who else is in the photo?"

Ethan: "Thomas, Thomas, Thomas." (pointing to a boy in a hooded jumper with his back turned to the camera).
Me: "I think that might be Lucas."
Patrick: "Where's Thomas?" trying to move the conversation on I ask.
Me: "And who's in the middle?"
Very long pause … (silence and children looking around the room)
Me: "Who is this in the middle do you know who that is Patrick?" (my direct question and pointing finally resulted in Oliver's identification)
Patrick and Michaela: "Oliver." (Field Notes, 25/5/12, S1, p. 69)

The children in this conversation seemed to work hard to avoid identifying, or saying Oliver's name. The awkwardness and discomfort about naming Oliver, at the beginning of this conversation, is palpable. The long pauses, the uneasy movement of the children's bodies, as they squirm in their seats, and the many "ummm's" in the children's responses, makes visible the taboo around the marked child. This child's name cannot be spoken. In between the silences, the children look in other directions, as I ask them to identify Oliver. Some look away from the computer screen and out into the room. Oliver's location, in the photo in the centre of the frame, is 'obvious', as his wheelchair is large and cumbersome. My questions presented the unmarked children with an awkward brief. The physical signs of their discomfort took me by surprise. They tried to name everyone else in an attempt to avoid using Oliver's name. The children it seems did not have the words to talk about Oliver. Things that are unsaid remain that way because in some ways they are forbidden (Foucault, 2008). Naming Oliver was hindered by the available discourses, and possibly forbidden by the taboo, that surrounds the marked child in the 'inclusive' classroom. By remaining silent and not naming Oliver, all the while naming everyone else in the photo (and even those not in the photo), the unmarked children perform their adherence to the taboo, confirming that certain things need to be left unsaid. Conceivably they may wish to avoid mentioning Oliver as any questions about him might produce more uneasiness, as the answers are inaccessible and unavailable. If they name *the elephant in the room*, it would no longer be *the elephant in the room*, the taboo would be broken and they would not know how to speak of it, and so, they avoid saying Oliver's name.

Using Reflexivity…

I took this photo of Oliver in his large wheelchair and placed him in the middle of the frame to elicit comment and conversation. I wanted to construct some understanding of how the children thought about Oliver, the 'disabled' boy, within the circulating discourses. The marked child was being conceptualised by me as a catalyst to procure data related to in/exclusionary practices. I wanted the children to talk about the Other in the classroom as I wanted to be able to describe and analyse discourses. My power as a researcher was being exercised as I provided the children with this photo. The awkwardness that surrounded this encounter was not what I expected. I don't know why. As the conversation progressed (or faulted) I persisted in asking the children to talk about something that they did not seem to want to speak of. My questioning I think made everyone uncomfortable. Looking back I 'forced' the words and the silences as I exercised my power as the adult researcher. My photo and questioning positioned Oliver as the Other. What was the effect of my questioning on the subjectivities of Oliver and the children? Did I produce the awkwardness? Did children feel uncomfortable because they expected me to ask about Oliver? Did they want to avoid my questioning? How did this uncomfortable scene happen?

The teachers in this classroom refer to Oliver as a very disabled child. His diagnosis and impairments define who he is, and what he does, and not only pathologise him, but also inadvertently objectify and de-humanise him. The director and teachers on several occasions referred to him as 'the boy with cerebral palsy' before using his name (Field Notes, S1). This could explain, in some ways, why the children could not recall his name immediately in our conversation. Oliver is described by his pathology and via medical discourses, as an 'object of concern' and often as an 'object of sympathy'. The teacher's frequently express a sense of remorse in comments such as 'the poor thing' and 'the poor family'. A discourse of personal tragedy is taken up by the adults in this classroom, particularly for this child, Oliver, but also for the other marked children. Statements such as "I don't know how the parents cope" and "Can't imagine what it must be like for his poor parents" (Field Notes, 4/6/12, S1, p. 134) draw on tragic discourses.

Oliver is talked about mostly by the teachers in terms of the severity of his impairments and his need for specialised equipment and constant supervision. Non-human actors, in the form of specialised pieces of equipment, including the wheelchair, leg splints, and headphones, all powerfully contribute to the discursive production of Oliver as a subject. His subjecthood is created via a long list of deficits that equate with tragedy. The children use developmental and sanctioned discourses to describe Oliver, "he can't walk", "he can only talk like a baby" and "he always cries". In this classroom, the discourses produce an objectivisation of Oliver, as well as an infantilisation (Robey, Beckley, & Kirschner, 2006) of him, by both the children and the teachers. The teachers respond to Oliver as one would an infant. Oliver's 'noises', as with the other marked children inside the 'inclusive' classroom, produce a cause for concern and stopping the noise is a matter of urgency. Although Oliver is four years old, the teachers respond to his communications by offering him food, a nappy change, or a walk around the yard in his wheelchair, to settle him and stop his 'noises'. The teachers on several occasions decided that Oliver was tired and in need of sleep (Field Notes, 18/5/12, S1, p. 42) early in the day. On other occasions when he makes noises, headphones are placed on his ears to minimise the classroom sounds he can hear, as music is thought soothe and quieten him. His 'noises' are not interpreted by the teachers or the children as a different way of communicating, but instead are responded to in a way that positions Oliver as an infant.

Oliver is subjected by discourses that judge his embodied physical differences as a failing, incomplete and inferior and "not so much for what it is but what it fails to be" (Shildrick, 2005, p. 756). Shildrick (2005) argues that the anomalous disabled body represents an "uncomfortable reminder that the normative, 'healthy' body, despite its appearance of successful self-determination, is highly vulnerable to disruption and breakdown" (p. 757). Shildrick goes on to say that as "disability is viewed this way it is always the object of institutional discourses of control and containment" (p. 757). The 'normal' from this perspective, feel threatened by Oliver's disabled body and the risk to their own body's vulnerabilities. It seems that there are traces of historical discourses in the classroom that produce the threat of contagion (Foucault, 2006). Oliver is mostly ignored by the children, as they experience a level of discursively produced anxiety. There is similarly a sense of fear about the possibility of contagion assembled around this marked subject.

The nuanced silences, shared among the unmarked children, teachers and parents, as they sidestepped interactions with the marked child, by ignoring, avoiding, moving away from, or speaking about them in sanctioned and acceptable terms, have been deconstructed in this chapter. The notion of a taboo around the marked child, as a discursively produced subject, has been shaped by the shared avoidance of the 'obvious'. The taboo, adhered to via the social and discursive practices of the classroom, creates an unaddressed anomaly, the 'inclusive' classroom's version of *the elephant in the room*.

References

Althusser, L. (1984). *Essays on ideology*. London: Verso.

Arthur, J., Powell, S., & Lin, H.-C. (2014). Foundations of character: Methodological aspects of a study of character development in three- to six-year-old children with a focus on sharing behaviours. *European Early Childhood Education Research Journal, 22*(1), 105–122.

Blaise, M. (2005). *Playing it straight; Uncovering gender discourses in the early childhood classroom*. New York, NY: Routledge.

Blank, J., & Schneider, J. J. (2011). "Use your words": Reconsidering the language of conflict in the early years. *Contemporary Issues in Early Childhood, 12*(3), 198–211.

Burman, E. (2008). *Deconstructing developmental psychology*. East Sussex: Routledge.

Butler, J. (1993). *Bodies that matter: On the discursive limits of "sex."* New York, NY: Routledge.

Butler, J. (1997). *The psychic life of power: Theories of subjection*. Stanford, CA: Stanford University Press.

Cadwallader, J. (2007). Suffering difference: Normalisation and power. *Social Semiotics, 17*(3), 375–394.

Cannella, G. S. (1997). *Deconstructing early childhood education: Social justice & revolution*. New York, NY: Peter Lang.

Carrette, J. R. (2000). *Foucault and religion: Spiritual corporality and political spirituality*. London: Routledge.

Davies, B. (1989). *Frogs and snails and feminist tales: Preschool children and gender*. Sydney, NSW: Allen & Unwin.

Davies, B. (1993). *Shards of glass: Children reading and writing beyond gendered identities*. Sydney, NSW: Allen & Unwin.

Davies, B. (2006). Identity, abjection and otherness: Creating the self, creating difference. In M. Arnot & M. Mac an Ghaill (Eds.), *The Routledge Falmer reader in gender and education* (pp. 72–90). London: Routledge.

Derrida, J. (1992). Passions: 'An oblique offering'. In D. Wood (Ed.), *Derrida: A critical reader* (pp. 5–35). Oxford: Blackwell.

Douglas, M. (1966). *Purity and danger: An analysis of concepts of pollution and taboo*. London: Routledge.

Dreyfus, H. L., & Rabinow, P. (1982). *Michel Foucault: Beyond structuralism and hermeneutics*. Brighton, Sussex: The Harvester Press Limited.

Ferfolja, T. (2008). Discourses that silence: Teachers and anti-lesbian harassment. *Discourse: Studies in the Cultural Politics of Education, 29*(1), 107–119.

Foucault, M. (1967). *Madness and civilisation: A history of insanity in the age of reason*. London: Routledge.

Foucault, M. (1977). *Discipline and punish: The birth of the prison*. London: Penguin.

Foucault, M. (1982). The subject and power. *Critical Inquiry, 8*(4), 777–795.

Foucault, M. (1984). What is enlightenment? In P. Rabinow (Ed.), *The Foucault reader* (pp. 32–50). New York, NY: Random House.

Foucault, M. (2006). *History of madness*. Oxon: Routledge.

Foucault, M. (2008). *The history of sexuality: The will to knowledge volume 1.* U.S.A.: Penguin Group.

Froebel, F. (1974). *The education of man* (W. N. Hailmann, Trans.). Clifton, NJ: A.M. Kelley.

Gordon, C. (2013). History of madness. In C. Falzon, T. O'Leary, & J. Sawicki (Eds.), *A companion to Foucault* (pp. 84–104). West Sussex: Blackwell.

Grace, R., Llewellyn, G., Wedgwood, N., Fenech, M., & McConnell, D. (2008). Far from ideal: Everyday experiences of mothers and early childhood professionals negotiating an inclusive early childhood experience in the Australian context. *Topics in Early Childhood Special Education, 28*(1), 18–31.

Harwood, V. (2006). *Diagnosing 'disorderly' children: A critique of behaviour disorder discourse.* London: Routledge.

Hekman, S. J. (1990). *Gender and knowledge: Elements of a postmodern feminism.* Boston, MA: Northeastern University Press.

Jarrett, O., French-Lee, S., Bulunuz, N., & Bulunuz, M. (2010). Play in the sandpit: A university and a child-care center collaborate in facilitated-action research. *American Journal of Play, 3*(2), 221–237.

Laws, C., & Davies, B. (2000). Poststructuralist theory in practice: Working with "behaviourally disturbed" children. *International Journal of Qualitative Studies in Education, 13*(3), 205–221.

Leavitt, R. L., & Power, M. B. (1997). Civilising bodies: Children in day care. In J. Tobin (Ed.), *Making a place for pleasure in early childhood education.* Michigan: Edward Brothers.

MacLure, M., Jones, L., Holmes, R., & MacRae, C. (2012). Becoming a problem: Behaviour and reputation in the early years classroom. *British Education Research Journal, 38*(3), 447–471.

Mazzei, L. A. (2007a). *Inhabited silence in qualitative research: Putting poststructural theory to work.* New York, NY: Peter Lang.

Mazzei, L. A. (2007b). Toward a problematic of silence in action research. *Educational Action Research, 15*(4), 631–642.

McDevitt, T. M., & Ormrod, J. E. (2007). *Child development and education* (3rd ed.). Upper Saddle River, NJ: Pearson.

Millei, Z. (2005). The discourse of control: Disruption and Foucault in an early childhood classroom. *Contemporary Issues in Early Childhood, 6*(2), 128–139.

Millei, Z. (2011). Thinking differently about guidance: Power, children's autonomy and democratic environments. *Journal of Early Childhood Research, 10*(1), 88–99.

Nutbrown, C., & Clough, P. (2009). Citizenship and inclusion in the early years: Understanding and responding to children's perspectives on 'belonging'. *International Journal of Early Years Education, 17*(3), 191–206.

Pillow, W. S. (2003). Confession, catharsis, or cure? Rethinking the uses of reflexivity as a methodological power in qualitative research. *Qualitative Studies in Education, 16*(2), 175–196.

Purdue, K., Gordon-Burns, D., Gunn, A., Madden, B., & Surtees, N. (2009). Supporting inclusion in early childhood settings: Some possibilities and problems for teacher education. *International Journal of Inclusive Education, 13*(8), 805–815.

Robey, K. L., Beckley, L., & Kirschner, M. (2006). Implicit infantilizing attitudes about disability. *Journal of Developmental and Physical Disabilities, 18*(4), 441–453.

Rose, N. (1999). *Governing the soul: The shaping of the private self* (2nd ed.). London: Free Association Books.

Schegloff, E. A. (2007). A tutorial on membership categorization. *Journal of Pragmatics, 39,* 462–482.

Shildrick, M. (2005). The disabled body, genealogy and undecidability. *Cultural Studies, 19*(6), 755–770.

St. Pierre, E. A. (2000). Poststructural feminism in education: An overview. *International Journal of Qualitative Studies in Education, 13*(5), 477–515.

Walkerdine, V. (1999). Violent boys and precocious girls: Regulating childhood at the end of the millennium. *Contemporary Issues in Early Childhood, 1*(1), 3–23.

Wankoff, L. S. (2011). Warning signs in the development of speech, language, and communication: When to refer to a speech-language pathologist. *Journal of Child and Adolescent Psychiatric Nursing 24,* 175–184.

Ward, J., & Winstanley, D. (2003). The absent presence: Negative space within discourse and the construction of minority sexual identity in the workplace. *Human Relations, 56*(10), 1255–1280.

Watson, K. (2016). 'Silences' in the 'inclusive' early childhood classroom: Sustaining a 'taboo'. In E. B. Petersen & Z. Millei (Eds.), *Interrupting the psy-disciplines in education* (pp. 13–31) New York, NY & London: Palgrave Macmillan.

Winderlich, K. (2012). *Sensory play and learning* (Vol. 10). Deakin West, ACT: Early Childhood Australia.

Wohlwend, K. E. (2007). Friendship meeting or blocking circle? Identities in the laminated spaces of a playground conflict. *Contemporary Issues in Early Childhood, 8*(1), 73–88.

7

Fear, Separation and Asylum-Like Practices

Fear of 'Disability'—The Embodied Abject

> Oliver (a child with a diagnosis) is lying on his back on a mat in the yard. A younger child George (without a diagnosis) from the other classroom sits next to him with me and his teacher. He stares at Oliver as if he has not seen him before, his eyes wide and his body pensive and uneasy. He is closely watching Oliver's every move. The teacher comments that Oliver has kicked off his socks and while putting them on remarks in a playful way that Oliver's feet are very cold. She says to George, "Feel his toes, they are so cold". George shakes his head, and with a look of shock, moves his body further away. (Field Notes, 15/6/12, S1, p. 152)

George does not wish to touch Oliver's feet. He sits and stares at Oliver for a short time looking somewhat apprehensive. Oliver is positioned as the anomaly in the classroom and the 'abject' (Davies, 2006) in this encounter. Young (1990), following Kristeva (1982), posits that abjection brings about feelings of aversion and animosity, while at the same time, the abject is seen as fascinating, it draws the subject in, in order to repel it (Young, 1990). The separated self that abjection creates, needs to keep the border firm for fear of disintegration. Young (1990) writes, "The abject must not touch me for fear that it will ooze through, obliterating the border between inside and outside" (p. 207). The abject provokes fear because it exposes the border between self and other, constituted and fragile, as it threatens to dissolve the subject, by dissolving the border. The abject poses a threat to identity itself, as "people from groups marked as different fulfil the function of what lies just on the other side of the borders of the self, too close for comfort and threatening to cross or dissolve the border" (Young, 1990, p. 208). The fear and threat of the abject can and must be managed by maintaining a level of separation.

George is drawn to Oliver but looks at him as though he is scared of him and when asked to feel his cold feet, he looks panicked. Oliver's positioning as the 'disabled' boy, whose body functions in 'different' ways, might seem fascinating to George, but at the same time Oliver is the abject and remaining separate is vital for maintaining one's own subject positioning. George's interest in Oliver, in moving over to the mat initially, was somewhat unusual in this classroom, as most of the children did not seem to engage with Oliver at all.

Fear, awkwardness, silence and abjection are again observed in the following observation.

An Uncomfortable Fear of 'Madness'

> Hugo (a child with a diagnosis) approaches the small trestle table to have his fruit break. He sits down with his banana shaped container but as he cannot open it he hands it to me without a word. I open it for him. As the other children at the table continue to eat Hugo turns himself around so that his back is now facing the children opposite and he begins to make loud roaring noises. Sitting at the table with the pre-schoolers is a child who is having an orientation visit with his parent. Hugo stands and walks toward the parent roaring loudly at them with his face very close to their face. The parent, eyes wide and mouth open, and then frowning, turns her body away from Hugo and looks around her. She does not respond to Hugo. The other children at the table look at Hugo and then at the parent, with wide eyes and open mouths also. All continue to eat their fruit. (Field Notes, 17/10/12, S3, p. 13)

At fruit break the unmarked children sit quietly and eat their fruit. They do not make unnecessary noises or play while sitting at the fruit break trestle. If they do they are usually disciplined by the other children or teachers. Eating your fruit has regulatory norms on one's body and the space provided by the small trestle table restricts what can be done.

When Hugo 'roars' into the face of the visiting parent, his 'noise' and uninhibited actions are met with silence. Silence is constructed by the discourses that surround it, but also constructs discourse in return (Ward & Winstanley, 2003). Neither the children nor the visiting parent say anything. The parent's immediate response is to turn her body away. She looks outward, anywhere other than at Hugo, appearing very uncomfortable in the presence of his 'roaring'. She looks around the playground possibly scanning for someone to help her, to explain. She cannot deal with the potential danger that Hugo poses to the dissolution of order, and the border that separates the self from Other (Young, 1990). Hugo's 'noises' and his 'roaring' into the face of a visiting mother, is an act that positions him, in this discursive context, on the "other side of the border" (Davies, 2006, p. 75). The 'roaring' noises reinforce Hugo as the irrational subject, as the 'unreasonable'. There is no explanation offered about Hugo's behaviour, no diagnosis heard, but Hugo is nevertheless positioned. In another reading of this scene, Hugo could have been playing a particular game, or creating a character using his imagination. He could have been attempting to invite the others to join in his game, or he may have been using his roar to welcome the parent, or extend an invitation to play. But his actions are not read this way and Hugo is positioned as the opposite to the 'normal'. Hugo's performance is considered an act of 'unreason,' and as such, a threat to 'reason' (Foucault, 1967).

Foucault's (1967) asserts that there is an awareness and alarm around "the precariousness of reason that can at any moment be compromised, and definitively, by madness" (p. 201), and so the 'normal' must be vigilant as not to become compromised. He refers to a growing fear of madness in the 16th century and suggests that the threat of 'madness' resumed its place among the emergencies of that century (Foucault, 1967). Historical reactions to 'madness', closed the possibility of a dialogue between reason and unreason due to fear, and what followed was isolation and confinement. Here in the playground at the morning tea table, there was no dialogue between Hugo and the parent, or the other children. Was it because no one knew what to say, or was it due to fear? Hugo's loud roaring seemed to create a level of apprehension, in particular for the mother, who had no experience of Hugo. The discomfort of everyone at the table was tangible.

Using Reflexivity…

I watched on and made a mental note. I thought that the parent's response was unusual at the time. I felt uncomfortable and constrained by the 'normal' being performed by us all at that moment. I wondered why the mother did not roar back at Hugo or respond to him in some 'playful' way. To respond to him in this way would have been very familiar. My reading of the mother's response could be viewed as constructed to support my argument, as I was looking for these kinds of responses for my data collection. Her lack of response left me with many questions. I use reflexivity to question the construction of my representation here, as there are potentially many other ways to create and read the data. I may have looked at this scene with too much familiarity. I may have been the only one positioning Hugo as the Other in collecting this observation. Nevertheless the press of the 'normal' in performing the 'right' way it seems is inescapable for us all in this scene.

Foucault (1977) maintains that the mechanisms of power that uphold the 'normal' produce a constant division between the 'normal' and the 'abnormal' to which every individual is subjected. Normative forces of subjection and performativity work through exclusion (Butler, 1993). These normative forces powerfully excluded and delegitimised Hugo's performance as not acceptable, deviant and alarming. Hugo, positioned as the 'mad', is silenced by the 'normal', reinforcing the taboo that contains and separates him. Hugo is obvious, *'the elephant in the room',* everyone at the table knew he was there, but he could not be looked at or addressed; the demand for conformity here leaves *'the elephant in the room'* well alone.

'The Elephant in the Room'

There is something in the classroom that cannot be addressed. What is it that cannot be spoken of? There is arguably a tangible link that endures in this context between the contemporary discursive construction of what we today call 'disability', the diagnosed, and the historical construction of 'madness'. Despite well-intended people, employing well-intended policies and practices, 'disability' in the early childhood classroom, cannot be addressed directly and can only be addressed in particular ways, and within particular discourses. 'Disability' in these classroom is at best tolerated while often silenced, uncomfortably navigated and often made separate, although not always physically. Understanding these connections with the past, are central in helping to explain how 'disability' in the classroom persists as *the elephant in the room'.* What historical remnants might shape our understandings of the diagnosed, those who are Othered, today?

Fear and Separation

How society experiences and defines its limits and what a 'culture' rejects and makes exterior was of great interest to Foucault (Gordon, 2013). He scrutinised the history of places of otherness and in particular the establishment of asylums.

Places for those deemed as diseased, and later those subjected to discourses of 'madness'. Foucault's thesis (2006) is described "as a history of the other: the forms of its delineation as other, of its exclusions, its expulsions and/or closure into dedicated spaces of otherness" (Gordon, 2013, p. 89). He reflects at length on how fear became pivotal in societies exclusions and expulsions.

Fear and separation have been constitutive of 'unreason' and 'madness' over centuries (Foucault, 1967, 2006). The contemporary exploits of medical and psychological sciences, to pathologise, objectify and categorise as deficient, those individuals who do not conform to the 'normal', is arguably similar to practices that occurred in past centuries where the 'diseased' and/or the 'mad' were produced as deviant and separated from the 'normal'(Foucault, 2006). The marginal Other has been produced in numerous gestures of segregation, and "the fact that the internees of the 18th century bear a resemblance to our modern vision of the asocial is undeniable" (Foucault, 2006, p. 79). Assorted 'modern' terms such as 'disabled', 'disability', 'diagnosis', 'additional needs' and 'special needs' are firmly attached to the subjecthood of the marked child, and the positioning of this child as different to the 'normal', and as such, in need of separation from it.

Fear

> Suddenly, in the space of a few years in the mid-eighteenth century, a fear emerged. It was a fear formulated in medical terms, but deep down it was animated by a moral mythology. People were in dread of a mysterious sickness that apparently emanated from houses of confinement and was soon to spread throughout the cities. (Foucault, 2006, p. 355)

Fear of the diseased developed over time, into a fear of 'madness'. Originating in stories about how disease is spread, of prison fevers, and of men in chains moving through cities, leaving diseases behind them as they went, leaving the air tainted and contaminated (Foucault, 2006).

Historically, fear of contagion and deviation led to the establishment of places of otherness, where the limits imposed by society were upheld. The leprosarias were the first dedicated Western spaces of exclusion (Gordon, 2013). The lepers were deemed to be dangerous and treated as plague victims, they were excluded and "cut off from all human contact" (Foucault, 2006, p. 199). Subsequently new asylums, created for 'madness', "were built on the same spot where lepers had previously been kept, and it was as though centuries later these new tenants brought a new form of contagion" (Foucault, 2006, p. 356). The fear of contagion, associated with leprosy, stayed with the residents of these confinement houses. Foucault saw that 'unreason' became marked with an imaginary stigma of disease, which he believes "lent it its power to terrorize" (p. 358). The former exclusionary treatment that had been applied to the lepers, now pertained to 'madness'. All forms of 'unreason' took the place of leprosy and disease, and became banished to the margins (Foucault, 2006, p. 357).

Fear in the Classroom

Fear of disruption and risk to the 'normal' infiltrates and saturates the data created in this project. The wrist band and the lock, in their assemblages with the teachers and the marked child, emerge as ways to 'guard' the 'risky' deviant from a possible escape. The child is subjected as a 'flight risk' and there is fear for his safety, fear for the safety of the 'normal', and fear for the teachers, who must accept responsibility as 'guards', and avoid the possible consequences of the child's escape, and/or the possibility of disruption. The non-human and human assemblages produce fear and provide a visual reminder of the danger and threat. Fear, or being fearful, defends the 'normal', safe from corruption.

Fear creates exclusionary practices and actions as the children become tolerators, as tolerance is a way to sustain a threatening entity (Brown, 2006). Tolerance also works to dampen the fear, as it is thought to manage 'dangerous' difference in society. There is a fear of those who are positioned as 'uncivilised' (Brown, 2006), those who cannot abide by timetables, the correct use of space, the rules of play and other regulations. 'Civilising' them becomes the imperative of the 'normal', and via tolerance, some corrections can be crafted and imposed, but a discursively produced fear remains palpable. Tolerance produces and maintains subjectivities of virtue, those positioned as the 'normal' are shaped by fear and act through it. In reinforcing their category membership, and the need for protection, they further create a divide between themselves and the Other.

In this reading of the data, fear similarly produces silence as a practice in the classroom. In silence, the unmarked children's acts of ignoring and separating from the 'not normal', illuminate fear of the Other, along with fear of the 'risk' they pose. Separation and/or preserving a distance, are discursive practices enacted to manage the fear, and reduce the 'risk' to the 'normal'.

Separation

The notion and historical practice of confinement, allowed the 'normal' to expel heterogeneous elements that could be considered harmful (Foucault, 2006). The confinement of 'madness' was an instance of order, and the community acquired the ethical power to eject from the world of the 'normal', all forms of the 'abnormal' (Foucault, 1967). The separation from 'unreason', witnessed inside the classrooms in this project is performed to avoid the risk of a scandal (Gordon, 2013) and conceivably the possibility of contagion. Confining and separating 'unreason' from 'reason' in the past generated places of purification, where the intention was to prevent the spread or risk of disease, or at least achieve its neutralisation.

The specialised confining institution of the asylum, exercised its power with its medical curative authority, and offered a place that could dispel the fears of reason and contain 'unreason': "an asylum where unreason would be entirely contained and offered as a spectacle, without threatening the spectators; where it would have all the powers of example and none of the risks of contagion" (Foucault, 1967, p. 196). These places were isolated from the population so that they could be surrounded by "purer air" (Foucault, 2006, p. 359). To achieve this purer air, a distance had to be fashioned between the threat and the population. These historical reforms envisioned a 'cure', some degree of purification for 'unreason', achieved by creating a distance between the two.

Separation in the Classroom

In the project's early childhood classrooms, the noises made by the marked child, are responded to as if they are 'scandalous' and need to be stopped. They activate practices of silence and/or avoidance. As non-speech sounds are thought to be produced by 'unreason', they are often awkwardly ignored by the unmarked children. Teachers attend closely to stop the 'noises' and avoid any risk of scandal. At other times, the 'noises' are dismissed as 'immature', but nevertheless regarded as a 'not normal' way to communicate. Separation, avoidance, and the quietening of these noises, are all read as attempts to minimise the impact of 'unreason' in the classroom. The marked child's noisy and obvious disturbance requires an active effort on the part of the members of the 'normal' to maintain their position. Avoiding the obvious, sees the emergence of '*the elephant in the room*', as taking notice of the anomaly is taboo. A shared silence becomes a strategic response and in its many nuanced forms, it is read to explicitly exclude those who do not fit in.

In the discursive context of the early childhood classroom, the imperative to 'cure' the diagnosed child is overwhelming. To achieve a cure, some level of separation is deemed necessary. The unmarked children and their teachers, engage in practices that are designed to cure and remediate the marked child, with the legitimised authority of educational, medical and scientific discourses. Helping those who are 'just learning' or 'haven't learnt yet' is necessary to move them closer to the 'normal' or those who have 'already learnt'. Current everyday practices of remediation in the classroom, reveal resilient connections to the past. Practices of special education, most often delivered with the best of intentions, are exercises that confine and isolate the diagnosed child, and when read from a poststructural perspective, they work to correct the child's body and mind, using constant surveillance.

More recent policy reforms in education have halted the practice of segregating and isolating children with special needs in separate institutions and/or classrooms. Nevertheless the discourses that inform practices in 'inclusive' education have not undergone parallel reform (Slee, 2011). The unrelenting scrutiny and surveillance, sanctioned in segregated special education classrooms, is still regarded as crucial for the child in mainstream education, as reaching a prescribed level of development is obligatory. This remediating work is no longer carried out in a different institution, or within a special unit in the school. It is now accomplished *in* the classroom and viewed as 'inclusive', but how can that be? The discourses and practices of special education separate and isolate *in* the classroom and actively create a 'somewhere else' for the marked child to 'be' and 'be cured'.

Places of confinement were crafted with multiple purposes in mind: to silence by isolation, to dispel any fear or threat to the 'normal', and to 'cure' what was created as 'unreason'. Even though those diagnosed 'disabled', or constituted as 'madness', no longer live or are educated in the asylums, like the ones described by Foucault, what form does their liberty take? Foucault argues that "the liberty of the madman was given free reign, but in a space that was more enclosed and more rigid, less free than the always slightly indecisive space of confinement" (Foucault, 2006, p. 514). Even though the walls and chains that thwarted the madman's free will have been removed, the 'mad' have been stripped of any free will, by the rigorous mechanism of determinism, and the doctors and other professionals that uphold it. The madman is now seen to be "free in the open space where his liberty had already been lost" (Foucault, 2006, p. 515).

As the psychiatrists and doctors of history imposed freedom on the 'mad', as they released them from 'walled' confinement, they then went about locking them into certain truths about 'madness', about who they were, and what they could, and could not do. The walls of the old asylum are now removed but today's confinement is different, it is multiple, and moving, and individualised *with* the child. This confinement is produced and reproduced as an effect of both historical and contemporary discourses. It is not addressed, it is overlooked, ignored and invisible. It remains unchallenged for the most part, but it is nevertheless insidious. How can the notion of inclusion be spoken of when exclusion and confinement are re/produced in the discursive context and social practices performed in the 'inclusive' classroom?

Asylum-Like Practices

Images of confinement and asylums disrupt the taken-for-granted idea of inclusion, as they create visions of exclusion and isolation. "Asylum is a loaded word" (Boldt & Valente, 2014, p. 202) as it conjures up the inhumane treatment of children and adults with disabilities. The notion of the asylum has undoubtedly been consigned to narratives of history. For the most part, it is no longer contemplated as a part of present practice. Nonetheless, traces of the past linger and are made visible in this project. In taking an alternative interrogatory look at the 'normal' inside the 'inclusive' early childhood classroom, the powerful and productive effects of its operations become conspicuous.

Practices of isolation, separation and exclusion, endorsed by the 'normal', as they encounter the 'not normal', exhibit an inescapable semblance to the confinement practice of the asylum. Our contemporary classrooms and ways of knowing and understandings of those positioned as 'not normal', are imbued with vestiges of a by-gone era. The fear produced around 'madness' and 'unreason' in past centuries, encircles modern constructions of the pathologised, those with a diagnosis or 'disability'. 'Asylum-like' practices operate in the classroom, to remediate the diagnosed and to act as a protection for the 'normal', without the need for solid and fixed walls.

While ever individuals are made subjects in the classroom, by the 'truth' and power of psychopathology and medicine, the psycho-pathologisation of the individual will continue to produce a "personal, portable, and psychiatric prison" (Harwood, 2010, p. 437), where the marked child is separated and guarded in the classroom. In educational institutions, Harwood recognises the production of the 'mobile asylum' (Harwood, 2010, p. 438), a portable creation that moves with the marked child, encircling and entrapping them. A produced effect that remains covert and precarious, as it is maintained within the prevailing discourses. It is a space of separateness, an insistent marginalising space that remains unaddressed and unchallenged in early childhood classrooms.

Exploring the discursively produced obscure nature of the mobile asylum in the classroom, "permits a view [that] has the potential to ascertain the workings of power, and thereby more closely appreciate the experiences of the child" (Harwood, 2010, p. 445). The experiences of the marked child bring into focus how exclusive 'inclusive' practices can be, as the marked child is contained, limited and fixed by a category dispensed to them. The asylum can no longer be thought of as distinct from the world of the everyday as it was historically. We need "to look instead to the exercising of power that produces asylum-type effects" (Harwood, 2010, p. 447).

The asylum, mobile and personal, exists in the classroom as a social mechanism and its asylum-like effects have been exposed in this project. The asylum is not distinct from the everyday. It can be made visible every day, when 'practice as usual' is challenged, and the 'normal' is investigated and interrupted. The 'mobile asylum' is continuously created, as practices of the 'normal' are readily and repeatedly, taken up by the children and their teachers. Assemblages of human and non-human actors also emerge, contributing to the constitution of becoming subjectivities in the classroom.

This notion of the 'mobile asylum', creates an imperative for 'inclusive' early childhood education to insist on a continuing interrogation of the 'normal' and the power it exercises. In chapter two, I made the comment that the marked child was not the focus of this project but instead an important catalyst for viewing the constitution of the 'normal'. Nevertheless, the alternative understandings presented in this book, have implications for the marked child, for the unmarked children, and for the 'inclusive' classroom. In questioning and examining the position and power of the 'normal', and its part in 'inclusive' and exclusive processes, we can see how it operates as a mechanism in the subjection of all individuals in the classroom. Fear, separation, and 'cure' are produced as effects, as the children take up subject positions, defining and defending the category boundaries of these positionings. The 'normal' exercises its 'muscles' as it maintains itself, by staying away from, and by not recognising the discursively produced Other. '*The elephant in the room*' endures, unaddressed in the 'inclusive' early childhood classroom.

References

Boldt, G., & Valente, J. M. (2014). Bring back the asylum: Reimagining inclusion in the presence of others. In M. N. Bloch, B. B. Swadener, G. S. Cannella, & M. N. Bloch (Eds.), *Reconceptualizing early childhood care and education: A reader* (pp. 201–213). New York, NY: Peter Lang.

Brown, W. (2006). *Regulating aversion: Tolerance in the age of identity and empire.* Princeton, NJ: Princeton University Press.

Butler, J. (1993). *Bodies that matter: On the discursive limits of 'sex.'* New York, NY: Routledge.

Davies, B. (2006). Identity, abjection and otherness: Creating the self, creating difference. In M. Arnot & M. Macan Ghaill (Eds.), *The Routledge Falmer reader in gender and education* (pp. 72–90). London: Routledge.

Foucault, M. (1967). *Madness and civilisation: A history of insanity in the age of reason.* London: Routledge.

Foucault, M. (1977). *Discipline and punish: The birth of the prison.* London: Penguin.

Foucault, M. (2006). *History of madness.* Oxon: Routledge.

Gordon, C. (2013). History of madness. In C. Falzon, T. O'Leary, & J. Sawicki (Eds.), *A Companion to Foucault* (pp. 84–104). West Sussex: Blackwell.

Harwood, V. (2010). Mobile asylums: Psychopathologisation as a personal, portable psychiatric prison. *Discourse: Studies in the Cultural Politics of Education, 31*(4), 437–451.

Kristeva, J. (1982). *Powers of horror: An essay on abjection.* New York, NY: Columbia University Press.

Slee, R. (2011). *The irregular school: Exclusion, schooling and inclusive education.* Oxon: Routledge.

Ward, J., & Winstanley, D. (2003). The absent presence: Negative space within discourse and the construction of minority sexual identity in the workplace. *Human Relations, 56*(10), 1255–1280.

Young, I. M. (1990). Abjection and oppression: Dynamics of unconscious racism, sexism, and homophobia. In A. B. Dallery & C. E. Scott (Eds.), *Crisis in continental philosophy.* New York, NY: State University of New York Press.

8

Rethinking 'Inclusive' Practice

Shifting the Focus

A disillusionment with inclusion policy and 'inclusive' practice is widely recognised (Allan, 2010; Armstrong, Armstrong, & Spandagou, 2011; Boldt & Valente, 2014; Graham & Sweller, 2011). This dissatisfaction and concern about inclusion comes from multiple stakeholders. From teachers in the classrooms, where a child with diagnosis is viewed as a concern, an added responsibility (Macartney, 2012), and extra support is seen as crucial, but difficult to come by. Parents and caregivers are often disappointed with the 'inclusive' experiences of their diagnosed child, as they feel they are seen as a burden. The parents of undiagnosed children also often report concern about the presence of a diagnosed child in the classroom and the potential risk to their own child and their learning. Inclusion in education generally "appears to be in something of a sorry state, characterised by confusion, frustration, guilt and exhaustion" (Allan, 2008, p. 3).

Following this line of thinking, Warming (2011) draws attention to the idea that inclusion has occurred in quantitative terms, but in qualitative terms 'inclusive' practices are still challenged, as issues of equality, social justice and participation have not been addressed, nor have classrooms eliminated all forms of exclusionary assumptions and practices. How to do inclusion better, Slee (2013) argues, is not the challenge. It is instead recognising and understanding that inclusion is framed by the political predisposition of exclusion. Learning "how to detect, understand and dismantle exclusion as it presents itself in education" (p. 905) provides a different insight and some promise for future practice.

This classroom project has offered a way to detect and better understand exclusion by exposing how the undisrupted 'normal' operates, within the authoritative and sanctioned discourses of the classroom. As the 'normal' enacts and endorses exclusionary practices, its political legitimacy is maintained. Dismantling exclusion, as it presents itself in the classroom, begins with an interrogation of the 'normal'; what constitutes it, and what power it exercises. Thinking about how we can disrupt it's taken for granted constitution and its continual reproduction and maintenance is the challenge for early childhood education.

Shifting the Focus of Inclusion Away from the Diagnosis

Initially what motivated this project was a feeling of frustration with the unfair way diagnosed children were often excluded in 'inclusive' settings. A child's physical presence in the classroom did not always entail full participation. As a teacher, I struggled with the 'diagnosis', as it simplified the complex child in my care, and knowing this child and introducing this child to a mainstream setting, seemed to reduce them to a list of diagnostic characteristics. A diagnosis had the information, knowledge and power to describe who the child was and prescribe their future relationships with others. The child's diagnostic characteristics, produced a fixed understanding of them and their potential. It declared that all children with the same diagnosis were part of a homogenous group. Many children, in my teaching experience, have been introduced to me as *their* diagnosis and not by their name; the child with autism, the child with cerebral palsy, the ADHD child, etc. A diagnosis defining the child's identity. The diagnosis declares the child as a pre-determined entity, and coming to know this child in other ways, is obstructed from view. The diagnosis, and the discourses that constructs it, keeps us blind to the possibilities of difference in the classroom.

I acknowledge that many children and families experience success with 'inclusive' education, and that most classrooms are very welcoming, and teachers and children work very hard to include diagnosed children. The early childhood classroom is not a place where exclusion is consciously and purposefully enacted. Teachers working diligently to help all members feel included. For the mainstream classroom, procuring a diagnosis for a child is considered necessary and constructive, as the diagnosis and its defining characteristics, provide a sense of certainty about how to help the child and how to explain the child and their behaviours. A diagnosis can assist in securing extra funding support, to assist the child in becoming part of the educational program. Teachers feel that they have a responsibility to act on the knowledge that the diagnosis gives them. However, accepting and acting on a diagnosis, as a descriptor of the child, does have consequences. Perhaps we do not consider often enough that a diagnosis for a child is a 'social disease' they will bear for the rest of their lives (Billington, 2000).

In the introduction, I related a story about a boy called David. His story represents one of my many experiences in an early intervention service. A global endorsement of early intervention presents it as a high priority (Guralnick, 2011) for children like David. He was constituted as a problematic subject and *his* diagnosis, and accurate knowledge of it, was presented as providing a way of solving *his* problem. Understanding the diagnosed child through this lens is widely accepted in education, it is a powerful and well-resourced practice that continues to saturate our early childhood classrooms and education systems more broadly (Ballard, 2013). Can we think otherwise?

Special education, is argued to be experiencing a global expansion, described by Tomlinson (2012) as the growing 'special educational needs industry', where rapidly growing assessment and accountability frameworks are being validated and maintained by education systems. The diagnosed or deviant child has become a valuable commodity (Allan & Hamre, 2016) with more and more children being assigned to diagnostic categories. There has been an expansion of professional groups who have a vested interest in increasing the numbers who might be in need of special and 'inclusive' education. New categories of therapeutic and neuro-science professionals, as well as allied technical experts, including pharmaceutical companies, all have interests in assessing, diagnosing and treating those who are presented as problematic for the classroom (Tomlinson, 2012).

A shift in focus away from thinking about the child as *his/her* diagnosis is necessary, as it is the diagnosis that contributes to their isolation inside the early childhood classroom. It is the diagnosis that draws on and privileges special education strategies to create a 'cure', or at least manage the difference. It is the diagnosis, as a comparison to the 'normal' that separates them and excludes them from participating in the classroom. It is the diagnosis that creates fear. Can we shift our understandings to see that the diagnosis is not *in* the child? Can our educational practices cease to assume a 'within-child' factor (Harwood, 2006)? Just as this project has made visible the construction of the 'normal', the knowledge that creates a diagnosis is a questionable construct, and the assumption that it is a truth, needs to be troubled. Is it possible to disrupt the power of this knowledge in our classrooms and the way it produces difference?

Shifting the focus from diagnosing and pathologising difference, has the potential to interrupt the propagation of fear, traced from centuries past. Difference has a long association with something dangerous. Foucault's *History of Madness* (2006) has steered and enriched this analysis establishing connections between past and present practices with regard to those who are regarded as "the 'asocial'" (p. 78). Produced out of fear, separation, confinement and 'cure' were measures taken up in the past to deal with 'madness'. Our contemporary practices in the early childhood classroom have manifest similarities. There is an association of fear with behaviours that are considered anti-social or low achievement (Tomlinson, 2012). In this investigation, effects such as silence, anxiety, fear and separation were repeatedly observed, along with the imperative to tolerate, 'fix' or remediate.

Historically the protection of the 'normal' generated the demand for the development of places of isolation like the asylum (Foucault, 2006). In examining these links between past and present, attention has been drawn to the 'dangerous' limitations and cruelty (St. Pierre & Pillow, 2000) of scientific discourses. The 'regimes of truth' of the past and present, re/produce the 'normal' and position individuals as fixed and deficient (Cannella, 1997) and potentially dangerous. As researchers and teachers "we have to know the historical conditions that motivate our conceptualization. We need a historical awareness of our present circumstance" (Foucault, 1982, p. 327). An awareness of the past has the promise to teach us that there are options that we are free to choose, that there are other possibilities, and that we do not have to merely adapt to the continuities of the past (Hutton, 1988).

Shifting the Focus to the 'Normal'

The manoeuvrings of the 'normal' are not always recognisable, consciously enacted or explicit. This classroom project has put the spotlight on the 'normal', the invisible and often difficult to pin down centre and its operations. Inclusion as is, veils the 'normal', as it works to secure its position and its invisibility at the centre (Ferguson, 1990). The 'ideological fog' (Freire, 1998) of the 'normal' prevails in schools and society, "despite incremental societal advances away from the demons of our past" (Annamma, Boelé, Moore, & Klinger, 2013, p. 1283). The discursive 'normal' remains embedded in the cultural milieus, with the outcome being an unconscious division of the population, into those who are 'normal', and those who are not (Annamma *et al.*, 2013). A disruption of the 'normal' is necessary, as it operations deny inclusion, as they continually reinforce existing power relations.

Foucault's (1977) incitement to question what we think we know, and to trouble the 'regimes of truth' that govern and subject us, provides a framework to critique the science and medical disciplines, and the practices of special education in the classroom. In education, the unrelenting reliance on the knowledge made available via the psy-knowledges and the medical model of disability needs to be troubled. I still grapple with my previous knowing, continually questioning the ideas that over many years gave me certainty about myself and the children I taught. This is work that must be done. This has been a genuine and difficult project and has required an intensive examination of my own historical, social and cultural meanings, a reflection on my own personal subjectivity, and a continuing wondering about whose interest is served in the way the present system exists.

The importance of troubling the certainty of the discourses that dominate 'inclusive' education, is central to this work. There is a desire to arrest "inclusion's need to speak of and identify otherness" (Harwood & Rasmussen, 2004, p. 5), as this shapes both the margins and a centre, through the 'privileging of "universal categories and a romanticised, universal subject" (Lather, 2003, p. 260). The idealised 'normal', created in the humanistic tradition, as progressive, and superior, and serving as a method of social regulation (Cannella, 1997), needs interrupting. The delusion that the norm is natural and true, because it is scientifically and statistically derived, needs to be exposed. The idea that this comparative measurement does not consider the naturalness of diversity (Graham, 2006) requires further consideration. Is there some potential for future 'inclusive' research and education in further scrutinising the power exercised by normative discourses?

It is not my intention to disparage the actions of individuals who position themselves within the accepted and available classroom discourses. I do not want to represent the research participants as being, in any way 'bad', in the way they go about their daily lives. The point is that "not everything is bad, but that everything is dangerous, which is not exactly the same as bad. If everything is dangerous, then we always have something to do" (Foucault, 1997, p. 256). This project gives us 'something to do' in the classroom. The 'inclusive' classroom has revealed itself as somewhat dangerous for the subjectivities of its participants. The discourses of the 'normal' are now on 'notice'; 'new', different and multiple discourses need to be valued and constructed in the classroom. Not enough has been deduced from the 'normal' concerning the ambiguity of its meaning. As classroom teachers, we can no longer just be happy to point out its existence, but we must look further to see it as a problem in itself (Canguilhem, 1991).

Interrupting Business-As-Usual with and Among the Children

Turning our attention as teachers and researchers, to how inclusions and exclusions are enacted by the children in their daily, continuous, and 'unremarkable' performances, has the potential for alternative understandings. Children in the early childhood classroom have been, for the most part, overlooked in these processes. Young children are not passive in their negotiations with each other. We would be wise to be attentive to how knowledge operates and how power is exercised (Foucault, 1982) *among* the children in the classroom. In this project the social and discursive practices of the children have been explored over several months. What has become noticeable, is how powerfully and actively children's words, actions and silences, legitimise and delegitimise certain ways of being for themselves and for others in the class group. The discourses of development, that view children as merely passive recipients of adult socialisation or imitators of adults, are disrupted in this project, as children demonstrate how active they are, in this positioning work, as they take up available discursive understandings. 'Inclusive' education research can no longer overlook the children who are 'already included', as they are implicated and enmeshed in how these processes operate.

How the undiagnosed children come to position themselves as 'normal', performed in their actions and words, is worthy of a more critical focus. Exploring the micro-workings of power among the children, illuminates the macro-discursive formations that contribute to the subjecthood of all classroom participants. An educational methodology that focuses on the processes of discursive in/exclusion, is a productive way to view how "some acts, articulation and bodies 'make it'" (Petersen, 2004, p. 199), as they are constituted as a successful individual in the context, while others 'don't make it', as they are constituted as "not getting it right" (p. 199). Challenges to the production of a right or wrong way to be, involve thinking outside the binary divides that structure our thinking in simplifying and reductive ways (Lenz-Taguchi, 2010). Is this possible in the classroom? While ever binary thinking continues to shape classroom understandings—normal/not normal, good/bad, big/little, able/disabled—possibilities are limited, as one quality in the binary, is the opposite and exclusive of the other, and anything in between, impossible.

Rethinking Funding Philosophy

In our everyday interactions as teachers with children and parents, we could do 'better' by remaining vigilant and critically reflexive about how we speak of ourselves and others, and how we act and 'be' with each other. Funding structures that uphold special education practices in the 'inclusive' classroom, need to be 'shaken up', rethought and de-naturalised, as they continue to rely on the identification of deficits *in* the child. In Australia, in July 2016, a government policy refurbishment produced the Inclusion Support Program 2016–2019 (AGDET, 2016), which states that its aim is to improve access for all children with additional needs, not just those diagnosed with a disability. Its goal is to see an increase in the number of children with additional needs attending mainstream early childhood services.

Access to funding has previously focused on a child's diagnosis, and their level of need, or disruption to the classroom environment. Funding often secures an additional educator for the classroom. The educator's role has not been to work solely with the child with a diagnosis, but instead to improve the educator-child ratios, where educators work as a team for the inclusion of all children. In this project, the diagnosed child seemed to typically be the responsibility of the additional educator. The new policy again describes the additional educator's role as being part of a team. Unfortunately, this document does not consider the difficulty in changing entrenched behaviours, while ever classroom discourses of developmentalism, special education and regulation, remain unchallenged. It does not recognise the premise of exclusion in the classroom. It does not take into account the experiences and negotiations of the children in classroom processes. It does not consider the operations and power of the 'normal'.

There seems to be no proposal to contest embedded understandings of a diagnosis and the truth it bestows. Educators will continue to focus on the child's diagnostic deficits, the need for remediation and the importance of special education strategies, which inadvertently but powerfully, marginalise particular children. The policy document requires educators to create a strategic plan for inclusion, and lists multiple possible barriers that a classroom needs to identify in their unique context (AGDET, 2016). Most of the barriers describe the limitations and failings of individuals in the context. The list however does not include the barriers created by the discursive 'normal' in the classroom. Whilst policy, and its funding structures, continue to naturalise ways of speaking about the diagnosed child, or the child with additional needs, difference will continue to be positioned as a defect, as a comparison to an unquestioned and unscrutinised norm.

Participation, Belonging and Difference

Participation in the classroom comes with constraints and limitations for those who are Othered. For the 'normal' it seems, participation is taken for granted. In early childhood classrooms, the Other is expected to conform and their participation is often dependent on compliance. As the 'normal' continues to operate in the classroom unchallenged and un-interrogated, *'the elephant in the room'* remains unaddressed and participation for the diagnosed child is inhibited. As the child's diagnosed otherness defines them, their relationships and connections within the classroom, will continue to be limited. The unmarked children and teachers are enabled by the 'normal' to abdicate their responsibility for developing relationships with the Other, as they view them as in need of special attention and care (Macartney, 2012). Participation, and any sense of belonging, is limited to the child's physical presence, and for the most part, exclusionary practices go unnoticed. Deconstructing the 'normal' renders more obvious and uncomfortable the unaddressed nature of *'the elephant in the room'* within existing discourses. Exposing the 'normal' makes the constraints on participation conspicuous, and the 'reality' of belonging, seemingly out of reach in this context.

Is it possible to create other discourses, that critique deficit driven constructs that continue to present predetermined homogenised ways of thinking and being? While difference continues to be constructed as problematic in our classrooms, inclusion will remain tenuous, as children and teachers come to learn that dealing with difference is oftentimes difficult. As young children continue to learn not to ask questions, not to protest, and not to offer alternative positionings, exclusionary practices will endure.

Is it possible to change the way we think about difference? What would happen if difference was not expected to conform? And rather than ignoring it, silencing it, or tolerating it, difference could be recognised and responded to it. Would it be possible to construct alternative discourses that expect, encourage and invite difference, ambiguity and uncertainty? This would require a significant paradigm shift for teachers and for children in the classroom.

Focus on Subjectivities

Could an emphasis on the constituted character of the subject, and the fluid nature of subjection, offer us in 'inclusive' education, an alternative? Could a greater appreciation of one's subjecthood provide us with a less limiting understanding of ourselves and each other? Would it be possible in 'inclusive' education to suspend the take up of dominant circulating normative discourses, and attend more to "the way a human being turns him or herself into a subject" (Foucault, 1982, p. 327), via the interactions between the self, truth and power (Harwood, 2006)? Could this provide a way to understand and negotiate difference and appreciate multiple ways of being in the classroom? By refusing to accept, and entertain as 'truth', the psychologising and pathologising stories, that are assigned to children, it may be imaginable to think and act differently within education, and see the child as a becoming subject.

I have come to realise, that my perpetual questioning has been concerned, to some extent, with how we come to know ourselves, and how we come to know others. As Foucault (1984) contends, "the critique of what we are is at one and the same time the historical analysis of the limits imposed on us and an experiment with the possibility of going beyond them" (p. 50). I have examined the limits imposed on subjects in the 'inclusive' classroom by the discursive 'normal', its historical construction, and its effects on inclusionary and exclusionary processes. I have analysed and scrutinised the re/construction of these limits, with the idea of hopefully 'going beyond them'. But rather than seeing this research as a body of new 'stable' and long lasting knowledge, I see it as continuous, as we are always in the process of beginning again (Foucault, 1984). I think this classroom project has introduced other possibilities for viewing the 'inclusive' classroom, and as a whole I hope that it creates promise for a shift in focus and practice.

My former knowledge as a mainstream and early intervention teacher has been vigorously questioned, and my previous practices robustly challenged. However, this is important work and I agree with Laws when she writes:

> For, once coming to a kind of agency where one is able to see the discursive practices that hold us in one place, we are better able to shift to another place—still within discourse but better able to see the ways we are bound and to loosen those ties even for small moments in time. (Laws, 2004, p. 126)

This classroom project has allowed me to examine the discursive practices that hold me in place, as I continue to wrestle with my shifting understandings and my own subjection. Right through this project and the writing of this book, I have attempted to be cognisant of my own positioning in troubling my take up of 'normal', while at the same time feeling the gravity of it on me, to perform in particular ways. The 'normal' is not a neutral instrument in the early childhood classroom, it is a social mechanism, a technology of power that is productive while also limiting and constraining for children and adults. As a reflexive self, subjected to and within the available discourses, I have tried to account for my own becoming. I recognise unambiguously my serious limitations in doing this work.

A Continuing Struggle

As a teacher, I wondered how I could have done things differently. Even though I have come to see this as an ongoing challenge and a never-ending process, I think this book has some implications for how we, as teachers, could do things differently, if not 'better'. I think as teachers we need to consider some of the things that we could stop doing straight away. We could stop applying labels, and stop looking for new labels, for children who do not conform. We could stop creating difference as problematic, and something that needs to be changed or fixed. We could stop using the norm as a measurement to privilege those who conform. We could stop speaking of 'otherness', and instead, challenge 'sameness'. We could stop ignoring or overlooking the unfair encounters we witness between children and adults and between children and children, where some children are isolated or separated. We could stop avoiding *'the elephant in the room'*, start discussing difference, and be curious and open to the unknown. Above all, we could stop our incessant obsession with developmental and psychological discourses that construct and maintain the privileged 'normal' and the subjugated 'not normal'. For policy makers and professionals, who assume inclusion is complete and a finished product (Slee & Allan, 2001), this research draws attention to how difficult, unfinished and exclusive it is, not just for the young children in our classrooms, but for society more widely.

According to Foucault (1988), it is not our role as researchers to propose alternatives to others that we imagine could be useful to them, as this can only have effects of domination. Instead Foucault proposed that "what we have to present are instruments and tools that people might find useful" (Foucault, 1988, p. 197) for their own investigations. Following this I am not presenting 'solid' proposals or new 'strategies' for working in the 'inclusive' classroom. This book is not a 'how-to-do-it' manual. What I am offering is a productive approach which attends to the continuous, never ending work done in the classroom, towards the production and maintenance of the category of the 'normal'. This exploration of the discursive 'normal', using poststructural 'tools', might be useful for others who may wish to also interrogate and trouble the 'normal'. Combining Foucault's conceptualisations of discourse, power and subjectivity, along with Harré and van Langenhove's (1999) analytical tool of positioning theory, and Davies' (1989) concept of category boundary work, has opened up other ways of viewing the operations of power in 'inclusive' education. Butler (1997) also adds to the tool box with her work on performativity, and recognisability of the subject, to illustrate how the children get this work done.

By problematising everyday practices and understandings in the classroom, I, like other Foucauldian researchers (if I can be so bold), seek new understandings, enabling a 'practice of freedom', by opening up possibilities for thinking and acting 'otherwise'. In thinking otherwise would it be possible to give up all references to things being 'normal' or 'natural'? Would it be possible to take seriously the notion that everything (people, categories, classrooms, diagnoses, etc.) is continually made, and that we are all implicated in this making? Would it be possible to interrupt the privileging and power of cultural and historical discourses? Could this provide new understandings for 'inclusive' education? There is promise if we can begin to shift the focus from the 'objectifying' of the subject, toward a discursive understanding how "human beings are made subjects" (Foucault, 1982, p. 326), and begin to grasp how the operating power of the 'normal' creates effects for subjection inside the classroom. There is promise if we can come to accept that we are all implicated and complicated in our own making as discursive subjects, and also, in the making of others.

References

Allan, J. (2008). *Rethinking inclusive education: The philosophers of difference in practice* (Vol. 5). Dordrecht, the Netherlands: Springer.

Allan, J. (2010). The sociology of disability and the struggle for inclusive education. *British Journal of Sociology of Education, 31*(5), 603–619.

Allan, J., & Hamre, B. (2016). Guest editorial: Special education and the deviant child in the Nordic countries—The impact of Foucault. *Nordic Journal of Social Research, 7,* 1–5.

Annamma, S. A., Boelé, A. L., Moore, B. A., & Klinger, J. (2013). Challenging the ideology of normal in schools. *International Journal of Inclusive Education, 17*(12), 1278–1294.

Armstrong, D., Armstrong, A. C., & Spandagou, I. (2011). Inclusion: By choice or by chance? *International Journal of Inclusive Education, 15*(1), 29–39.

Australian Government Department of Education and Training. (2016). *Inclusion Support Programme User Guide 2016–2019.* Retrieved September 22, 2016, from https://docs.education.gov.au/system/files/doc/other/inclusion_support_programme_user_guide_-_release_2.pdf

Ballard, K. (2013). Thinking in another way: Ideas for sustainable inclusion. *International Journal of Inclusive Education, 17*(8), 762–775.

Billington, T. (2000). *Separating, losing and excluding children: Narratives of difference.* New York, NY: Routledge Falmer.

Boldt, G., & Valente, J. M. (2014). Bring back the asylum: Reimagining inclusion in the presence of others. In M. N. Bloch, B. B. Swadener, G. S. Cannella, & M. N. Bloch (Eds.), *Reconceptualizing early childhood care and education: A reader* (pp. 201–213). New York, NY: Peter Lang.

Butler, J. (1997). *Excitable speech. A politics of the performative.* New York, NY: Routledge.

Canguilhem, G. (1991). *The normal and the pathological.* New York, NY: Zone Books.

Cannella, G. S. (1997). *Deconstructing early childhood education: Social justice & revolution.* New York, NY: Peter Lang.

Davies, B. (1989). *Frogs and snails and feminist tales: Preschool children and gender.* Sydney, NSW: Allen & Unwin.

Ferguson, R. (1990). *Out there: Marginalization and contemporary cultures* (Vol. 4). New York, NY: MIT Press.

Foucault, M. (1977). *Discipline and punish: The birth of the prison.* London: Penguin.

Foucault, M. (1982). The subject and power. *Critical Inquiry, 8*(4), 777–795.

Foucault, M. (1984). What is enlightenment? In P. Rabinow (Ed.), *The Foucault reader* (pp. 32–50). New York, NY: Random House.

Foucault, M. (1988). *Politics, philosophy, culture: Interviews and other writings of Michel Foucault 1977–1984.* New York, NY: Routledge.

Foucault, M. (1997). On the genealogy of ethics: An overview of work in progress. In P. Rabinow (Ed.), *Michel Foucault: Ethics, subjectivity and truth, the essential works of Michel Foucault* (Vol. 1). New York, NY: New York Press.

Foucault, M. (2006). *History of madness.* Oxon: Routledge.

Freire, P. (1998). *Teachers as cultural worker: Letters to those who dare to teach.* Boulder, CO: Westview Press.

Graham, L. (2006). Caught in the net: A Foucaultian interrogation of the incidental effects of limited notions of 'inclusion'. *International Journal of Inclusive Education, 10*(1), 3–24.

Graham, L. J., & Sweller, N. (2011). The inclusion lottery: Who's in and who's out? Tracking inclusion and exclusion in New South Wales government schools. *International Journal of Inclusive Education, 15*(9), 941–953.

Guralnick, M. J. (2011). Why early intervention works: A systems perspective. *Infants & Young Children, 24*(1), 6–28.

Harré, R., & van Langenhove, L. (Eds.). (1999). *Positioning theory: Moral contexts of intentional action.* Oxford: Blackwell Publishers.

Harwood, V. (2006). *Diagnosing 'disorderly' children; A critique of behaviour disorder discourse.* London: Routledge.

Harwood, V., & Rasmussen, M. L. (2004). Studying schools with an ethic of discomfort. In B. Baker & K. Heyning (Eds.), *Dangerous coagulations? The uses of Foucault in the study of education* (pp. 305–321). New York, NY: Peter Lang.

Hutton, P. H. (1988). Foucault, Freud, and the technologies of the self. In L. H. Martin, H. Gutman, & P. H. Hutton (Eds.), *Technologies of the self: A seminar with Michel Foucault.* Amherst, MA: The University of Massachusetts.

Lather, P. (2003). Applied Derrida: (Mis) reading the work of mourning in educational research. *Educational Philosophy and Theory, 35*(3), 257–270.

Laws, C. (2004). Poststructuralist writing at work. *International Journal of Qualitative Studies in Education, 17*(1), 121–134.

Lenz-Taguchi, H. L. (2010). *Going beyond the Theory/Practice Divide in Early Childhood Education: Introducing an intra-active pedagogy.* Oxon: Routledge.

Macartney, B.C. (2012). Teaching through an ethics of belonging, care and obligation as a critical approach to transforming education. *International Journal of Inclusive Education, 16*(2), 171–183.

Petersen, E. B. (2004). *Academic boundary work: The discursive constitution of scientificity amongst researchers within the social sciences and humanities.* (PhD), University of Copenhagen, Copenhagen.

Slee, R., & Allan, J. (2001). Excluding the Included: A reconsideration of inclusive education. *International Studies in Sociology of Education, 11*(2), 173–191.

Slee, R. (2013). How do we make inclusive education happen when exclusion is a political predisposition? *International Journal of Inclusive Education, 17*(8), 895–907.

St. Pierre, E. A., & Pillow, W. S. (2000). *Working the ruins: Feminist post-structural theory and methods in education.* London: Routledge.

Tomlinson, S. (2012). The irresistible rise of the SEN industry. *Oxford Review of Education, 38*(3), 267–286.

Warming, H. (2011). Getting under their skins? Accessing young children's perspectives through ethnographic fieldwork. *Childhood, 18*(1), 39–53.

Watson, K. (2016). 'Silences' in the 'inclusive' early childhood classroom: Sustaining a 'taboo'. In E. B. Petersen & Z. Millei (Eds.), *Interrupting the psy-disciplines in education* (pp. 13–31). New York, NY & London: Palgrave Macmillan.

Index

CHILDHOOD STUDIES

Gaile S. Cannella, *General Editor*

For many years, the field of Childhood Studies has crossed disciplinary boundaries that include, but are not limited to, anthropology, art, education, history, humanities, and sociology by addressing diverse histories, cultures, forms of representation, and conceptualizations of "childhood". The publications in the Rethinking Childhood series have supported this work by challenging the universalization of childhood and introducing reconceptualized, critical spaces from which increased social justice and possibilities are generated for those who are younger.

This newly named Childhood Studies series in the global twenty-first century is created to continue this focus on social justice for those who are younger, but also to broaden and further explore conceptualizations of privilege, justice, possibility, responsibility, and activism. Authors are encouraged to consider "childhood" from within a context that would decenter human privilege and acknowledge environmental justice and the more-than-human Other, while continuing to research, act upon, and transform beliefs, public policy, societal institutions, and possibilities for ways of living/being in the world for all of us. Boundary crossings are of greater importance than ever as we live unprecedented technological change, violence against living beings that are not labeled human (through experimentation, industrialization, and medicine), plundering of the earth, and gaps between the privileged and the marginalized (whether rich/poor, human/nonhuman). Along with continued concerns related to social justice, equity, poverty, and diversity, some authors in the Childhood Studies series will choose to think about, and ask questions such as: What does it mean to be a younger human being within such a world? What are the values, education, and forms of care provided within this context? Can/how should these dispositions and practices be transformed? Can childhood studies, and the diverse forms of representation and practice associated with it, conceptualize and practice a more just world broadly, while avoiding utopian determinisms and continuing to remain critical and multiple?

For more information about this series or for submission of manuscripts, please contact:
Gaile S. Cannella
gaile.cannella@gmail.com

To order other books in this series, please contact our Customer Service Department at:
(800) 770-LANG (within the U.S.)
(212) 647-7706 (outside the U.S.)
(212) 647-7707 FAX

Or browse online by series at:
www.peterlang.com